Magic Made in Mexico

*Live Your Dream...
in Mexico*

Joanna van der Gracht de Rosado

Editorial Mazatlán

MAGIC MADE IN MEXICO: Living Your Dream ... In Mexico
D.R.©2011 Mary Joan van der Gracht Powell
editado por

Editorial Mazatlán

David W. Bodwell, Editor y Director

matriz:
calzada Camarón Sábalo no. 610
centro comercial Plaza Galerías, local no. 11
fracc. El Dorado C.P. 82110
Mazatlán, Sinaloa, México
Tel: (+52 o en U.S. o Canada, 011-52) 669-916-7899
email: mazbook@yahoo.com

sucursal en los Estados Unidos de Norte America:
6917 Montgomery Blvd. NE
Albuquerque, NM, U.S.A. 87109
Ph: (001) 505-349-0425

diseño del libro por: 1106 Design
cubierta ilustrada por: 1106 Design
compuesta en Adobe Garamond Pro por: 1106 Design

fotografías interiores por autor, por Carlos Rosado y de uso libre del Internet

U. S. Library of Congress número de control: 2010937619

catalogación de la editorial en la fuente de datos:

Van der Gracht de Rosado, Joanna.
    Magic made in Mexico : living your dream ... in
Mexico / Joanna Van der Gracht de Rosado.
    p. cm.
    ISBN 978-0-9816637-2-2
1. Van der Gracht de Rosado, Joanna. 2. Mexico—Guidebooks.
3. Mexico—History. I. Title.

F1209 .V36 2010
917—dc22   2010937619

primera edición
10 9 8 7 6 5 4 3 2 1

IMPRESÓ en MÉXICO / Printed in México

Table of Contents

Introduction: ¡Bienvenidos a México! viii

JOANNA'S STORY . . . . Chapters 1 through 18 . . . 1 to 113

THE ALPHABET 114

   A is for... ATTITUDE .117

   B is for... BEHAVIOR .123

   C is for... COMMUNICATION 129

   D is for... DRIVING 145

   E is for... ENTITLEMENT. 151

   F is for... FAMILY 155

   G is for... GIFTING 160

   H is for... HEAT 169

   I is for... INSECTS 177

   J is for... JOURNAL 183

   K is for... KISSING 189

   L is for... LOVE 195

   M is for... MÉXICO 199

   N is for... NETWORK .207

   O is for... OFF CENTER 213

   P is for... PEOPLE 219

Q is for... QUALITY 223
R is for... RESPECT......................229
S is for... SETTLING IN..................239
T is for... TIPPING 247
U is for... UNDERESTIMATE...............253
V is for... VOLUNTEER...................261
W is for... WORK.........................267
X .... MARKS THE SPOT! 274
Y is for... YOUTH........................278
Z is for... ZERO – ZIP – NADA 285

OUR COUNTRY – OUR STATE – OUR CITY...... 289
OUR COUNTRY – MÉXICO.................. 290
  I: Pre-Columbian México 290
  II: The Colonial period in México............292
  III: The Independence of México 299
  IV: The Mexican Revolution 305
  V: The Era of the PRI in México.............311
  VI: The Twenty-first century in México 315
OUR STATE & OUR CITY – Yucatán & Mérida 319
A TIME LINE OF SIGNIFICANT EVENTS........347
BIBLIOGRAPHY.............................353

The TTT Story 355

ACKNOWLEDGEMENTS...................... 367

JOANNA'S RECOMMENDED READING LIST 369

Have you ever thought about picking up and moving to another country?

Joanna and Jorge Yesterday...

...and Today!

To Jorge

You are here for me always – in every way
I thank you for the life you've shared with me
And for being
Mi amor, mi cómplice en todo…

¡Bienvenidos a México!

H AVE YOU EVER THOUGHT ABOUT picking up and moving to another country? To a place where you could rediscover your passion, learn a new language, meet intriguing people and in a sense, re-invent yourself?

Whether you are contemplating a move to México or have already taken the plunge, *MAGIC MADE IN MEXICO* vividly describes the country and explains its nuances. This information will increase your comfort on many levels. It will allow you to see the humor, revel in the wonder and at the same time, realistically examine the challenges this change of lifestyle will bring to you.

MAGIC MADE IN MEXICO consists of three main sections—each almost a book in itself. It also features a condensed account of how my husband and I started and, although "officially" retired, still successfully run our own business in México.

To further increase your enjoyment and knowledge, a suggested reading list provides the names of other informative and interesting books about the country.

In the first part, "JOANNA'S STORY", you will read about how I met the man who would become my husband and how I moved to México to be with him. That happened more than 35 years ago and in the process I became part of the magic that encompasses this corner of the world. I've lived such amazing adventures and yes, from time to time have struggled with homesickness and cultural clashes. I'm certain that reading about my life will validate some of the doubts you may have and at the same time, will strengthen your resolve to forge a new path and build a completely different, exciting life for yourself.

The second part of the book is a detailed guide that will shed light on many of the cultural shocks you might experience or are already experiencing as you start your new life. "THE ALPHABET" features anecdotes and practical tips that will both increase your appreciation of, and ease your way in adapting to the unique culture and customs of México…from A to Z.

In the third section of this book, "OUR COUNTRY – OUR STATE – OUR CITY", you will find a condensed, concise history of México (and the Yucatán). Many of your questions about pre-Columbian México, the Spanish Conquest, Independence and our Republic up to the modern day will be answered while reading through its easy-to-follow pages. Learning about the past, in turn, will increase your understanding of present-day México.

Settling into life in this very diverse country is full of fun and feistiness. México seduces like a Latin lover, and every day you'll be surprised by the people's warmth and kindness; the vibrant music; delicious cuisine; sultry climate; and vivid colors of this land—a feast for every one of the senses.

I moved to México in 1976—it certainly was a very different place all those years ago. Reading about how my life has evolved will provide you with the time perspective that is necessary to truly understand its day-to-day culture and customs.

I feel lucky to live here. Although I love the country of my birth, here I feel more alive. For me, moving to México was like waking up from a long sleep.

Such a change…at any age…is a very good thing!

México is romantic candlelit nights…

...and long-shadowed afternoons.

Joanna in 1976

JOANNA'S STORY
Chapter 1

I'VE OFTEN WONDERED what would happen if we could recognize pivotal times in our personal journeys—the forks in the road that present themselves. Do we ever see them coming? Does a vague premonition warn us that certain decisions are destined to truly change our path? If we could anticipate these critical junctions, would we have the nerve to follow through?

In 1976, I surely did not sense that my life was about to veer radically off course. I had no idea what lay in store for me for the rest of my days. I ambled along, completely unaware and tumbled headlong through the door that opened.

My home in Vancouver, British Columbia, Canada was near Stanley Park in one of the lovely old ivy covered buildings that have since been torn down to make way for sky scraping glass and concrete towers. Although it seemed small, there was always room in my one bedroom apartment for friends and family who visited on the weekends, and whenever possible I'd drive two hundred miles in my powder blue Honda Civic to see my parents who lived in Princeton, a small interior town. I dated guys I'd meet through girlfriends but at the time, there was no special romantic interest in my life.

A few years previously, I had learned Spanish while teaching English in Peru. I felt lucky that my recently acquired language helped me to land a job with a company that pioneered Canadian tourism packages in Latin America. As part of my customer service position, sometimes I'd be asked to guide familiarization groups of travel agents, journalists and other media types to the company's vacation destinations. I agreed immediately when asked to take thirty people on a seven-day swing through Cuba, followed by six days in Mérida and Guadalajara, México. What a great gig in the middle of the west coast Canadian winter!

Prior to leaving, I remember going shopping with my best friend Mary. "You'd better buy a couple of bikinis," she said. We'd both heard that the beaches were beyond compare in Cuba. I can still remember those two suits, one red and one colorfully striped – both, very daring at the time. "You'll need something sexy for the discos," advised my more experienced friend. A teal blue mini dress and a tropical print halter top with a matching long skirt seemed perfect. Cotton day dresses, tops and skirts; some strappy sandals and two last minute prudent purchases, a beach cover-up and hat—I was ready!

To call the fledgling Cuban tourism industry Spartan would be a generous critique. I had been warned that the usual amenities were probably going to be in short supply, but my many previous travels had not prepared me for what we experienced.

Upon arrival, the Cuban authorities asked for our passports and dollars then exchanged money for us. We held the frayed Cuban currency in our hands and tried to discern why our precious identity documents weren't returned. No satisfactory explanation came forth. The official firmly told us, "Your passports will be returned when you depart Cuba." Everyone on the flight felt somewhat nervous but we all resigned ourselves to the requirement.

Our hotel in downtown Havana provided a trip back in time—all the furnishings, appliances, decoration and (I suspect) the staff, were of early fifties vintage. We always felt we were being watched and in fact, this proved to be true.

At the hotel, I learned of a floor declared: *Prohibido* – out of bounds – but I managed to get a glimpse of it. It was the casino!

Intact since Batista's fall from power, all the gaming tables were draped with frayed velvet coverings and the crystal chandeliers were coated with at least twenty years of dust. My mind filled with images of Hemingway, the mobsters and their platinum blond, baby-doll girlfriends. An elderly elevator attendant sneaked me in there and I asked him if he'd seen the place in its heyday. His bony black body seemed to slump submissively and his ebony eyes became furtive, "No señorita, people like me couldn't come in here."

In Havana, we were not allowed to take city transportation and explore on our own. No out-of-the-way restaurants existed. No tours could be purchased that would take us off the beaten track. Only the government-run tourism stores offered shopping options. No artisan markets, no sidewalk vendors, no private commerce of any kind. Our official Cuban guide, Veronica, accompanied us everywhere. She would count us as we entered the elevator to go to our rooms at night and she'd be waiting patiently when we descended for breakfast the following morning. We began to suspect she slept in the lobby. She took us to see many monuments of *la Revolución,* including a cigar factory where men and women labored in an impossibly hot, humid warehouse-like building, all the while listening to patriotic Cuban music.

During the time we visited, the workers had wide smiles glued on their faces. People on the street would not (could not?) talk to us, and even the children avoided our attempts at making eye contact.

The faces and famous quotations of the world's socialist leaders had prominent places on thousands of gigantic billboards around the city. Day and night, the radio played recorded speeches by Fidel Castro interspersed with Latin rhythms.

Now all this was fine with me. Every country has its own customs and ideology. But for me, the cuisine has always provided a paramount component of traveling, and I felt severely challenged by the food we were served. In Havana, we ate rice & beans…beans & rice…one day we got ham hocks! No one offered us regular coffee or black tea, just chicory or chamomile – *manzanilla* – tea. However, we did have a choice of alcoholic beverages—Cuban beer or Cuban rum. I drank neither of these, so found myself forced to abstain and believe me, I needed a drink! For some odd reason, not even fruit was available.

We spent the second part of our Cuban vacation at a beach development. The brand new property, located in the middle of nowhere, sat smack-dab on one of the most incredible beaches I'd ever seen. Every day at the resort Playa Sur, I tied on one of my new bikinis and strolled for kilometers along the sparkly sand. By the end of the week, all but a few tiny triangles of my formerly aspirin-white skin were toasted to golden brown.

Our group sure couldn't go anywhere *prohibido* from where we stayed (unless we'd had the ability to walk on water all the way to Florida). But good news came at dinner time, the Havana rice & beans rations were a nightmare of the past. We were supremely content after feasting on seafood harvested right from our shore. We delighted in the day and night entertainment provided by excellent Cuban musicians, and by this time I had learned to drink *ron con limón* – rum with lime. Our group swooned and swayed into the wee morning hours.

I had the opportunity to speak with the hotel staff, band members and other people I met. I applauded what they told me about their health care and educational systems and was further pleased by the evidence of social equality I could see all around me. Yet I picked up on their frustration.

Being exposed to western tourists did not encourage blind allegiance to *la Revolución*. Women wanted me to give them my clothing and the men asked for Canadian cigarettes. Human nature is hard to deny; people are people all over the world.

So as interesting and educational as our week had been, none of us regretted getting on board the Mexicana Airlines plane bound for southeastern México.

We cheered out loud when a flight attendant announced, "Once we reach cruising altitude, steaming hot Mexican coffee and complimentary cocktails will be served." Lord be praised! Just what we needed. We relaxed and smiled happily at one another as we flew over the turquoise Caribbean towards our next destination, Mérida, Yucatán.

Arriving in the Yucatecan capital was such a contrast to our previous touchdown. As we disembarked, the sultry tropical air enveloped us like a summer blanket. Smartly uniformed, lacquered-haired Immigration officials greeted us and looked puzzled when I enquired if they'd need to keep our passports. Off to one side, a white-clad guitar trio strummed a romantic welcome. No travel agency representative met us, but a young airline employee assured me the bus waiting on the curb had to be the one we should file onto. We obliged and after a circuitous drive through skinny streets, we were dropped off in the historic center of the city. At the fully-appointed Hotel Mérida, the receptionist promised that our guide would be in the lobby the following morning at 8:30 to take us all to Chichén Itzá, an hour and a half drive from town. We spent the evening walking in the streets and people watching in the plazas. Almost immediately I longed to belong in Mérida. From a pleasant, plump vendor, I bought a big crimson-colored balloon, shaped like a heart and a bag of salty popcorn. I felt that something very magical and meaningful was in store for me in this place.

Chapter 2

IN THE MORNING we assembled in the reception area, then collectively smiled at the handsome man in a red shirt who came rushing through the door. We figured he must be our tour guide. Jorge was his name, and did he do a double take when he saw me! Gazing into my eyes he crooned, *"Estoy a tus ordenes."* – "I am at your service." Things were getting better and better!

Sitting beside him in the bus on the way to the archeological site, I learned that Jorge was single (promising…), had a law degree (how interesting…), and he spoke five languages (Good God!). He had worked for two years in a Mexico City legal firm but missed Mérida and his work as a guide. He returned home and never looked back.

The next three days brought one enchanting surprise after another. Jorge initiated us to the pleasures of México but somehow led us to believe that we were the ones discovering the rare treasures. We devoured delicious Yucatecan delicacies—fragrant *poc chuc* – Yucatecan marinated pork – crispy fried plantains and creamy caramel-topped flan. We imbibed considerable amounts of a wide variety of potent spirits and afterwards were revived by drinking rich, aromatic coffee…gallons of it.

A woman from the group remarked giddily, "You and Jorge are like Suzanne Pleshette and Ian McShane in that movie 'If This Is Tuesday, This Must Be Belgium'." She proved to be right on.

On our last night together, my teal dress and deep Caribbean tan set off blue sparkles in my infatuated eyes and Jorge's chocolate colored ones totally melted. Sitting closely together in a romantic patio restaurant he took my hands, kissed them both and asked, "Do you realize that we are going to get married?"

I nearly fell off my chair and yet, somehow as outlandish as it sounded, I knew what he said had to be true. Flattered but flustered, I mouthed, "How?"

"We'll find a way," he said and kissed me. At that moment, all the prudence I'd once possessed morphed into "the ghost of good sense past".

The following three days in Guadalajara were full of Mariachi music and tasty regional fare: *pozole* – Mexican hominy stew – *tortas ahogadas* – a sandwich on a roll drowned in a piquant sauce – and *churros* – crisp-fried dough sticks served with various sweet accompaniments. I also shopped seriously in the artisan markets of Ajijic and Tlaquepaque (two onyx chess sets and blown glass stemware for eight), but much of the time all I could think of was Jorge and his pronouncement.

Seriously, could I really call it a proposal? On the way home, my arms groaned as I carried my weighty purchases through the long airport corridors. But the load seemed light compared to the heaviness in my heart as each flight took me further and further away from México.

Upon my return to Vancouver, my boss congratulated me. Despite the adverse conditions in Cuba, the group enjoyed the people and the experience. Many of them were spreading the word that Canadians should travel there and to México. This kind of publicity was exactly what the company wanted. I was asked, "Would you consider taking six more back to back groups?"

Six more trips to Cuba? Six more three-day stays in Mérida? *¡Sí, sí, sí!* As I'd be leaving in just two days, there was no way to let Jorge know I'd be returning so soon. I took another shopping trip with Mary and this time purchased souvenir gifts for Jorge—Purdey's chocolates, a Vancouver T-shirt and a Canucks cap. Mary seemed worried, "Are you sure about this?" she asked.

I definitely had big reservations because there didn't seem to be a way to let Jorge know I would be returning to Mérida so soon. In 1976, the Internet could be found only in the pages of science-fiction novels, so the options we had were telegrams that were notoriously unreliable; mail, that was hopelessly slow and telephone calls that were prohibitively expensive.

I figured that if Jorge seemed less than pleased by my surprise arrival, I would have the necessary answers to some hard questions. Maybe I would find he was less than fully available to me? My anxiety knew no limits as I took my new group through the paces in Cuba. The week's scenario mimicked the previous one. I wondered if the Cuban tourism department figured we were all actors in a Kafka play.

Finally the day arrived. I would travel to Mérida again and to my knowledge, Jorge had no idea I was coming. I second-guessed my decision over and over again. What would he think? Would he view me as a naïve girl who believed all his flowery words and made too much of them? Would he be put-off by my almost immediate return? Did I look too eager? I reviewed different scenarios over and over in my head. It seemed like torture to be so unsure! Never in my life had I acted like this…what could I be thinking? During the entire flight from Havana to Mérida my heart pounded.

As I walked through the Customs area I could see into the main terminal and who did I see? I saw Jorge…waving with flowers in hand and blowing kisses! How did he know I'd be here?

I smiled straight into his eyes and walked entranced into his arms. We kissed as my group looked on. They'd heard little confidences about Jorge for a whole week and I know they were as relieved as I that he seemed to be on the level. Once settled, they waved us away, and we went for a long walk along the Paseo de Montejo "boulevard".

"How did you know I was coming?" I asked.

Apparently, just that morning while reading the passenger manifest, he saw my name listed as tour conductor. He confessed to being as overwhelmed as me. Things were certainly moving very fast and yet he sensed our chance meeting had to be destiny at work. "We are meant to be together, it's as simple as that!" said Jorge.

He suggested many scenarios that would help to make this happen but none of them involved him moving to Canada. A true *Meridano* – citizen of Mérida – to the core, he'd lived away once and didn't like it. He really hoped I didn't expect him to uproot his life. Fine with me! I readily agreed to live in México. I well remembered the time I had spent teaching English in Peru. I figured that compared to the services available in that Andean country, México would not be challenging at all. Certainly my future involved a perfect life with Jorge!

While on the city tour that included a stop at the zoo, I watched a couple of swans turning together in perfect circles. I thought they were like Jorge and me. In my besotted state, I grasped only one absolute certainty. I had fallen over-the-top in love. At the time I totally rejected the possibility that any serious difficulties could possibly lie ahead.

Just before Easter I finished with my sixth group. It had been an idyllic three months with me traveling back and forth between México and Cuba. Our time together had certainly fulfilled every one of my romantic fantasies. Now though, decision time loomed. Jorge had seen the light and had begun to consider all the complications coming into our lives. He urged me to honestly and carefully assess the next step. I refused. We were totally in love; what could beat that?

Later in my life, my great friend Jo, whose marriage had a similar start said, "México enhanced everything about our relationship!" I nodded my head and remembered how I told Jorge I would go to Vancouver, say goodbye to my friends and family, quit my job, let go of my apartment, sell my car and be back in a month; which is precisely what I did.

And what did my loved ones make of all this? They tried to dissuade me; they delicately suggested I give this idea more thought, more time and more deliberation. When I wouldn't change my mind, they asked how I would ever manage without my culture, my language, my comforts, etc., etc. With tears in her eyes, my sister Barb asked, "Won't you miss Mom?" That proved very tough to toss aside. I hugged her close. I would miss Mom, I'd miss her, I'd miss them all but was absolutely stone deaf to their pleas.

Finally, one by one, they decided to support me and for this, I will be eternally grateful. They felt somewhat comforted by the few things I had in my favor. As the eldest of eight children, I had learned responsibility at an early age. I'd lived in Latin America before, so I had experience with the culture. I spoke enough Spanish to communicate with people I'd meet and having been raised Catholic, I would have an understanding of this integral part of Mexican life. Knowing they respected me enough to let me go without a scene made my exit much easier and allowed me the security I was certainly going to need in the coming weeks, months and years.

The brothers and sisters I left behind in Canada – 1976

Chapter 3

I FELT LIKE I WAS on a roller coaster! Delirious about being with Jorge again, I likened myself to a romance novel heroine. On that first evening, just as I remembered from previous visits to Yucatán, the heat was diffused by refreshing breezes that swept into the city from the Gulf of México bringing the early evening dew. The moon tipped at a different angle than up north and familiar constellations looked higher in the sky. Fallen Royal Poinciana blossoms carpeted the ground reminding me of saffron. I perceived a tangy smell everywhere.

As I settled in, my sensible side began twigging to the fact that adjusting to life as full time a resident of Mérida would be more than I had allowed myself to consider.

One morning, sleepily rubbing my eyes, I padded bare-footed into the kitchen looking for coffee. I felt something slimy ease between my toes. Confused and distressed, I was confronted by six large white ducks in our living room. They'd wandered over from the neighbor's yard and in through the open back door. Freaked-out by duck droppings—everywhere—I was down on all fours with Clorox™ and a stiff brush. To his credit, Jorge quickly saw he was going to have to help me—and with a lot more than simply cleaning up after the wildlife!

Our little house was tucked away on a quiet street in the García Ginerés neighborhood. Before I got here, Jorge assured me I'd find it fully furnished. And it was...for his needs. A new bed and a cane rocking chair in the master bedroom; no furniture in either of the other bedrooms; a vintage fridge, a miniscule stove, an old wooden table and two mismatched chairs in the kitchen; a Formica-topped dinette suite in the dining room; a lime green couch, two matching armchairs and a cast-off coffee table in the living room. No curtains, no lamps, two towels, no art, no decorations of any kind...and no toilet seat! One set of pink sheets, cutlery, china, and glassware for four, two pots, a can opener, a corkscrew, a cutting board, one knife and oh yes, two hammocks and two ceiling fans! That was the entire household inventory.

Nonplussed, I figured I would soon acquire the other things I'd need. I had no way of knowing that many items I felt were indispensible were hard to come by or terribly expensive. I did manage to overcome the dearth of necessary basics, but parked outside, I spied my Waterloo. Jorge had a brand-new canary-yellow VW bug that he expected me to drive. I had never driven a stick-shift in my life!

I did not want to drive—not ever—not for anything in the world! I quickly learned to take the bus downtown and all the shake, rattle and roll endured on rock-hard bus benches was preferable to putting my life in the hands of all those wannabe Formula One racecar drivers!

I observed that the locals were truly split personalities...so polite...until they got behind the wheel of a vehicle! But Jorge didn't accept my absolutely valid arguments. He cajoled me and finally resorted to bribery. He said if I'd go with him to get my driver's license, afterwards he would buy me whatever I wanted. He assured me the process would be a mere formality; I had a Canadian license, so I'd automatically get one here.

Ha! Not so! "You know I can't drive a standard!" I hissed at him as the officer escorted us to the waiting VW. Reluctantly, I got in—the policeman beside me and Jorge in the back. We lurched and squealed around a few blocks and when we returned to the starting point, the examiner turned to Jorge and said sternly, "You have to let her practice more." Then he smiled at me and said, "You've passed." If it was that easy to get a license, I truly understood why the majority of the people drive badly.

But before long I could maneuver that little bug with the best of them. I mastered all the México moves: I resolutely held my own at intersections, spun around traffic circles and parked any-which-way on any-old-street. Once I got used to it, driving in Mérida wasn't that difficult or scary and many possibilities opened up to me. That sunny Beetle became my ticket to freedom. I could go wherever I wanted to, whenever I chose.

Sometime during my first summer in Mérida, Jorge had to spend the night with a Swiss group in Chichén Itzá. I missed him and thought, *Well Joanna, you could drive there.* I reveled in the mental image I had of myself driving through the Mexican countryside to meet the love of my life...talk about romantic! Delighted with my surprise visit, Jorge encouraged me to do this again and arriving spontaneously became somewhat of a pattern during my first months of living in México. I saw wonderful places and met literally hundreds of memorable characters, including Jorge's fellow guides, the hotel employees, the bus drivers and the workers at the archaeological sites.

Three and a half decades later, I can remember some of those people as clearly as if I'd seen them yesterday. Marisol, the electric blue-eyed bus driver; Catherine, a Swiss tour conductor who said she kept fit chasing Italian men through the Alps and Jack Sosa, a senior guide who counseled me like a father.

There was great camaraderie amongst the group and I soon became accepted as one of them. My Spanish kept improving, although later on I'd realize how poor it still was. Once I confused the word *cebolla* – onion – with *caballo* – horse – and asked the perplexed waitress for some French Horse Soup.

In those days, travel in México presented an experience and a half! The roads were very, very narrow and bumpy at best. The buses belonged in a classic car museum and if they had air-conditioning, it was really rudimentary. In fact, every time the vehicle would take a curve, ice-cold water spilled out of the AC drip pan and soaked the unsuspecting persons sitting in the vicinity – we always knew what was happening when we heard, "Ee-ee-ee-eek-k-k-k!" coming from the back.

The archaeological sites were not nearly as restored and maintained as they are now but you could climb anywhere and explore every nook and cranny. On the ground, Jorge often spied small pottery shards and once, a Mayan mother-of-pearl button in the shape of a flower.

The amenities were minimal. Even at Chichén Itzá, the major tourism destination, a simple hut served as the entrance/ticket booth. You had to pay to use the grungy washroom but no toilet paper or soap was ever provided. I carried my own, just as experienced Mexican travelers still do today.

The only two commercial enterprises were a Coca-Cola™ stand that stocked chips as well as soft drinks and a dusty curio shop.

The ocean waters, both on the Gulf and the Caribbean, ranged in hue from emerald green to bright turquoise. Again,

Jorge at Chichén Itzá in 1976

a Coca-Cola™ stand and some sort of makeshift bathroom area comprised all of the facilities at most destinations.

Sometimes, on the beaches, an enterprising fisherman would gather up dried coconuts and fronds, build a fire and prepare part of his catch for the privileged tourists who were on hand that day. Swaying palm trees, strong surf, white sand, blazing sun, cold beer and grilled-to-order snapper. The memories of those days still make my mouth water, my heart gallop and my hormones soar! We were young; we were in love and life tasted good—very good!

We traveled often to the villages. Nearly all of the women still wore the traditional *huipil* – a white cotton shift with bands of brightly colored embroidery around the neck and hem. The dwellings were thatch-roofed. The people we met were gracious and laid-back. They had such dignity and generosity. Many would actually invite Jorge and his groups into their homes to show them the way of life in rural Yucatán. Some tourists came away saying, "Oh, those poor villagers look how they live!" But most were impressed with the ingenuity, simplicity, and the sweetness of their lifestyle. Foreigners absolutely loved Yucatán; not many complained about the heat or any other discomfort. As long as they were provided with a good bed, a tasty meal and a couple of margaritas at the end of the day, they were happy.

The late seventies marked the end of México's romantic tourism era. In those days everything the tourists saw was served to them, à la mexicana – with Mexican flair. The amenities and services were simple but tasteful and no one ever worried about personal security, not even for a second! Fresh flowers, not big screen televisions, brightened the hotel rooms and the staff was accommodating, never condescending. The guides were educated gentlemen and the shopkeepers provided the visitors with items and souvenirs they wanted, without gouging them. Most vacationers seemed informed, polite and respectful. Many had read a lot about México before coming and their manners were lovely. They felt like ambassadors of their home countries. I feel very blessed to have witnessed and participated in the Mexican tourism industry's *época de oro* – the golden age.

Chapter 4

FROM THE BEGINNING, we always had lots of company from abroad. Jorge welcomed them all and many years later, he still does. In 1976 my best friend Mary and her husband Rick came "on inspection". The four of us spent three amazing weeks together.

Being with Canadian friends again made me feel lonesome for more of the same, but the visit did much to allay Mary's worries about Jorge, the mystery man who had swept me away to México. I didn't want to reignite her anxiety because of a little homesickness.

Later, I was glad that I didn't confide my concerns because as soon as she returned to Vancouver she was on the phone reassuring everyone we knew that I was indeed very much in love, and that Jorge was all I'd said he was.

My sister Anne had just finished high school and also came to see us that year. She was the first family envoy, and she also went home to Canada with positive reports.

When there was a lull in Jorge's schedule, we would sometimes take the opportunity to visit other nearby places. I particularly remember our first trip to Isla Mujeres. To get there we had to drive for six hours through about twenty-five small villages. The highway felt similar to washboard roads that connect Canadian backwater towns. Hot and tired, we stopped in several of the *pueblos* – villages – for oranges, soft drinks, anything to quench our thirst! At the time, all of these hamlets looked much alike.

Usually, an impressive seventeenth century Catholic church and much less imposing *presidencia* – town hall – faced a dusty plaza. A community water well, a tortilla mill and a small store or two made up the business district. Oval-shaped, thatch-roof homes were grouped in family compounds and a colourful *campo santo* – graveyard – lay on the outskirts of town.

I cried at the sight of many mangy, hungry dogs and laughed with the throngs of curious half-naked children. Shy women dressed in brightly embroidered huipiles and men stretched out in hammocks, taking their siestas – life seemed to be completely on hold.

We also visited Cancún, but since it was in the first stages of development, it just looked like a huge construction site.

As a new tourist resort development, it received lots of press, especially because much of the land was owned by México's politicians and their cronies. Hotels and golf courses, shopping centers and marinas were all part of the grand scheme. In 1976 three hotels were finished and open for business; others were nearing various stages of completion. Everything was booked solid for the Christmas season. I wondered what the future occupants of the still-in-progress properties would say if they could see what I was seeing?

A hideous shanty town that housed the workers had sprung up outside of the tourism zone. Some of Jorge's guide friends had moved there in order to be part of the boom. They were buying up available land in the hopes that one day it would be worth a bundle. I determined I would not like to live in Cancún. It seemed such a plastic place, as though taped together. Little did any of us imagine it would become what it is today!

We drove another ten kilometers along the palm-lined coast to Puerto Juárez and caught the ferry to Isla Mujeres. It had grown dark by this time and we opted to lie out on the deck, under the canopy of stars. The sultry Caribbean breeze, the phosphorescence and the crystal-clear sea reflecting all those stars, the gentle rocking of the boat and Jorge beside me...I wondered if this could be Heaven or what? Times like this were intoxicating but not a reality we could sustain. Both Jorge and I knew I'd have to get on with developing the life I had envisioned several months back. This proved to be a lot more than I'd reckoned with.

Summer in Mérida always felt scorching and humid. Sometimes, when a breeze blew, someone would mention that it was "cool". What were they talking about? The heat just never let up. I hardly had the energy to get through the daily cleaning, cooking and shopping. There were bugs everywhere and within half an hour dust seemed to settle on every recently polished surface. The newly-planted garden needed hand-watering, and since I had no washing machine, I did the laundry at Jorge's mother's house. It quickly became apparent that this full-time *ama de casa* – housewife – routine was not going well. I felt frustrated with just housekeeping. I wanted to work, be with people and earn money! When a friend of Jorge's brother offered me a job teaching English at a secretarial college, I danced for joy!

La Academia had been a Mérida fixture for decades and taught all the skills necessary for employment in an office. The owners—two buxom, middle-aged sisters—definitely seemed more practical than pedagogic. They gave me no course outline or syllabus. I had to simply wing it in the classroom. In the face of this, I took the approach that the students would tell me what they needed to know, and I'd provide the instruction. This actually worked very well. I really liked the girls and they adored me.

After some more experience with México's very structured educational system, I understand why they enjoyed my impromptu classes. But the sisters didn't appreciate our boisterous back-and-forth sessions and soon presented me with a volume entitled, *English for Bilingual Secretaries*. (*Lesson One: A Dialogue: "María, I will dictate now!" – "Immediately Mr. López; I am at your command."*)

I was expected to impart this outdated material and to make a long story short; it was the beginning of the end. My teaching career seemed to be over in one semester. Or so I thought.

It didn't take much time for the word to spread that I would give *clases particulares* – private classes. Few native English speakers lived in Mérida, and I soon had an eclectic array of students – young children, housewives and businessmen. I did some translation; I made crafts and baking for sale. Friends and neighbors liked my banana bread, carrot cake, apple pie and other home-style Canadian goodies. I made an income and had something to fill my days but this was a far cry from the career I'd envisioned. I wanted to work for an airline or as a tour guide or as a hotel rep., but without permanent residence papers (that took ten years to get) these jobs were unavailable to me. Except for being a tour guide, it's much easier today.

Despite my frustration with the work situation, I found myself adapting to my surroundings and new people kept coming into my life.

Antonia, the cleaning lady, assisted me with a lot more than keeping the house in order. I had no experience with domestic help and she had no knowledge of non-native Yucatecans. Antonia looked very small. I wondered how she'd be able to reach high enough clean my house? Easy—she cleaned what she could reach, and the rest she forgot about.

About thirty-five years old when she came to work with me, she'd already lost many of her teeth and lacked a good bit of her hair in front. Her weathered skin and lined face showed that she was accustomed to long, hard labor under the hot Yucatecan sun. Home was a one-room *chosa* – a palm-thatched hut – in the nearby village of Cholul, where she lived with her husband and two daughters.

We had quite a time training one another. She did things pueblo-style. I did not feel satisfied with that but could not get her to understand what I needed; she seemed to be completely unable to comprehend my Spanish unless it was to her advantage. But little by little we worked things out and began to accommodate ourselves to one another. I felt honored when she requested I be *la madrina* – the godmother – at her daughter's Confirmation. I attended the *fiesta del pueblo* – a big party her village held every year – and she invited me to her cousin's wedding. She prepared hand-made tortillas and taught me how to cross-stitch. Antonia also showed me how tough a poor woman's life is and made me feel very grateful for the many privileges I mistakenly thought were my rights.

There was little time for fun in her life, and with an unhappy look on her face she showed her disapproval of my penchant for entertainment. She said I acted like *una niña rica* – a little rich girl.

I protested about this to an acquaintance who asked, "Do you have more than one pot, one towel, and one plate?"

"You know I do!" I answered hotly.

Holding up her hands with a resigned gesture, my new friend said, "Then to her, you are rich!"

Material comforts aside, I was rica in many other ways as well. I had an education, knew my rights and knew I would be listened to with respect in stores, offices and by the authorities.

Antonia did not receive the same treatment. She had never been to school and couldn't read or write; she had to wait while patrons with more status were served first and when a pickpocket stole her change purse the police made light of her pleas. Antonia taught me to be very grateful for my accident of birth. Since meeting her, I am keenly aware of my fortune.

Antonia taught me to be very grateful for my good fortune – 1978

Chapter 5

TO JORGE'S FAMILY I remained an enigma. They were most pleased he showed signs of settling down. After all, he had turned thirty-two and never been married. But did he have to be interested in me? They couldn't get their heads around my unconventional ways. I acted too young and too carelessly and failed to recognize that much of what I did seriously affronted established Mexican traditions. The correct way of doing anything would usually be prefaced with the expression, "*Es costumbre...*" – "It's customary to..." Usually, if I heard those two words strung together, I'd dig my heels in.

I now feel embarrassed when I remember the way I dressed. Short wrap-around skirts, tube tops, a puka shell choker or peace sign pendant and flat sandals were as much as I could bear in the heat. To Jorge's family I looked very unacceptable to say the least. In their opinion, I did not know how to behave. I refused to sit with the women at parties (all they talked about were *telenovelas* – Mexican style soap operas – or the problems with their maids and their children.) I preferred sitting with Jorge and the men. Not socially correct behavior. Worse yet, I did not like going to Jorge's parents' house for lunch every Sunday. I wanted to be alone with him and do our own thing.

Again I was rejecting the habits of most established Mexican families. I only went to Mass on the occasional Sunday. I dared go to the store, pay bills and even go to the movies unaccompanied. They couldn't believe I'd never heard of chaperones until I came to live in México. And the final affront? I spent far too much money fixing up the house; money that Jorge no longer generously handed over to his brothers and their families.

Obviously my living arrangements with Jorge were also very frowned upon in 1976. In fact it was such a quantum leap for everyone that the subject entered the realm of, "Things we just won't talk about." It wasn't what we preferred, but I felt I couldn't get married before being reasonably sure I would be able to adapt to living in México.

Of course most people couldn't begin to fathom why I thought this was even an issue! They figured I'd moved to Paradise; what was I thinking? I agree with them now, I did move to Paradise, but it didn't seem that way to me at the time. I felt strongly that if we married before I was ready, I'd feel trapped and become resentful. I knew myself well enough to be certain that such feelings would be the beginning of the end.

Looking back, I know I should have been more culturally aware but I was young, just twenty-three. To my mother-in-law's credit, she always acted in a pleasant way when I was a guest in their home. But in my absence, open season resumed, and I was the main topic of gossip between her and the other women in her world.

They saw me as an exotic. México had very established social conventions, and in those days Yucatán's population showed little tendency towards ever changing. Few people from other parts of

México had settled here, much less foreigners. But Jorge's friends seemed to enjoy getting to know me and I certainly liked having other people around.

The wife of one of Jorge's friends, Amira, came from Belize and spoke English. I felt grateful for her company, but despite sharing a language, our lives were worlds apart. I needed to talk with someone who understood my points of reference. Sixteen months passed before I actually met another native English speaker. Lynne came from California and had little time to spare on the day we started speaking in the aisle of the little grocery store. When she turned to leave, I wanted to hang onto her ankles and not let her go!

I felt closed-in by all the formality in Mérida. When I'd meet new people, they would always ask the same questions:

"Do you like Mérida?" (¡Sí, mucho! being the appropriate answer.)

"Can you tolerate the heat?" (I'm adapting!)

"What about the mosquitoes?" (Now really, what nice comment can you make about venomous insects that leave huge welts all over your body?)

The drill seemed always the same. I told Jorge I should pass out my bio every time we went somewhere new. I missed the way Canadian men and women banter easily back and forth and I felt irritated by some of the women's scornful scowls. "They're just jealous." Jorge would say. Now I realize they thought I acted too forward.

Generally speaking, Mexicans are very warm people but they have to get to know you first. One well-meaning dowager aunt advised me, "Strangers are suspect and you need to be more prudent!" With my natural curiosity and my enthusiasm, this presented a tall order indeed.

As much as I loved the archaeological sites and going to the beach I also enjoyed late nights, dancing, drinks.... Mérida, the one city of any size in all of south-eastern México, had lots of nightclubs but not like I was used to. Yet there was one I really liked. I think the Barry Manilow song, "Copa Cabana"—you know, "Her name was Lola, she was a showgirl..."—could have been written for our favorite nightspot, El Aloha, atop the Hotel Montejo Palace. The first time I went there with Jorge was to celebrate getting my driver's license. A great dance band played, and the line of coochie-coochie chorus girls surprised me when they stripped down to pasties and g-strings.

Big Mexico City headliners came to play. I saw Emanuel, Napoleon and other favorite recording artists. Though an evening there broke our budget, we made a point to go as often as possible. I wish it was still open because it was just too much fun!

There was also an amateur theater group, and we looked forward to their performances. The director, Eric Renato, and our favorite cast member, José Antonio López Lavalle, always made sure we got good seats at Teatro El Mural in the Hotel Panamericana.

Right through into the eighties our city had, at most, five international restaurants. Our favorite was Alberto's Continental Patio. The flamboyant owner, Alberto Salum, knew everyone there was to know in México's entertainment and tourism industries, and we'd often dine in the company of the country's most innovative artists.

The regal Teatro Peón Contreras, down on its luck, had been turned into a billiard hall. Many of the elegant mansions on Paseo de Montejo and in the historical center were also in bad repair, covered by creepers and garbage. I never imagined it would be possible to restore them to their former glory.

We had one large grocery store (Gran Komesa) and a few smaller ones like Rosales. Almost all my shopping happened in the outdoor city markets. I enjoyed the markets but I longed for the convenience of American-style supermarkets.

The plethora of the cultural activities Mérida has now were in very short supply then, but first-run English-language films played in the many cinemas. We escaped to the air-conditioned theaters a lot!

I recall the night we watched "Close Encounters of the Third Kind". As we exited the theater, the Milky Way blazed brightly across our night sky. Jorge looked upwards and began to hum the tunes we heard all through the film, "Dah-dah-dah...dah-ah... dah-dah-dah...." I smiled and felt a bond with Richard Dreyfus and all the others who'd been looking for something elusive all through the film. Like them, I'd found my special place. It was not always an easy space to be in but I increasingly knew it was the right one for me.

Chapter 6

THE LACK OF PLENTIFUL ENTERTAINMENT compelled us to improvise our own. We invited friends over, and Jorge's family visited frequently. They often appeared unexpectedly—people thought nothing of just popping by. They didn't call first because few of us had phones—Jorge and I were on a waiting list for four years before we finally got one! If someone came over, you dropped what you were doing and made them feel welcome.

Jorge explained that of all the rude things I might mistakenly do, the worst would be my failure to extend a full welcome to whoever came to our door. It didn't matter what I might be doing or what I had plans to do. He said Mexicans feel it's unpardonable not to be a good host.

Sometimes, we would invite people over and to my extreme annoyance they wouldn't show up. He'd tell me later they couldn't come because someone dropped by to see them – "*Me cayó visita.*" – and to say they had another engagement would in fact be like saying, "I prefer to spend time with other people...so away you go!" Even after his explanation, I had great difficulty with this concept. I also judged the Mexican custom of showing up two or even three hours later than the appointed time, to be equally strange. How many ruined dinners I served in those days!

An English class or two during the mornings; writing letters to my mother, sisters, and friends; cleaning some more after Antonia had finished and reading paperbacks were my main pastimes. Jorge usually spent the day guiding and the weeks stretched out...I felt lonely sometimes. But his mother did provide a diversion I blessed her for. She taught me new ways to cook. In my previous life, I'd considered myself to be reasonably accomplished in the kitchen but in Mérida, I couldn't get many of the ingredients I needed for my tried-and-true recipes. On top of this, Jorge couldn't eat dairy products, so I had to change much of my repertoire.

México's reputation for fire-hot food is somewhat exaggerated. In Yucatán the cuisine tastes very flavorful but it is not all that spicy – hot. To liven things up, cooks do use some dynamite chiles called *habaneros*. These are almost always made into a sauce and served on the side, so you can choose to singe your throat or not! Jorge's mother, Doña Bertha took justified pride in her reputation as an excellent regional cook and seemed pleased to teach me her way around *la cocina* – the kitchen.

I learned how to make typical dishes like *Frijol con Puerco* – Beans and Pork (do not confuse this with the mushy brown stuff that comes in a can); *Chancletas de Berenjena* – Pork-stuffed Eggplant; *Pescado Ticinxic* – Annatto Seasoned Fish Baked in Banana Leaves and *Pollo en Escabeche* – Chicken in a Savory Onion & Garlic Broth. The food is delicious and wholesome. She never touched packaged seasoning mixes, canned goods or anything that had not been bought fresh that very day. I really liked the cooking lessons. They provided Doña Bertha and me with a non-conflicting setting and helped us establish some rapport.

I wanted to learn from Doña Bertha, and she worked very hard to understand me, but we had so little in common. She had been raised to obey her father and then give the same allegiance to her husband. Her life involved service to her family and she felt totally happy with this. Admirable, but in no way could I become just like her. I wanted to make her son happy but when he wasn't around, I needed to have other distractions and activities.

She thought I acted very spoiled and it irritated her that I needed constant entertainment. She would tell me that I should learn to be *tranquila* – calm – and that I should learn to *aguantar* – to put up with things. Just hearing her say that would make my blood boil!

However, I did work at **seeming** to conform. "*Sí, Doña Bertha*," I'd say when she wanted me to do things in a certain way. As soon as she left I'd turn around and reestablish my way. I know we both tried, but neither of us could change how we felt; and that usually seemed like polar opposites.

Doing laundry at Jorge's mom's house a couple of times a week was truly a Herculean task. She had an automatic washer but first she insisted I scrub every single piece of clothing with bar laundry soap (Jabón Zote™); soak the whites in bleach and boil the kitchen linens in borax! My hands were like dry parchment after one of these sessions.

The wicker basket of extremely clean, dripping laundry then had to be balanced on my right hip as I climbed a precarious ladder to the roof, where everything was hung to dry. The items needed to be very securely pinned on or they'd quickly fly away. The wind blew really strongly up there!

On laundry day I would also go with her to the main city market. What an adventure! We would head off four blocks up the street, each carrying two empty *sabucanes* – Maya for shopping bags. In Yucatán, Mayan words and expressions are used in everyday speech; just as Náhuatl ones pepper the central and northern Mexican lexicon.

We'd always be greeted upon our arrival by a young boy, Manuelito, whose broad smile showed his excitement at seeing Doña Bertha. Out of the depths of her purse, she'd pull out a huge napkin-wrapped meat sandwich or some other food item.

The poor boy would devour whatever she gave him. She'd smile and tell him to look for us again in an hour or so. This is one thing my mother-in-law did successfully teach me—the importance of kindness and charity. Doña Bertha could not tolerate seeing anyone in need. Her kitchen table often had hungry strangers sitting around it and she unfailingly made them feel like welcome guests.

The market excursion always began with her errands. Often she needed to pick up something from the shoemaker, the merchant who repaired metal pots, the lady who sold natural beeswax candles or the flower sellers. In the produce section, we bought onions, chilies, garlic, peppers, tomatoes, other vegetables and luscious fruits such as pineapple, papaya, *marañon* – cashew fruit (we make juice out of the fleshy fruit to which the nut is attached. The nut itself is encased in a thick skin and is poisonous until roasted) – and *zapote* – sapodilla, a native Yucatán fruit now grown world-wide in the tropics.

Then we'd move on to the spices & herbs: *achiote* – annato – *cilantro* – fresh coriander leaves – *yerbabuena* – fresh mint, etc. She liked to purchase other ingredients like smoked ham, spicy sausage and beans or grains from a special *marchante* – a vendor in the market. Our last stop (my least-favorite) was to the meat, fish and fowl.

There, on display, lay whole fish with bulging eyes and red-red gills. A few stalls over were chickens hanging from poles with their heads still attached and entrails oozing out. Still further along slabs of pork, beef, and organ meats were laid on open counters and sometimes there would be venison or other game. The flies swarmed all over the place and the smell…*¡Díos mío!* Doña Bertha didn't seem to take any notice of the blood and entrails, and I tried to be equally stalwart.

However, it was extremely trying for me because I could see no evidence of refrigeration, or standards of cleanliness and food sanitation in the meat displays of the market. Doña Bertha claimed that as long as we bought early enough in the day, all would be well. She knew I wasn't convinced that she was right but I had to admit no one ever got sick from any kind of food poisoning in her house. Nonetheless, I seriously considered becoming a vegetarian and I certainly wasn't going to buy any meat to take to my house. I would continue to patronize the butcher in the town's one and only sizable supermarket.

Fortunately, food handling has improved greatly since my early days in México. If I choose, I can now buy FDA approved cuts of meat at our nearby Costco! Eventually the meat ordeal would end, and at this point, our bags groaning, Manuelito would miraculously reappear. Doña Bertha would give him a few *centavos* and he would heft the bags in his two spindly arms and carry them to a waiting *calesa*. We'd get up into the horse-drawn taxi and clip-clop back to the house.

We usually conversed somewhat but never about anything of much importance. By now I'd learned that most members of my husband's family are not big communicators. They quite honestly prefer to ignore unpleasantness and controversy. This was their way and I tried to be accepting. Later I discovered that this was typical of nearly **all** Mexicans.

However, I wished that Doña Bertha could realize how I felt…so much seemed to go right over my head. For example: women's attitudes. I tried hard to comprehend how husbands, children and family were absolutely their whole world. They didn't seem to want to travel, except to Miami for shopping… they loved that! They had no interest in a career, just a job until such time as they married. And they never went out without a chaperone! It seemed that every female in Mérida knew just how to behave in any given situation…everyone but me.

I must say though, Doña Bertha would explain when she realized I might not be catching what was going on. But, much of the time it never occurred to her that I wouldn't be in the know. At festive events, the expectation was for me to be an active (and socially appropriate) participant. My first *Quince Años* party turned out to be just such an occasion.

Chapter 7

THE ENTIRE EXTENDED FAMILY (ages: three months to ninety-one years) received an embossed invitation to a *Quince Años*. I knew this signified a special occasion—a birthday party for a fifteen-year-old girl named Martha, who somehow belonged to the family. We left at 7:30 p.m. and after driving out of town, we arrived at a church. A church! What were we doing at a church I wondered? Not wanting to appear ignorant (again), I opted to say nothing and trooped in with the family.

Yellow and white flowers festooned the immense church. They hung everywhere—on the altar, up the aisles and trailing down from the chandeliers. Yellow ribbons and white lace streamers adorned everything that could be nailed down.

The congregation, dressed in jewels, sequins, brocade and satin made me feel out of place in my tropical print halter top dress and go-go beads! I wanted to ask Jorge what we were doing here, but he had sneaked out of the church and joined a few of his brothers and male cousins who were standing around outside. It appeared perfectly acceptable for the men to do this during any religious ceremony, but the ladies, no way! So I sat there with all the other women and children.

The choir began to sing and everyone stood up to turn and look towards the back of the church. In came Martha, walking alone, dressed in the most magnificent yellow chiffon, high-necked, puffy-sleeved, bell-skirted dress I'd ever seen. She wore a twinkling rhinestone tiara in her upswept ebony hair and carried a small bouquet of yellow sweetheart roses. She looked beautiful, in a Barbie doll kind of way. As she passed by, I heard unmistakable oo-oos, ah-ahs and other sounds of full approval. I looked to the front to see if there was a groom. No, this appeared to be a groom-less ceremony. What the heck were we all watching?

As the ceremony progressed, I realized this Mass indeed celebrated Martha on the occasion of her fifteenth birthday. The priest said, "Martha has reached the age of illusions." I could sure see that! Now that she was no longer a child her parents wished to present their daughter to society. They beamed, she beamed, everyone beamed, so I beamed too; what else could I do? Remember, I needed to strive for socially appropriate behavior.

Once the religious celebration had finished, Martha placed her bouquet at the feet of the statue of *La Virgen de Guadalupe,* the patron saint of México. I watched as she crossed herself and the tears welled in her eyes. She had a beatific smile on her face. It touched me to see her so happy.

Soon I caught up with Jorge outside, who far-too-belatedly explained the Quince Años tradition. In México it is almost a sacred duty for parents to throw as huge a party as possible for their daughters when they reach the age of fifteen. He told me that while Martha's parents could well afford this celebration, many families incur serious debt in order to do so.

He told me about a village family he knows. They raised four pigs and twelve turkeys and then slaughtered them all for the feast in honor of their fifteen-year-old daughter. The entire clan willingly went for months without any meat on the table, so as to be able to afford great quantities of it on her special day.

The mother and her daughter, the aunts, sisters and the grandmothers spent months planning the affair. No detail escaped their full attention. They ordered an elaborate dress; chose jewelry, hairstyles, makeup and nail polish; they debated the color scheme and decided on the guest list. The young girl chose her music, and she practiced endlessly with her friends— she wanted her dance to be perfect. Mamá carefully thought out the menu. As well as the food, Papá bought *aguardiente* – raw sugarcane liquor – in prodigious amounts for the men who would attend the party.

Bewildered neophytes have often asked me about the Quince Años ceremony. When seeing this fiesta for the first time, many are dumbfounded by what they perceive as excess and extravagance. How can families who have so little, spend so much money on a girl's birthday party?

I feel fortunate that my friend Susi explained the whole tradition to me. She comes from Mexico City and says the tradition is the same all over the country. When she talked about her own Quince Años, she described it as nothing short of magical. "Many times, this is the one night in a woman's life when she is truly special. The birthday girl is a queen, a goddess—she's like a movie star!"

Susi went on to say that as little as a year after the big event, many girls are married and pregnant. From this point onwards, they'll permit themselves no illusions—their lives will be hard. Seen in this context, she asked, "Isn't it important that a woman has at least one occasion that she can look back on and remember that she was outstanding?"

For the families, the night is equally special. They look upon the extravaganza with pride and feel the satisfaction that comes from doing something out of the ordinary for their child. It is difficult not to be critical when we witness what looks like poor judgment but the Quince Años is a time-honored institution. It may be modified over the years but it will not disappear.

Now, back to Martha's Quince Años: from the church we drove to an elegant reception facility. I had never been there before and could see most of the others were also new at this. Yet nothing short of splendid would do on this day; in we filed as though we did so every day of the week. Here again, more is better seemed the predominant theme. The banquet room, set up for at least five hundred people, glowed golden. Yellow and white flowers, ribbons, lace and swan-shaped centerpieces adorned every flat surface. As we entered, the band played soft background music.

An hour or so later the rhythm changed and a classical violin recording filled the room. In came Martha, this time accompanied by six young men in tuxedos! They danced a choreographed waltz that lasted at least fifteen minutes. Once more lots of approving sounds came from all the ladies gathered together. The swains left the floor; Martha stood alone curtsying for a full minute, and then her father took his place at her side. More violins, more waltzing...following the proud papa, all the other men at the party, including Jorge, took their turn dancing with the radiant birthday girl. She was having, literally, the time of her life! With my newly acquired insight, I felt great affection for sweet Martha.

Meanwhile conversation took the usual turns. The women, all congregated at one end of the table, spoke of their children, difficulties with the maids, the intricate plot of the currently popular soap opera and they gossiped about all the other women they knew who didn't happen to be present. As usual, I contributed nothing because I had no experience with anything they enjoyed talking about. They figured I didn't understand Spanish, and I let it go at that. I'd tired of trying to introduce other topics.

The men, at the other end of the table, laughed and carried on about the good old days, local political scandals, current movies, and they too gossiped about all the other men they knew who weren't there. Jorge and I had worked out a system. I would sit at the far end of the ladies' enclave and he would sit at the junction of the two groups; this way we would be seated next to each other and yet neither of us was out of bounds, so to speak.

Needless to say, I didn't find the evening's conversation in either camp to be very stimulating. I wanted Jorge to take me home.

"No", he said. "We can't go until after the meal has been served, it would be very rude."

My wristwatch read 1 a.m. by this point and I felt hungry and tired. All of a sudden, the band changed tempo. Food time, I wondered? No such luck…

Martha appeared again with the six boys. This time they all sported tight, bright outfits and danced to a medley of popular disco tunes. They performed very well.

Although it could not have been her parents' intention, when Martha changed from her demure yellow chiffon creation into a foxy, hot pink double knit jumpsuit for the disco number, every male mind shifted into overdrive!

A murmuring of hearty approval ran throughout the crowd. This number took a good half hour and I began to wonder if her father would also participate? (What a sight that would be!) But the dance finished and the waiters brought out the dinner.

What a meal! It looked like a buffet on a plate: three meats, two salads, a rice pilaf, two savory pastries and garnishes. Everyone dug in with gusto! The three-tiered cake was cut and served. What a cake! It was called *Torta del Cielo* – Cake from Heaven. Never was anything more aptly named.

La Quinceañera – 1976

Chapter 8

MY FIRST CHRISTMAS IN MÉXICO was not lonely because my aunt came to stay with me for a month. Auntie Missy had recently lost her husband and we kept each other's spirits buoyed. We had some great laughs, especially when cooking the Christmas turkey. My friend from Belize was very keen for us to prepare a traditional Canadian Christmas feast; she said she'd get the turkey and we could cook it at her home.

This all sounded good but when we asked her how big the bird was, she said, "You'd better come and see it." We did and found it gobble-gobble-gobbling out in her backyard! I knew nothing about killing a turkey but Amira quickly reassured me it would be all ready for us on December 24th.

On the appointed day, we showed up with the ingredients for stuffing, mashed potatoes and "all the fixings". The turkey indeed seemed dead, but Amira had not set it...the wings and legs were sticking straight out. We couldn't believe it! We had to break the limbs and truss mightily, in order to get that stuffed turkey into the roaster. Nevertheless, it turned out very tasty and I have prepared the "Canadian Christmas Feast in México" every year since then. It is one of our great family traditions.

As the months slipped by Jorge and I found we'd grown more and more devoted. We understood the challenges we faced, but we were both certain it would be impossible to live without each other. On Valentine's Day 1977, Jorge gave me a ring, a baroque pearl surrounded by small diamonds and he formally asked me to marry him. My answer was an unequivocal *"¡Sí!"*

Extending my left arm, turning my hand at different angles, I admired my gorgeous ring. I felt every obstacle we had before us would somehow be overcome and our life together would be perfect. Jorge said, "I am absolutely crazy in love with you." I believed him totally and looking back, I can see that if we hadn't started right there—with crazy love and a total desire to make each other happy—things would have been very, very different.

However, many practicalities needed to be addressed. The legal prerequisites for my eventual permanent residency papers included a civil marriage, the only legally binding one in México. We decided this could be held in Mérida in late May.

Both our families wanted a Catholic ceremony and, even though Jorge and I weren't regular attendees at Mass, we also wanted a traditional Church ceremony. We decided to have the religious wedding in Canada in July.

Little did we realize the bureaucratic nightmare we stood poised to embark upon. At the time, a foreigner needed "permission" to marry a Mexican citizen; something still true, but more easily handled at local offices of *Migración* – the Mexican immigration office – today. There were endless forms, affidavits, testimonials, blood tests and X-rays. When everything had been gathered, compiled, and stamped—many, many times—we sealed the two inch thick envelope, mailed it to the Immigration office in Mexico City and the wait began.

The Catholic Church also required that banns be posted, and we committed to attending the prenuptial gathering with other engaged couples. The fortyish husband and wife team who led the marriage course had sensible advice to pass along. The three sessions placed little emphasis on religious aspects and focused on how we could be positive role models for future children, who we promised would be raised Catholic.

Future children? This started sounding a little scary. It began to really dawn on me that I would soon be making a life commitment. There would be no more abstract plans for the coming years; a permanent pledge would be made. I could no longer view my move to México as a romantic fairy tale.

At what point had this turned serious? Yes, I felt very nervous, and Jorge actually suggested that maybe we should just leave things as they were. We both stood quietly for a while but then he took a deep breath and declared that the marriage needed to happen. We loved one another so much; surely we'd be able to overcome the jitters we both had?

In March, my parents came for a visit. Prior to this they had never taken an international trip together and it was certainly a testimonial of their love and concern for me.

Dad had always said, "If you've seen British Columbia, you've seen the best there is; why would you want to go anywhere else?" But before the wedding(s) they had to meet Jorge and see where I'd be living. Then they'd be able to feel more confident that getting married was the right decision for me.

After nearly a year without seeing my mom, I totally lost my composure when she and Dad arrived at the airport...all I could do was cry and this certainly didn't do too much to reassure my parents! I hung onto my mother and once again wondered if this rollercoaster I rode was good for me. Then I saw Jorge's concerned face and knew that I needed to go over to him. I regretfully let go of Mommy and took his hand. No one seemed very comfortable.

By the next day my emotions had come into line and Jorge diverted any more possible tears by taking us on a city tour that ended up at the Café Colón for coconut ice cream. We visited a different place every day, but my parents were mostly interested in getting to know Jorge's family, seeing our house, walking around town and meeting our friends. My father-in-law-to-be spoke excellent English and took on the responsibility of showing my parents that I was in good hands.

My mother expressed some dismay over how bare our home was. What if she'd seen it ten months earlier! Since moving into the place, I had added items (mostly small) and features daily—posters, pillows, curtains, folk art, plants, a little furniture and yes, a toilet seat! The house gradually took on some more personality and although it could not be called elegant, I didn't think it looked bare.

Mom also commented on how complicated the simple chores like washing dishes seemed to be. "You have a lot to take in here," she told me. It made me realize that I no longer required all the stuff I'd seemed to need in my former life. I liked this about myself.

"Mom" I said, "To be happy we don't really need electric juice squeezers, dish washers and air conditioning...do we?"

She looked wise and hugged me, "Not now dear, you don't now. Later you will want these things. Now all you need is to be loved and I can see that you are."

The three weeks sped by, and before I knew it Mom and Dad had to return to Canada. They loved Jorge and gave their blessing to our marriage. But when they boarded that plane I was absolutely bereft.

Jorge did all he could to comfort me, and now I can admit we both secretly wondered if this was going to work. My family was important to me; how would I live the rest of my life with them so far away?

We pushed the private misgivings to the back of our brains, and with the confidence of youth we continued with our plans to be married. Weeks and then a couple of months went by and still we had no word from Immigration. We wanted to be married on the 24th of May. That idea quickly faded from the realm of possibility, but then on May 14th we received the authorization; the letter from Mexico City, postmarked April 30, explained that we had just thirty days in which to become man and wife or we'd have to start the whole process again. Ten days to plan a wedding!

To my surprise, no one else seemed particularly fazed by this. We quickly determined that we'd have the ceremony performed at the Civil Registry on the morning of May 24th, and the marriage celebration would take place that evening in our garden.

Jorge's mom announced that she'd do all the cooking. We would have recorded music, and the seamstress said she'd get a dress made on time! We drove to the card shop, ordered the invitations, and then three days later we hand delivered every one of them.

The frenzy of preparation that ensued exhausted me. But everyone else seemed energized and excited. I felt relieved that they seemed glad about the marriage.

Chapter 9

Waking up on May 24th I felt overwhelmed by the step I'd soon be taking. Today I would marry Jorge and we would begin a whole new chapter of our life together.

I put on a mint green cotton dress that had been made from the same fabric as the gowns my bridesmaids would wear at wedding Number Two in Canada. Today's wedding would be the legally binding one, and no one from home was here to share it with me. I would be doing this alone and it hit me hard that this would be true of much else from here on.

Jorge called out from the car, "Are you ready?"

I smoothed down the folds in my dress, swallowed hard to keep my voice from catching and called back to him, "As ready as I'll ever be!"

As I slid into the passenger seat, Jorge seemed shaky. "Are you OK?" I asked him.

He blinked his eyes hard. He smiled his wonderful smile, took my hand and told me he felt he was bursting with love. "I can't believe this is happening," he said.

Having just dealt with the jitters produced by the enormity of what we were about to do, all I could do was squeeze his hand. I looked straight ahead and went with him to the *Registro Civil* – the local government civil registry office.

As we walked through the door of the tired old government building I grew even more apprehensive. *This was not a good place for a wedding*, I thought, and the soon-to-be-pensioned looking bureaucrat made no effort to make the occasion special in any way. There were no vows exchanged, there was no pomp; we simply filled out and signed forms as though this day had no importance whatsoever. I mentally steadied myself. *This is how it is here*, I reasoned, and I refused to be sullen.

The actual celebration we'd been planning would be held in the evening, so Jorge and I drove home to rest and get ready. No special lunch, no flowers…this was it. I didn't feel married at all! To top things off, the 24th of May seemed to be the hottest day of 1977; we all shone with sweat. So much for looking like a **perfect** bride…what had I gotten myself into?

But relief was on the way. That afternoon, the customary cool breeze wafted in from the Gulf of México and blew soothingly through our lush, tropical garden. We festooned little fairy lights all through the plants; candles and flowers adorned the tables and the recorded music was augmented by our neighbor's son practicing with his band next door. We got a good laugh out of their rendition of "You're such a sexy lady…oh won't you be my baby?"

Many of Jorge's relatives I hadn't met came to the party and acted most graciously. My mother and father-in-law smiled nonstop and officially welcomed me into the family. We ate, drank and danced until late, and my earlier disappointment definitely lifted. After everyone had headed home, I unquestionably felt like *una Señora* – a married lady!

One wedding down and one to go! I had a steady flow of correspondence going on with Mom, my sisters and my matron of honor, Mary, in Canada. When Mom visited us in Mérida, she and I bought fabric and had the bridesmaids' dresses made; we also bought *guayaberas* – Mexican Wedding Shirts – for the best man and ushers. My dress of sheer white cotton and lace fit me perfectly and I decided to use a Spanish mantilla as my veil.

Without an on-site bride, all manner of decisions had to be made on my behalf. The invitations got mailed and the flowers decided upon without me. My mom, Mary, and my sisters did everything. They made bright paper blooms and I carried other handmade favors up to Canada that would be used to decorate the reception hall. The caterer prepared a "Mexican" buffet and we brought the recorded music from wedding Number One. Non-traditional ceremonies were not common in 1977 but ours was to be a "Mexican wedding in Canada".

Jorge's parents would be joining us for the Catholic rite which greatly pleased me. I thought that when Doña Bertha saw my home and met my whole family, she would better understand why I missed them so much. Hopefully, this would lead to a better relationship between us.

Doña Bertha and Don Humberto loved the British Columbia scenery. "Look at all the pine trees," Doña Bertha exclaimed, "It looks like Christmas trees have been planted all over."

The weather cooperated fully, providing us with long sunny days and cool star-filled nights.

Princeton, the small interior town in British Columbia where my parents lived, was abuzz over the theme wedding to be held on July 2nd. My guests occupied a lot of the hotel rooms and many of the campsites around town. Of the one hundred and fifty invited, only five could not attend. The rehearsal dinner, the wedding itself and a brunch the following morning made for three days of festivities.

Unlike my disappointing experience at the first wedding, Father Conalan performed a full ceremony in the tiny Catholic chapel, and life-long vows were exchanged. Auntie Missy flew from Toronto to give the toast to the bride. She read from Kahlil Gibran's *The Prophet*, and there was not a dry eye. The food and dancing to Latin rhythms were a hit with everyone. In fact, more than three decades later, those who were there affirm that ours was one of the loveliest and most enjoyable weddings they have ever attended.

At the brunch the following day, Jorge and I had a chance to speak with all the out-of-town guests, and I basked in the glow of our beautiful wedding.

"Are you happy?" my mom asked me. I threw my arms around her and told her I had no idea how I could be happier.

Later I stood up and requested a round of applause for my parents. "Thank you for everything Mom and Dad. This has been the happiest weekend of my life." And with that said, Jorge and I set off on our honeymoon.

What a comedy of errors! I forgot to put Jorge's suitcase in the trunk, and when he discovered he had no clothes he asked, "Is this your way of telling me what you want?" I laughed as we headed to a local mall to buy the essentials for a week.

The honeymoon was our first and last experience at camping. Jorge absolutely hated the tent. He said he couldn't breathe in there and quite frankly, it had lost its charm for me as well. I figured the little walk-up motel we spied across the lake would be much more enjoyable and believe me, it certainly was.

Jorge and I were now as married as any two people could be—in the eyes of the Law **and** in the eyes of the Church. My emotions were not at their most stable and after returning from our camping/motel honeymoon, I became very pensive.

Joanna & Jorge on their Canadian wedding day – 1977

Then I panicked! Reality invaded my core. An undeniable truth needed to be realized—when Jorge and I returned to México, there'd be no turning back. My mind could not pretend this was a vacation or even an extended stay. This was forever. I confided in Auntie Missy and told her I didn't know if I could do it. She placed her hands on my shoulders, looked me in the eyes and said, "Oh yes you can! It won't always be easy, but you'll do just fine. You are tougher than you know."

I took her words to heart; I had always enjoyed challenges and that's what this would be but it could also be an amazing adventure; I had just become a little overcome by the magnitude of it.

Our first and last camping experience—on our honeymoon – 1977

We were very much in love – 1977

Chapter 10

ONCE BACK IN MÉRIDA, our life together settled into a rhythm. When Jorge took tourists on tour, often for several days, I'd go along if possible. If not, I filled my time with the same activities I'd begun months earlier and I started going to the gym. I tried mightily not to miss my family and friends. I wrote many letters and from the few that have survived, I now recognize this was a time of great personal growth.

When I think back, I realize my letter writing developed my interest in other kinds of writing. I found I enjoyed telling my stories and that everyone liked to read them. In some of them, I recorded everything I saw and developed a fondness for descriptive narrative. Many of the missives were emotional escape valves. They were the window I used to look out of my world and the door to bring others inside. I kept a journal and wrote a few short stories.

Jorge tried to be helpful. He showed me how to get along in a day-to-day way. Although he acted sympathetically to my adaptation issues and tried to be a compassionate listener, his life hadn't changed a lot from what it was before he met me. He couldn't fully relate to my challenges.

I now realize that I made the adjustment period harder and longer than it needed to be. I liked playing house but I didn't want to take responsibility. I did not want to come to terms with the key issues, yet unless I did so, I would never have a real life in México. Like it or not, fair or not, difficult or not...without the resources I was used to, I'd have to find new ones. Without my established network of friends, I'd have to form a new one. Without my family, I somehow needed to learn to love the one that was here.

I feel a certain emotional distance as I write the preceding words, and I am grateful that time is well behind me. But my heart has no trouble in vividly recalling how the loneliness and the feelings of separateness made me so vulnerable. I pined for what I did not have anymore. I longed for Vancouver's lifestyle, the shopping, the entertainment, the food, the climate and my former job.

"If you are so unhappy, come home!" advised one friend. But I couldn't. I loved Jorge and I knew that living without him in my life would be worse than what I faced here. I felt torn, but I also understood that if I persevered, this would pass eventually. I did not give up easily.

I realized that my heart was resisting change; I walked through the paces but would have to do better than that. I would have to stop comparing my old life to this new one and get with the program. I wanted to, but still...I resisted because I felt put upon.

I felt so jealous of Jorge because he had his roots here, his whole history. Mine were far away. No one understood how difficult this was for me. I endured endless hours of talk-talk-talk about "the good old days" and "remember when...?"

I'm embarrassed to admit that I often sat there with a look on my face that told the world, I'd rather be anywhere else. I contributed very little. Of course this behavior elicited little sympathy. I needed to stop resenting Jorge and remember it had been my choice to live here. Little by little, it dawned on me that I should listen closely and ask some questions because through these stories, I could learn so much about the Mexican lifestyle, and I'd fit in better.

I did not value my surroundings. I could not look past the peeling paint, the grit that held fast to every surface and the earthiness of the tropical climate. I spent so much energy trying to keep cool, to keep up the aesthetics and maintain order all around me. I needed to learn to appreciate the architecture and not focus on the lack of upkeep; I needed to revel in the texture of my surroundings and the sensuousness of the climate. I did not live in a scrubbed-clean, right-angled world anymore. I needed to get past that.

I had to stop looking back and develop some new interests. I needed to listen, learn and participate. I had to take responsibility for myself and stop leaning on and blaming Jorge. Indeed, I fully recognized my challenges, and I guess that my ability to isolate and identify what made me miserable did help my adaptation somewhat. But even so, it took at least two full years before my attitude shifted gears and I began to make progress.

Making friends was absolutely my salvation. A very eclectic bunch of women helped me to see my life in a more positive way. They were of many ages, backgrounds and citizenships and each one of them was kind enough to take me under their wing.

There were a few resident foreigners who faced similar issues and we commiserated. Some had lived here longer than me, and they taught by their example and experience. The Mexican women who befriended me were generous with their advice. They had the grace to guide me through my growing pains and taught me why things are done one way and why not another. This new understanding helped me to accept and embrace many customs I had rejected earlier. I know one thing for sure. Without my friends I never would have been able to stay in Mérida. Without them, I would have been absolutely lost.

One event that made a huge difference in my life was the arrival of my sister Barbara. When she finished high school, she came to Mérida for an extended stay. I felt responsible for her and wanted her to have a good time.

She left her boyfriend Craig at home and she pined for him. I did what I could to divert her thoughts and as I did so, my own melancholy lifted. Barb loved México from her first day here. Although I am seven years older, she and I are quite alike, and we had great times together. We spent a week in Mexico City and traveled to most of the signature spots in southeastern México. Through her wide eyes, I began to re-evaluate my environment. Actually, this was a very cool place!

She and I experimented with Yucatecan cuisine and exercised a lot so as not to gain weight from all we ate! Craig came to stay that Christmas, and since then the two of them have returned many, many times. To this day, whenever Barb and I are together—in México, Canada or wherever—we always spend at least a day cooking and then enjoying a long, luscious meal with our appreciative companions.

My mom's eldest brother Douglas was another frequent visitor to Mérida. Outgoing and generous, he was a big hit with everyone. *Tio Doug* came to Mérida every winter and rented a house on the beach for several months. This went on for almost twenty years. He was such a wonderful person to have in our lives.

In order to have official Mexican teaching credentials, I decided to take an ESL – English as a Second Language – teachers' training course at a local language institute. After graduation, I began working at a technical high school where I taught Food & Beverage as well as English!

Jorge also taught classes there. We really loved the work environment and we met many other young couples who were also "team teaching" as we liked to call it. These people are still our good friends and many of the students have kept in touch over the years.

I had to learn to appreciate the unusual beauty of my new environment

Chapter 11

A NOTHER MAJOR SHIFT OCCURRED that year; I started looking at babies in a different way and thinking that maybe I wanted one for myself! When I asked Jorge if he too felt the time had come to start a family, he seemed thrilled. "But you have to be sure this is what you truly want. You have to be positive you'll stay and live here with our baby. It would break my heart if you left me, but it would be even worse if you left with our child."

I did deliberate long and hard. I decided I was ready and in August, we found out I was expecting.

How all these changes had occurred in me was quite the mystery. In just four years I'd met the man of my life and married him. I moved to a México and after a very rocky start forged a new life; complete with a job I liked, good friends, a pretty house and now a baby on the way!

As the due date approached, we decorated the nursery and bought things for our baby. None of the hospitals in Mérida had ultrasound technology available, so we had no idea if we'd have a boy or a girl. I took the Lamaze prenatal class and on May 4, 1980, after a very normal labor (ten hours from start to finish), our son Jorge Carlos was born. Smitten at first sight, we could not believe the depth of our feelings for this tiny human being.

I remember hearing him mew like a kitten and holding him in my arms. I felt such a rush! Such instant, total love. Jorge was in awe. This man, who is so demonstrative and never at a loss for words, stood mute with the wonder of our son. The Apgar score showed everything was fine; Jorgito was weighed and measured: 3 kilos 500 grams, 52 cm. long. The whole experience seemed perfect to us.

We had three unforgettable days at the hospital. Jorge and Jorgito stayed with me the whole time, and we had a steady stream of family and friends who came by to share our joy. Jorgito looked beautiful, neither as blond as I am nor as dark as Jorge. He inherited his grandfather's ears, his daddy's hands and my eyes. He had such a clean smell. He tended to be quiet; he nursed and slept a lot. Then, the night before we were to go home, he became very agitated. He wouldn't stop crying. A nurse came to the room, "Your milk is coming in but perhaps there is not quite enough yet; maybe he is hungry? Let me take him to the nursery and you get a good night's sleep." I kissed him; little did I know that I was kissing him goodbye.

Our joy was short-lived. On the morning of May 7th, Jorgito had a massive cerebral hemorrhage and he was dead by that afternoon.

Losing a child is the loneliest thing that can happen to a person. Even after all these years, when I think of that day, I feel the shock. It seemed so sudden, so unanticipated and so definite. I can hardly remember what transpired over the next few hours, although I do recall the doctor giving me two shots; one to stop my milk and the other to keep me from getting hysterical.

He needn't have given me either, because as soon as I heard Jorgito had died, my milk completely stopped on its own, and I felt calm, dangerously calm. I understood what had happened was irreversible. No denial resided in me. I blindly accepted our loss but I couldn't even speak, let alone get hysterical. I seemed to be paralyzed. I didn't want food or drink or company. I just wanted it to be yesterday. I longed to hold my baby again and to feel his sweet little body. Jorge suffered in much the same way and he stayed like this for a long time. I think I grieved for him almost as much as I did for Jorgito.

There was such an outpouring of sympathy towards us, but we felt numb. Nothing made any sense at all. Before this, I thought adapting to a new life in a new country had to be the hardest thing imaginable. I had no idea what hard entailed; I was humbled by what had happened to our little family. Friends stayed with us and my mom came as well. She took me to Mass, and the familiarity of the Catholic Church seemed like a supreme comfort. I hadn't felt this anywhere else. Padre Manuel Ramos, was such a gentle man and, with love, he took me into his care.

I had not been a regular at Mass for years, but this priest welcomed me home. I felt grateful for his unconditional support because alone I could not bear the pain Jorge and I were going through.

No one and no test could determine why Jorgito had died. At first I wanted to know but after a while I didn't care. I just wanted to be left alone and yet people came to see me regularly. Some of them, like my friends Betty and Suzi were helpful and kind, but many others voiced such inappropriate platitudes and even admonitions.

"The nurses must have dropped him," or

"You shouldn't have been so physically active during your pregnancy," or

"It is God's way. You'll have more babies. Be brave for your husband's sake."

I wished they'd keep their theories to themselves. I truly appreciated that in their own inept ways they tried to help me. I knew they meant well but they had no idea how much they exhausted me.

Finally a cousin of Jorge's, who I had never met before, came to visit us. She'd lost her first child too. Hearing that was like getting a dose of pure oxygen. She could really understand how I felt! At first she just held my hand and when I started to cry, she said, "Tell me about Jorgito."

I did, I told her everything, and when I finished, I felt like a huge weight had been lifted from me. That sparked my recovery. I knew I had a long way to go but compared to those first days, I felt so much better.

My mother got me out of the house for the first time. It had been a month, but over and over again I refused to leave unless I had to go to the doctor or to see Padre Manuel. I thought I'd fall apart out there. I felt like everyone would be be staring and pointing, saying, "*Ahí va la pobrecita.*" – "There goes the poor (little) girl!"

Mom eventually wore me down, and we went to the movies. We saw a picture with Dudley Moore, Julie Andrews and Bo Derek called, "Ten". At first I couldn't believe that I'd been made to watch such a ridiculous movie, but after a bit I paid closer attention. I couldn't help myself; I laughed like crazy…what a release! I have often thought about writing to the producers of that movie to thank them.

Jorge and I dealt with our grief in very different ways. I wanted to talk about Jorgito, and I clung to his memory. Jorge could not; he couldn't stand the pain of remembering. I did not judge Jorge, nor did he judge me. Neither of us felt like we were much help to each other; yet we bore witness to one another's suffering and vulnerability.

Now I know that sharing that terrible pain strengthened our marriage. When two people accompany one another through such agony and somehow remain intact, they are better equipped to handle other difficult times and successive trials are less stressful for them.

Although we'll never be sure, I think this happened because I'd had dengue fever during the first weeks of my pregnancy. I took no medication during my illness, but I had a very high fever for several days. As dengue was a new, and yet unnamed, disease in the area, no one knew what the possible effects on pregnancy could be. We'll never know the "why" with certainty, but over the years we've grown to accept this tragedy and it is a bitter-sweet part of our family's history.

I did not seem to have any decision-making ability during the months following Jorgito's death, so when my gynecologist recommended another immediate pregnancy, I went along with the idea. When I found out I was expecting again, Jorge held out his arms and we wept. I don't know if we cried from happiness, fear, relief, sadness, or what?

During the second pregnancy, Suzi introduced me to the writers' world. She asked if she could show a few of my short stories to a friend of hers—Joe Nash, editor of the "Vistas" section of the largest English language daily in Latin America. Joe liked my work, and I became the Mérida correspondent for *The (Mexico City) News.*

The writing skills I'd been honing would actually be used for something besides letter writing and journal entries. I covered

all the events the international community held in Mérida. I
wrote about festivals, archaeological sites, unique customs, food,
art, concerts and local luminaries.

Jorge helped me with the research and we spent a lot of time
working on my articles. It was fun and a great distraction from
our worries. As the new life grew inside me, a new passion also
flourished. Writing became an integral part of me.

I noticed details that had completely escaped me before. I
was always on the lookout for a new twist, something to write
about. I read a lot of novels and observed how others played
with words. During the nine months I waited for the birth
I discovered that English is an incredibly rich and expressive
language.

On April 25, 1981—ten days before the first anniversary
of Jorgito's death—our second son Luís Carlos (Carlitos) came
into the world. He weighed and measured exactly the same as
Jorgito. He looked very much like some of my brothers.

When the pediatrician, Dr. Sergio Cano handed Carlitos to
me and I held him for the first time, he said, "This is a perfect
baby; don't be afraid of him, just enjoy him and love him." And
that's what he was—the sweetest baby!

I'm sure Jorge and I acted nervous and over-protective but
who cared? Carlos seemed to be absolutely healthy, cheerful,
and funny. We were finally a family. I had no spare time that
year; being a mom, teaching at the high school, writing for
the newspaper and looking after the house kept me occupied
and happy. Gone were the morose days of my early residence
in Mérida!

My sister, Cathy, added to my happiness. Like Barb had
done previously, she came to stay with us for a few months after
her high school graduation.

She and I enjoyed Carlos so much; we'd swing him in the hammock and sing the songs our mother sang to us. ("Are there li-lac tree-ee-ee-ees in this part of town? Do you hear a lark-ark-ark in any other part of town?") I remember a T-shirt she bought for him, with "Macho Baby" emblazoned on the front.

Unlike Barb, Cathy did not leave a boyfriend behind; she met her future husband Miguel, in Mérida. They dated for several

Joanna and Carlos, April 1982

months while he finished his degree in veterinary medicine and then emigrated to Canada.

I felt sorry to see her leave, but I believed it would prove to be the best decision for them. This has indeed happened; they now have a lovely family and a good life in Vancouver.

Jorge with his parents and Carlos – 1982

Chapter 12

ALL WAS RIGHT WITH OUR WORLD but not with the country. 1982 marked a devastating year for México's economy, so we did what had been previously unthinkable…we decided to move to Canada.

My dad had died the previous winter and Mom was happy that I'd be coming home. However, it turned out to be a brief experiment because Jorge never felt happy there. He is the most Yucatecan man I've ever met and he got depressed in cold, rainy Vancouver.

We returned to Mérida after a year *en el norte*. I tried to keep from feeling peeved. I really wanted to stay in Canada with my family but I soon got over it. I had adapted to life in México once before and surely I could do so again.

Jorge changed careers when we returned; a private university had hired him to develop the first Bachelor of Tourism degree in southeastern México. His experience in Education & Tourism and his training as a lawyer made him ideally suited to this. He had definitely found his niche!

For the next couple of years, I did not work much outside the home. My days were absolutely filled with Carlitos and all his activities; Jorge and I loved being parents. When Luís Carlos turned three, we figured it was time for him to have a sibling.

The next pregnancy was really rocky; I was sick a lot. The baby moved for the first time as we watched the Olympians running into the Los Angeles stadium on television...and that baby was never still for a minute after that!

In part to distract myself from the uncomfortable pregnancy, I acted on an idea I'd had brewing for many years. Since my first months in Mérida, I believed we needed an English speaking women's club where newcomers could meet and make friends. I also believed this organization would be a great venue for Mexican women who had spent time in the U.S. or Canada and wanted to keep up their English language skills.

Through the newspaper job, I had met the U.S. Consul in Mérida, Mrs. Ginny Carson-Young. She turned out to be a marvelously supportive person, and when I told her about my idea she immediately offered the use of the meeting facility at the U.S. Consulate.

In October 1984, I chaired the first meeting of The International Women's Club of Mérida. A friend from Cancún belonged to a similar group there and agreed to be our first speaker. We decided that we would have three aims: social, informative and community service. Twenty-two women attended that first meeting, and our club has grown ever since. I've been gratified over the years when members have approached me and said, "I don't know how I would cope with my issues if this club didn't exist!"

The International Women's Club (IWC) was an instant success. By 1984 many more foreign-born women had come to live in Mérida and Mexican women were now venturing out on their own. Chaperones were largely a relic of the past. Our club developed special interest groups: gourmet cooking, reading, women's issues and so on.

We raised money for needy groups in the community and visited orphanages and old-age homes. We involved our own children in these activities, and they learned to share with others. We had many interesting speakers at our monthly meetings and held many, many great parties! In very meaningful ways, we were like one another's family. My friends and relatives from abroad who have met these women always comment, "Do you realize what an extraordinary group this is?" Yes, I certainly do, and I am grateful to know all these women!

The IWC special interest group that had the biggest impact on me was the English-speaking children's play group. Through this activity I met some of the best friends I've had in my life. And the kids! My friends' children are my nieces and nephews; I no longer see a lot of them (they are now grown and on their own) but in my heart, I'll always hold such a special place for them all. I watched these children grow up, and I know more about them than they realize.

We moms would organize events to mark the special occasions from our countries that were not celebrated in México. We had Easter egg hunts and went trick-or-treating; we had a Teddy Bear's picnic and made Christmas cookies. We took the kids on many outings and taught them about helping others.

We read to them. I'll never forget Carlos' face as he listened to *Where the Wild Things Are* for the first time. Jo and her kids always came to play group, and she also formed the bi-monthly "Thursday group", which met at each other's homes, and where we talked about everything that came into our heads. Usually it turned really late before we'd force ourselves to go home. This friendship was vital to my very survival. The Thursday group doesn't get together as frequently anymore but nonetheless our bond is absolutely golden.

On January 18, 1985, our little Ana Margarita—Maggie—came hollering into the world…before the doctor could even get to the hospital! My mom—who worked as an obstetrics nurse for thirty years and is the mother of eight—assisted in the delivery of her granddaughter. Maggie's birth was such a high…"You have a girl!" Mom cried. It was the first of many emotional moments the three of us shared through the years.

Maggie looked as much like her dad as Carlos looked like me. With her gorgeous chocolate eyes, lots of downy brown hair and the longest fingers I'd ever seen on a newborn, I thought she looked like a Latin angel who'd one day play the piano!

Jorge absolutely loved having a daughter, but as he's from a family of all boys, he felt somewhat intimidated by her. The loud, constant screaming didn't help matters either! Yes, she made a lot of noise and wouldn't stop squirming around. As I cuddled her she tried to wiggle out of her swaddling. "This baby will not be as easy as your last one," said Mom.

Our tiny daughter quickly let us all know that she aimed to be the one in charge at our house. She demanded milk and undivided attention all the time. When she didn't get it, she wailed her head off and would not sleep. One day I ran into a neighbor whose forehead was knit into a frown. She said, "Your baby cries a lot."

Oh really, we hadn't noticed!

Maggie didn't want to miss anything. As soon as I'd go pick her up, she'd gurgle and coo and be sweet as can be…until I laid her down again.

With Jorge working most of the time, four-year-old Carlos had to help out a lot. He rocked her in the buggy, and he sang

Jorge and Maggie, 1985

to her. He ran to me with her talc, bottle or whatever else she needed. It became clear that we needed more hands. When she turned three months old, the doctor told me to quit breast feeding, to get some rest and to hire *una muchacha* – a live-in nursemaid!

For years, I'd listened to the gossip about these young village girls who were available to help out in the home. Many reports of their dishonesty, laziness and unreliability had me convinced that una muchacha would be more trouble than respite. But I desperately needed help.

The search began and eventually Estelita Santana showed up at our door. Just a kid with no experience, she seemed painfully shy yet willing to learn. Maggie terrified her but she fell instantly in love with Carlos. He didn't speak much Spanish and she spoke no English but they chattered away to each other and became wonderful friends. He showed her how to keep Maggie from crying and she complied—for hours on end.

The collection of toys we had fascinated her. Growing up, she'd never had any, and when I would buy things for my children I found myself wondering if Estelita would enjoy them too? She quickly became a part of our family.

A few words about las muchachas: when I came to Yucatán, I was told to never let them get the upper hand. I was told to be stern and not to give in to the demands for time off, a loan or whatever. I never followed that advice. I have always been open and honest with the women who have come to help me in our home and most times, I have been treated the same way. On occasion, a few have taken advantage but this is to be expected in any setting. I think having una muchacha is a responsibility that must not be taken lightly, but it is also a great perk, because it allows you time for other activities while still keeping things running smoothly at home.

What a lot of people fail to realize is that when a young woman from a village comes into your home—cares for your children, learns your family's routine and becomes part of your everyday life—it is an opportunity to learn as well as one to teach. Estelita and I have taught one another so much; after twenty-five years we are great friends.

When Maggie was six months old, I became very ill. I had a severe type of pneumonia that landed me in the hospital for ten days. I dropped ten kilos in that time and felt extremely weakened…it was impossible to walk even a few steps.

Once home and convalescing, the children and Jorge had to stay away from me, and I missed them terribly. It took months for me to get my health back. I only did so because of the excellent care I received.

This particular form of pneumonia has killed thousands of people all over the world, especially the very young and the elderly. Years later, one of the teachers at our school almost lost her little daughter to this terrible infection. She too said her child's recovery only occurred thanks to the medical intervention her daughter received. She is now an activist working towards making a vaccine for this frequently fatal type of pneumonia available to all.

In México, the doctors and hospital staff really care about their patients and they are not afraid to use controversial treatments when the conventional ones are not effective. Mind you, there is a dark side to the country's medical care. It is very different for those with means and those without. The government health system is terribly underfinanced and poorly managed. The frustration level of the practitioners is high, and this is often reflected in the treatment of their (usually poor) patients.

How thorough can a doctor be when he has to see so many people in an hour? How much patience can a nurse have when she is stretched to the limit? I have witnessed injustices and carelessness in the medical field and in other branches of public service. Why is it that some of those working in this sector somehow come to feel that they can grant or withhold their service at whim? Where did they get the idea that the public has to meet their needs and not the other way around?

This being said, it is also true that preventative medicine in México is excellent. Young nurses actually visit every home in their hospital's jurisdiction to inquire if there are children who need vaccinations. These are administered completely free to both foreign permanent residents and citizens in México. Even the controversial and expensive vaccine for cervical cancer is now given free to girls reaching their 10th birthday.

The HMO/public health (Medicare and Medicaid) medical systems in the U.S. and, to some extent, the public health systems in Canada seem much more interested in administrative procedures and billing than in their patients' wellbeing.

When I was ill the private hospital that treated me had state-of-the-art equipment, superbly trained doctors and medical personnel. The nurses were kind and attentive. In fact the absolute superiority and low cost of this country's private health system is one of the main reasons that some people opt to move to México.

Our first family portrait

Chapter 13

ONE MORNING DURING MY CONVALESCENCE, as I watched the program, *"Hoy Mismo"* – "Today" – I thought something seemed wrong with the screen. The light fixture above the newscasters was swinging wildly and the obviously terrified anchorwoman improvised, "It seems that we are experiencing tremors but please don't be frightened because we think that it will be just a small quake." Then the program suddenly cut off.

We soon learned the transmission had ended because a nearby ten story building doubled over and crashed into a section of Televisa's studios. Word quickly spread that the quake measured 8.1 on the Richter scale. The date was Thursday, September 19, 1985.

When the government finally gave estimates of the number of casualties, they vacillated between seven thousand and thirty-five thousand people. Consequently, most of the populace believed that the true numbers would never be revealed and could be as high as one hundred thousand.

Our friends Susi and Carlos kept an apartment in Mexico City; we were worried sick about them. Several days later we heard they'd survived but Susi was terribly shaken.

The entire country mobilized to help the hundreds of thousands of displaced people. But to me, the most moving story to come after the earthquake was the successful rescue of nearly all the newborns from the Capital's largest hospital.

A group of teenagers who called themselves *los topos* – the moles – explained how they had been walking silently through the hospital wreckage when one of them heard a faint whimper. Immediately the entire group began digging—some with their bare hands. No one who was present or who watched the coverage of the rescue on TV will ever forget the sight of the scrappy, scrawny boys pulling live baby after live baby from the rubble. They became known as the Miracle Babies of Hospital Juárez. And the Topos of Tlaltelolco became national heroes.

I could no longer remain in bed, as I figured that if those babies could survive then so could I. The pneumonia had weakened me, but when a friend offered me a part time job at his hotel representation agency, I accepted. My position at *The News* was enhanced by this, because I met many people from the Mexican tourism industry who provided plenty of fodder for my articles.

The latter half of the 1980s now seems like a blur. Opportunities and excitement never lacked. We had our work, lots of friends and ever-growing interests. After her initial temper subsided, Maggie grew into a curious, cute little girl and Carlos' outgoing, sunny personality captivated everyone he met. My Canadian family visited often and we went to see them every couple of summers.

Jorge and I had known each other for more than a decade and were still very much in love. However, our busy lives left little time for the intimacy we once took for granted. In those years, we were lucky to get out to dinner once a month.

I accepted the fact that Jorge's family and I were not ever going to be really close and I continued to feel uncomfortable when I was around them. This certainly was as much my fault as theirs. I balked at conforming to their expectations, and most of them viewed my habits as odd. The one exception was my sister-in-law, Lupita, who always championed me.

Despite the impasse with the family, I did feel very comfortable living in Mérida. This no doubt had a lot to do with the fact that I now understood the society better, I spoke Spanish proficiently and I had permanent residence papers.

Jorge helped me so much with my adaption to living in México by teaching me about the history, customs, art, literature, music and of course the archaeology. He always made sure I caught the nuances of the current political and social occurrences, but I also feel very grateful to other capable, generous friends who took the time to become my mentors.

Dalila showed me how to soften my straightforward North American style and how to make my points subtly—à la Latina. Susi taught me how to dress with much more flair and also how to cook many central México specialty dishes. Both of them helped me to understand Mexican women's spirituality and the ultra-close connections they have with one another and with the earth.

Nonetheless, despite all the changes I'd made over the years, I still retained a strong Canadian identity. Jorge supported me and encouraged me to pass this on to Carlos and Maggie, so they became completely bicultural. They gained an innate knowledge of both their heritages and languages. Jorge and I often say that we gave the world to our children. By this we don't refer to ownership, but rather to a sense of belonging wherever they go.

My father-in-law passed away very suddenly on September 13, 1988. Jorge was with him and said he went peacefully. Losing the patriarch was a blow to everyone, me included. We hadn't agreed on everything, but I admired Don Humberto's intelligence and wit.

As we stood outside on the terrace of the funeral home, I noticed the sky looked very odd. The clouds were swirling around in circles, flush with the horizon. They weren't traveling across the broad blue expanse as they normally did. There was a reason for this. Hurricane Gilbert was preparing to smack right into us.

In Yucatán, where embalming is not a common practice, it is customary for the burial to occur twenty-four hours after a death. But with the huge weather system approaching we were urged to have Jorge's father cremated as quickly as possible. By 11 p.m. the procedure was completed and we deposited his ashes in the family crypt. It had all seemed too sudden and rushed. But I was content after Jorge told me, "This is how he would have wanted to go. He hated sickness, hospitals and funerals."

How the wind howled! A hurricane is an awesome force to witness. We watched transfixed as tree after tree fell, and a neighbor's red tile roof smashed down into the street. We felt totally safe in our cement block house, but the many people who lived in flimsy little shacks suffered terribly. Hurricane Gilbert holds the record as the second most intense hurricane ever experienced in the Atlantic basin. The aftermath was a nightmare. It really took years to completely clean up and rebuild.

By 1990 Jorge had worked at the university for seven years. He'd gained a lot of experience and felt the time had come for us to have our own business. Being completely independent had always been his dream and he knew there was certainly a market for another tourism college. I readily supported him and Doña Bertha was willing to rent us her big colonial house downtown, a perfect building for starting the college.

The one catch was that she would need somewhere to live. We pondered the problem and finally came up with an unconventional solution, "a sabbatical year with our mamas". We thought it would be ideal if I could go with the children and live at my mother's place in Canada for a year. Jorge would remain in Mérida in our home, and his mom would move in with him, freeing her house for our venture. We approached our moms with the idea, and bless them, they said yes.

The children got very excited about going to see their Canadian cousins but Carlos felt extremely upset at the thought of being separated from his dad, though finally he went along with the idea. Maggie was too young to understand fully and her adventurous spirit seemed to be up for anything.

We spent an idyllic Vancouver summer, and in September Carlos started Grade 3 and Maggie entered Kindergarten. Both children soon loved their Canadian school, which offered greater freedom than the traditionally structured Mexican one they were used to.

I took a job as a waitress at a popular European-style restaurant. I didn't mind my job at all, although the owners could be a little testy at times.

On the whole, I considered it to be a good experience and working the busy lunch shift provided me with enough income to cover our expenses.

My mother loved having us at her house. Before we arrived my aunt said that Mom told her, "I feel as though I've won the lottery; my daughter and grandchildren will be living with me for a whole year!" In fact all my family and friends went out of their way to be kind. Carlos, Maggie and I had a great year.

Tongues were wagging back in Mérida of course. Many people thought I wouldn't return. I even received a postcard from Jo that read, "They say you're not coming back – Oh tell me it isn't so!" I laughed and penned back on a different card, "Oh Jo, ye of little faith!" We still joke about it.

Jorge and I wrote to one another, and we spoke on the phone as often as we could afford to. He came to visit us for two weeks at Christmas and again at Easter. Being together on these two occasions made it possible to be apart the rest of the time. When June rolled around, we couldn't believe how quickly the year had passed. But *Tecnología Turística Total*, our new private college venture, was off to a good start (see The TTT Story).

Of course I experienced mixed feelings. I had settled back in with my Canadian family and now I would once again have to adjust to being without them. This seemed to be the story of my life. Adapt, adapt, adapt!

The constant adjustments and need to reinvent my world every time the Mexican economy took a dive or Jorge made a career change or some other huge upheaval occurred did wear on me sometimes. Occasionally I wondered what it would be like to be married to someone from my own culture and to live in the country where I grew up. I pondered about how much simpler it would be if I didn't need to figure things out all the time. Such a life would have been much easier…that's for sure.

But it wouldn't be as rich. If we come into this world to learn, and I believe we do, then I was in absolutely the right place. While still conserving my Canadian identity and values I took on parallel Mexican ones.

When I entered Jorge's world I learned to love Latin ballads and late nights; sensuous salsa dancing; dramatic history and ancient civilizations; rich spicy food; the sweet romantic Spanish language; vibrant bold color and tumultuous passion.

It wasn't a one-way street though. Jorge learned to appreciate listening to Leonard Cohen on Sunday mornings, 1960s dancing, and my native land's stories of bravery and brute strength. He grew to love roast beef and hamburgers; my precise and descriptive language; colorful Canadian burnt fall tones and my unabated enthusiasm.

A price must be paid for everything in this life, and the ante in my case was constant change. My natural need for stability and security had to take a back seat. I wanted to support Jorge's dreams and I trusted him to make a success of our new venture.

Carlos, Mom and I in Canada – 1990

Chapter 14

BUT HEY! IN CANADA, big changes were also occurring. My mom, widowed for ten years, announced she planned to remarry! Shortly after my return to Mérida she'd been reunited with a man she knew in her youth, and after a six-month courtship George Norris was in line to become my stepdad. I felt very happy for Mom and very grateful when George sent me an airline ticket, so that I could be at their wedding in January of 1992.

Mérida must be the most inventive place on earth when it comes to creating fundraisers. At *Carnaval* – Mardi Gras – time that same year my friend, Dalila, wanted me to participate in a benefit dance for the Red Cross. I had no idea what this was about, so she explained it to me.

Every year the Mérida ladies have a pre-Carnaval dance, just for themselves. Thousands of women attend, all in lavish costumes and no men are allowed. The money they raise from the sale of the tickets, drinks and refreshments benefits the Cancer Hospital. As part of the festivities, there's a musical review and she insisted that I be part of her group's performance. The name of the number was, "Uncle Sam".

My part involved dressing up like the Statue of Liberty (complete with the huge pointed headdress and a lit torch). I agreed to do this and on the day of the show I found out I had to "glide gracefully" down a steep ramp with my flaming beacon held high and keep smiling!

"I'm going to fall and set the place on fire!" I wailed.

"You'll be fine!" Dalila assured me, so out on stage I strutted with the rest of the dancers following behind me.

Everyone knows I'm Canadian born but they said I looked every inch the part I played. I must say that I had a lot of fun and since then I've been a part of this show many, many times.

The Red Cross Carnaval Dance is not the only party for women only. In fact, even though the Mexican society is very family based, women spend a lot of time in one another's company. And men too have pastimes that they prefer to keep to themselves. Many new foreign residents in México look at this as sexist but really it isn't; most husbands and wives have different interests, so why should either feel the other must always be included?

One scorching summer day I headed for the beach with my friends Judy and Joanne. We'd all been under some stress and figured this day would be the balm we needed. The ocean looked beautiful, the drinks tasted cold, the food's flavor epitomized perfection and my friends' hilarious company topped it all off. We acted sillier than three grown women should, but I figure that cutting loose sometimes is good for the soul.

Our children were growing up quickly. They attended an afternoon school which enabled me to be with them in the mornings. They'd do their homework while I fixed lunch. At noon Jorge would come home and we'd all eat together. Carlos and Maggie started school at 1 p.m., so after getting them there,

Jorge and I would have an hour or so to rest before we had to get to our college. We usually finished by 9 p.m. and we would tuck our tired kids into bed with three songs and three stories.

During these years, we set the pattern for the relationship we have today—family life is our cornerstone. Jorge, Carlos, Maggie and I are a team.

Many of our friends were distraught when they learned that we had enrolled Carlos and Maggie at a public elementary school. They did not approve at all, "They won't be taught properly."

"They will make terrible friends."

"They won't be able to integrate back into the private school system later on."

It's true that in México the public school system is lacking but so is the private one. Rigid is the best word to describe both of them. At least in the public schools, especially the less-structured afternoon ones, the children are not expected to do such volumes of work. The axiom "more is better" doesn't sit well with me. In my opinion, very young children need to be nurtured and come to enjoy learning. They shouldn't be forced to regurgitate reams and reams of data.

At their school, the Cano y Cano, in Colonia Alemán, Carlos and Maggie had friends from diverse social groups. The school celebrated all the fiestas and festivals but it was all *más sencillo* – less flashy.

Years later, Carlos and Maggie went to private *secundarias* and *preparatorias* – junior and senior high schools. They had all the academic knowledge they needed, and Jorge and I were very pleased to see they had little trouble fitting in with their peers.

They definitely enjoyed the more sophisticated infrastructure—the labs, sports facilities, etc.—in their new schools. Both did well and we were glad that our decision to have them attend the government-run elementary school had been the correct one at the time.

Much later still, both of them graduated with first class honors from their respective universities.

The mid 1990s brought great changes. NAFTA was the buzz, and we were led to believe that globalization would result in wonderful improvements for all. Large national and international retail chains began operations in the city. We finally had some choices about what and where we could buy. In the "good old days", if you wanted to purchase sheets for example, you could choose from maybe two colors in *matrimonial* – double bed size – or king size. Now there seem to be hundreds of styles and colors available. There was plentiful entertainment, a wide variety of products, a rich cultural life, and great restaurants.

In the good old days, you didn't ask a person what kind of car they drove; you asked what color because almost everyone drove a VW bug! Now there appeared to be limitless models. Air conditioning, once very rare, had become commonplace. It got much easier to live in Mérida. All this seemed great, but I began to ask what was happening to our values?

We soon became aware of another reality. NAFTA did not produce the hyped-up benefits for everyone. The impoverished classes looked to be even worse off. On January 1, 1994, the very day that the tri-national treaty went into effect, a previously little known group, *los Zapatistas* protested the ratification by forcibly occupying San Cristóbal de las Casas and other smaller cities in the state of Chiapas. Their masked leader, Subcomandante Marcos said they wanted nothing out of the ordinary. They only wanted better education, healthcare and justice; rights that Mexicans in other states had enjoyed for decades.

The Zapatistas perceived that the accords would further exploit them and their region's natural resources. They wanted their basic human rights to be respected. Ineptly, the government tried to placate the group.

Jorge and I read a great deal about the movement, and I developed a tremendous interest in the region. I wanted to go there and see for myself. But because of sporadic violence between the "rebels" and the Army, it was quite unsafe to do so, and I had to wait.

Jorge and I both had very busy lives. Our growing college, children and our social activities left little time for "us". We missed the closeness we'd formerly enjoyed, so we made a pact to have dinner—alone—every Friday. Usually we would go to our favorite little bistro, Luigi's, in the Itzimna neighborhood.

Our handsome waiter, Alfredo, always made us feel welcome. The ground rules stood: no one could join us, and we could talk about anything except the college or the family.

At first we experienced embarrassed silence, as we had so little to say to one another. But we soon got "us" back and resumed the philosophical, cultural, political and comical conversations we used to take such pleasure in. We looked forward to Friday nights…and we still do!

Our Family in 1994

Chapter 15

IN THE SUMMER OF 1994 I went to Canada to see my family and friends. It had been more than two years since my last visit. Although Mom, George and other family and friends had come to Mérida several times, I could hardly contain my excitement about "going home." I'll always remember that summer as magical. But more changes and challenges were coming.

September to December 1994 saw the end of a very controversial Mexican presidency. Our country had fallen into economic ruin. The unrest in Chiapas and other economically disadvantaged states made the government more unpopular than ever. México sat on the verge of bankruptcy. Our college lost many students. They just couldn't continue paying for their studies. We helped as many as we were able to, but our numbers had dropped seriously.

We weren't the only ones in trouble. Many long-established businesses closed. People lost their homes. *La Crisis* had affected everyone—rich, poor and middle class. *El Boom* and the promised benefits of the new economic policies evaporated before our eyes. It was a disaster.

Personally, I was so angry I could have spit! Jorge and I had worked so hard and the corrupt, inefficient government was taking us down.

1995 sends a shiver through anyone who lived on a peso-based income during that devastating year, yet things were not so desperate that we lost all hope. We tightened our belts a little further and somehow managed to hang in there.

In the spring of 1996, I had lived in México for twenty years and I experienced what seriously needs to be called an Epiphany.

Out of the blue, Auntie Missy sent us a small cash gift – the caveat being that we needed to use the funds to buy or do something that would make us feel better. She stressed that paying the light bill was **not** an eligible choice. At Easter we decided to use the funds to take a little vacation and get away from our depressing situation.

We traveled to Cozumel, checked into a small hotel and headed for the water! The seductive Caribbean soon soothed us. Sitting on the blazing beach—with one of those huge balloon glasses full of a potent margarita—I fantasized about living in Cozumel. As soon as the bottom of the glass showed, a lithe, coconut brown waiter dressed in white Bermudas and a tropical print shirt smiled and set down a second bowl of the elixir. I hesitated but…what the Hell! Down it went—quite quickly I must say!

Carlos and Maggie continued to snorkel in a shallow tidal pool but my half-fish husband finally emerged from the surf. He guzzled some ice-cold beer, and we grinned contentedly at one another.

"Jorge, you and I could teach here and you could take a few tours as well. The kids could go to school on the island, and we could rent a little house not too far from the sea."

Even if he looked a little out of focus, I could see he loved the idea. Then it struck me that I was envisioning a life without our college! I decided right then and there that although I'd continue to work towards renewed success, I would no longer allow *la Crisis* to make me sick. I'd be pro-active and if things didn't work out, well...so be it.

Carlos and Maggie had seen enough colorful fish for a while and ran off to find some food. We continued our inner musing about a move from Mérida—something we never actually came even close to carrying out. That booze-sodden fantasy gave us the reprieve we needed.

Auntie Missy was one wise lady. This wasn't the first time she'd helped me with a huge dilemma. She died in 2008, but I know she's up there, still filling my head with little puffs of positive thought.

One of my new strategies was to "get out there". I figured I could initiate a direct high school recruitment program. This was "just not done" but I figured it would be worth a try. To everyone's amazement, it was extremely successful, so this became a part of my job. I continued doing the presentations on behalf of our college for ten more years.

On my trips to places with nearly unpronounceable names— Oxcutzcab, Timucuy and Cansahcab to name but three—I learned a great deal about the topography of southeastern México and I learned even more about village life. I also developed an appreciation for the progress in the infrastructure of the state.

Throughout the decade, I saw the roads improve and libraries, schools and clinics built. It was amazing to witness the spread of cell phone and Internet service and observe how the improved technology increased the mobility of the state's citizens and opened up government transparency.

Despite all the changes, the pueblo people retained their hospitality and charm. If I got lost looking for a school, someone would come along and explain the way or would even say, "Follow my motorcycle, I'll lead you there." They fed me and gave me little gifts like fresh homemade corn crackers and local honey. Those trips taught me to value the rural way of life. I never would have gained this appreciation had I not decided to "get out there".

In 1997 my mother became ill with Alzheimer's disease. It would take many pages to describe the devastation this caused our family. We all loved our amazing mother and to see her waste away was terrible. But what could be done about it? My stepfather cared for her at home as long as he could, but eventually she needed professional care.

The decision to take her there took a huge toll on us all, but we soon saw that she was happier once she settled in. She looked comforted by the routine and the loving professional attention she received. She had been a nurse for many years, so the clinical environment did not distress her.

There were many decisions to make, and I wanted to be near her and the rest of my family. This is definitely one of the hardest aspects of living internationally. When a faraway loved one becomes ill it is even harder to be away from them. I tried to keep myself focused on my work and my family here. Jorge insisted I see Mom as often as possible, and he did all he could to ease the situation. But still, I couldn't be with Mom nearly as much as she needed me to be.

Ever since Jorge and I had married, most of our travel budget had been allocated to airfare to Canada. Towards the end of the 1990s, Jorge and I decided it was time to start getting to know other states in México. When I asked him where he wanted to go first, there was no hesitation, "Joanna," he said "I want to take you to Chiapas!"

It was to be a modest trip and to this day, we like small hotels and eateries better than the large chains. We also prefer bus travel to driving. Maybe it's because my first travels—through South America—were by bus, riding for long distances never bothered me. I was a little uncomfortable after sixteen hours, but I felt exhilarated. Jorge said he was reminded of his days as a guide when he and I used to travel with his groups of tourists.

It had been too many years since we last passed along Campeche's long stretches of azure coastline, and we'd almost forgotten how lush the wetlands of Centla and the steamy tropical jungle of Palenque could be. Finally we began climbing through the arid highlands. Once again I felt awed by México's magnificence. As I looked out through the window the motor strained; we were in the mountain range known as *la Sierra Madre*.

I should have been scared senseless as the bus careened wildly around hairpin curves on what the driver euphemistically called a highway. It took seven hours to lurch over about two hundred *topes* – speed bumps – and ascend over two thousand meters to San Cristóbal de las Casas. But it didn't occur to me to feel afraid. I felt completely in awe of all I was experiencing.

During that ride, I developed clarity of vision I'd never known before. My eyes took in the high altitude green eucalyptus, the lanky canary-yellow flowers bending in the breeze and hundreds of thousands of plump, red coffee beans laid out to dry on hard-packed earth.

We passed minuscule settlements where time seemed to have stopped. Through the bus window, I caught glimpses of shy *Tzotzil* and *Ch'ol* Mayan women with their children. I smelled wood smoke on the wind and didn't give a thought to the groaning sounds of the luggage shifting in the compartments below.

On the edge of the road, pine trees and bananas were growing side by side. Apples and oranges were doing likewise. We spoke with one of our fellow passengers who worked for the national water commission and asked if he would explain how this could be? He answered, "The mountain ascent is so steep and fast that both the lowland and highland plant species have adapted to these less-than-ideal growing conditions, and so have the people. The region's Maya are small and compact, and they are resilient. Their remote towns and villages are extremely difficult to access, but in these places you will inevitably find the authentic contemporary highland Mayan culture you're looking for."

We found a delightful San Cristóbal hotel that had once been a monastery. As we walked the streets of one of the oldest cities in México, we reveled in the brisk high altitude air.

In nearby San Juan Chamula, we made our way to the town's church. I sensed an otherworld presence and felt compelled to stop. I gazed at the building, and an elder told us we could go inside. The heavy wooden door inched open and, as my eyes adjusted to the glowing interior, I knew the locals were observing my reaction to the scene arrayed before us. I had to put my hand over my mouth to keep from crying out.

This was like no sacred place I'd ever seen. No pews. No conventional main altar. Fragrant pine needles were spread on the floor and hundreds of multi-colored candles burned. Vases of flowers were everywhere. All around the perimeter, family groups knelt before a plethora of elaborately adorned statues.

But I heard no sedate murmuring and saw no reverent crossing of oneself. These people were yelling, stomping their feet and shaking their fists at the effigies. Men chanted and women keened. Little ones observed the elders, learning their ways.

They prayed in several Mayan languages I couldn't understand, but obviously they were begging for the saints' intervention. They set out food and *posh* – the traditional liquor – and it struck me that this was like "The Offertory" during Holy Mass.

I heard a rooster loudly protest as he was pulled from a sack. His neck was quickly wrung, and the twitching bird was laid down with the other gifts—"The Consecration".

They took bites of food and even the children were sipping the posh. There it was—"The Communion". I felt overwhelmed with emotion.

Jorge led me outside into the daylight. How long had we been in there? I wanted to ask him about what I'd witnessed but the words wouldn't come. I couldn't describe the confusion I felt. He could almost read my thoughts and told me, "This is an example of the syncretistic faith that is fundamental to the contemporary Mayan way of life."

I have returned to the mountains of Chiapas many times, and I feel if the culture is lost, a little piece of us all will die with it.

Chapter 16

THE NEW MILLENNIUM WAS UPON US. For the most part, Mexicans viewed all the Y2K hoopla with an amused eye. Our family spent the last minutes of 1999 and the first of 2000 in Santa Lucía Park, listening to the music of Luís Demetrio and gazing upward at a sky filled with exploding lights and smoke from the fireworks.

Less than three weeks into the new millennium, Maggie turned fifteen. I couldn't believe it, but I was orchestrating a Quince Años party. I still remembered attending one for the first time, as if it had been held yesterday, and since then I'd attended countless more. I learned that it is no mean feat to make your daughter's party a memorable one.

Fortunately, Maggie did not want the traditional Mass and *baile con chambelanes* – dance with her courtiers (royal attendants) – very formal. She didn't want a huge frilly dress, but she sure wanted a party—a big one! We rented a disco club, of all things, and by the time the count was tallied, we had invited three hundred guests.

I was overwhelmed at the excess, but this was what she wanted—lots and lots of people!

For most fourteen year olds, planning a Quince Años is very stressful. The birthday girl has to hope and pray a more popular friend won't have her party on the same day and she has to worry that maybe another one will have hers at a better place, and so on. But Maggie did not appear to be plagued with these doubts; she knew she'd have a great time, and that was all that mattered.

She wore a sweet, short white dress and had her lovely chestnut hair done up in a very elegant sweep. She toddled a bit in her first pair of very high heels but had a lower-heeled backup pair for when the dancing really started.

My sisters Anne and Barb, my niece Kelly and my ninety-year-old Uncle Doug came from Canada for the big day. They helped me make tons of food and in fact, none of us has ever eaten another cheese ball since!

The night was everything Maggie hoped for. Our friends and family had a joyous time and because the doors were wide open, other kids poured in from a different party nearby. Almost five hundred people ended up at the disco club! We were flabbergasted. They danced until 3 a.m. and every crumb was eaten. Good Lord, outside of a school setting, I'd never seen so many teenagers in one place!

After it was all over, Jorge and I felt relieved we had made a successful job of things…and grateful that we had only one daughter!

The year 2000 marked a new beginning for Carlos as well. He graduated from preparatoria. He then discovered a program that he wanted to take at university and moved to New Brunswick, Canada to do so.

What a turning point in his life and in ours! We'd always been "the four of us", and now one of "us" was far away. The

Jorge and Maggie dancing at her Quince Años

day he left, I felt as though I'd been kicked by a horse! But, we adapted (to yet another circumstance), and Carlos ended up living for five years in maritime Canada.

Following the terrorist attack of September 11, 2001, Mexicans felt great sympathy for their U.S. neighbors. The father of one of my daughter's friends (assuming I was a citizen of the U.S.A.) drove to our house and came to the door. With deep emotion he said, "I hope your family is safe."

I didn't have the heart to tell him that I'm actually Canadian and replied, "Yes, everyone is fine, thank you for your kindness."

But this date marked the birth of "Homeland Security", tighter border controls and increased xenophobia in the United States, things which have caused so much social upheaval in México.

The pattern of generations was broken. For decades, poor agricultural laborers would cross the border, work the growing and harvest season and send money to their families back in the villages; once the season finished, they'd return to be with their loved ones until the next year's farming cycle. But the trip to *el norte* became so treacherous, they stopped returning home for fear they'd not be able to get back into the U.S.

Thousands of men simply stayed on, waiting for the next crop. They no longer had the chance to renew their ties, and since then a serious breakdown in family values has occurred in México, and grave racial misunderstandings have become commonplace in the U.S.A. Meanwhile illegal drug and arms running have escalated and the immigration issue has been shelved in the U.S.

Foreign residents in México feared that this ill will might affect their status and comfort level—but no, their neighbors know the difference between politics and people. A friend remarked once, "While my country tries to keep Mexicans out, in Mérida

we are invited to participate in every aspect of community life…
even the Carnaval parade!"

On February 4, 2002 Mom passed away in her sleep. The
nurses said, "She just forgot to breathe." My sister commented
that this was just like our mom. We eight siblings attended her
burial, and the next day we went to Mass at her church. It felt
healing for us to be together saying goodbye to our mother in
this way.

When I returned home after her funeral I was comforted
by the many memories I had of her visits. Since 1977 she had
come to Mérida many, many times. She felt very comfortable
here and loved the warm weather.

Although she's been gone many years now, sometimes when I
turn around quickly I see her clearly out of the corner of my eye.

She loved to drink her coffee while sitting in one of the
white wicker rockers in our living room, and she'd always offer
to go out to the garden to pick lemons. She'd smile widely and
say, "Imagine, lemons right here in your garden!"

The next year, 2003, marked my 50th birthday. Me, fifty!
To celebrate (???), my sister Barb gave me a ticket to Holland, and
we traveled there to visit our 91 year-old Aunt Giséle. Actually
she is my dad's first cousin, but the two didn't know one another
until the end of WW II when his division of the Canadian Army
liberated Amsterdam. My brothers, sisters and I grew up with
stories of this amazing woman; finally I would meet her.

Giséle's life story reads like a riveting historical novel. She
has traveled and lived all over the world and speaks six languages. She's a renowned artist and a contemporary of Matisse
and Picasso. Her marriage and close friendship with many
European luminaries is the source of the animated anecdotes
she loves to recount.

Home for her is a tall canal house on one of Amsterdam's principal waterways. Her studio, located on the top floor of the same building, overflows with her art and memorabilia. But she waxes pensive when talk turns to the war years. For her bravery, she has been decorated by several countries including Israel.

The extraordinary energy of this woman, her childlike wonder, grateful demeanor and joyful expression made an indelible impression on me. After meeting Giséle, I realized that none of us can afford to waste one precious moment of our lives. She inspired me to use my gifts to the max. I concluded that I needed to encourage more artistic creativity in my life, and I began to work hard at improving my writing skills by reading writers' guides, attending workshops and by practicing, practicing, practicing.

The idea for a book began growing in my heart but I didn't feel quite ready. I decided to give myself more time. It turned out that I chose a fortuitous time to rekindle my artistic expression. In 2003 a lot of new foreign residents settled in Mérida, and among these were many artists of every discipline.

Innovative art galleries, restaurants, boutiques and studios opened. In February of 2004 the Yucatán Symphony Orchestra gave its inaugural performance in the renovated Teatro Peón Contreras. Mérida was certainly becoming a very different city than the one I arrived at in 1976!

Chapter 17

For our family, several momentous events occurred in 2004.

First of all, Jorge and I became empty-nesters when Maggie joined Carlos in New Brunswick. As this is the only bilingual province of Canada, she wanted to take French classes while immersed in the francophone environment of the city of Moncton.

Before she left I remember speaking with my friend Janet. "I am going to be lonesome," I confided.

She patted my hand and said, "Yes, yes you will be...for about two weeks. Then you'll rediscover the freedom of being on your own again."

She was right...we did enjoy having more time to ourselves but were also very thrilled when Mags came home to attend university in Mérida.

In the same year I applied for and was granted Mexican citizenship. I reasoned that after nearly thirty years in the country, I was certainly a citizen by every definition, and I wanted to officially state that fact. This has not diminished my Canadian identity in any way; I am a bicultural, binational person. I feel separate but equal loyalty to both countries.

Someone once questioned this statement and asked me, "OK, bottom line here...if Canada and México were playing against one another in the World Cup; who would you root for?"

I didn't hesitate and said, "It would depend on where I was, and who I was with." That's how it is, when I am in Canada I feel and act like a Canadian. When I'm in México I feel and act like a Mexican. However (and this is important), the imprint of the two nationalities is never totally absent, and I feel this enriches and enhances the perspective I have.

The months rolled quickly by and turned into years. Carlos and Maggie both graduated from university and did some travelling. Jorge and I visited several new destinations both in México and abroad. Our college continued to grow and diversify. There seemed to be something on every night of the week—and to think that at one time, I had nothing to do! The tables had certainly turned.

One late night in early January 2007 I simply started writing. The words practically tripped over one another. It was as though they wanted to be set down more quickly than I could type. A year later *Tomando Agua de Pozo – A Guide for the Neophyte Yucatecan* was published.

In 2008 the influx of new foreign residents continued to arrive in Mérida and the nearby beach communities. Many of these people read my book, and I was quite surprised by the positive feedback I got. I felt very satisfied when they told me that reading about my experiences helped to validate their feelings as they looked for their place in this community.

Jorge's mom was delighted with *Tomando Agua de Pozo*. Although she'd turned ninety, she still had a keen mind and sharp wit. When I opened the pages to the picture I'd included of her with Jorge and me, she scowled, "Why didn't you put in one of when I was young?" Then she took my hand and laughed.

Joanna and Jorge with Doña Bertha on her 90th birthday

After all these many years, we have come to an understanding. She loves me, I know she does. And I love her too. We've earned this sentiment through sheer fortitude. We have learned from one another. It's always the challenging lessons that are the most valuable, isn't it?

Although there is some age spread among the newly arrived foreign residents in Mérida, the majority are in their 60s, physically active and interested in learning about their new home. Initially most struggle with the language, but after a period of time they find they have learned enough "to get by". Others go past that point and take classes to further improve their Spanish. Many buy crumbling older houses and tastefully restore them, enriching our city.

The Santiago neighborhood is popular with this group, although they also buy houses in other parts of the city and on the coast. A host of new organizations, clubs and groups have been formed by and for the newcomers.

When asked why they chose Mérida, not many can give a succinct answer. Some of the responses I've been offered are:

"I came here in the 1970s and the place really never left my mind."

"I hate the winter, I love the sun – end of story."

"Here I can live well on my social security pension."

"Coming here was my husband's idea."

"I didn't choose Mérida, it chose me."

But no matter what reply I get, when these people hear how long I've lived in México, they inevitably ask, "How has Mérida changed through the years?"

It's hard to know where to start, but let's begin with what has not altered one iota…the heat! Our tropical climate is exactly the same as it was in 1976. All that this encompasses is also still the same—the insects, the humidity issues and the absolute necessity for a siesta during the heat of the day. Rudyard Kipling said of India, "Only mad dogs and Englishmen go out in the noonday sun." The same is true here!

The most obvious change in Mérida over the past thirty years is in the infrastructure. The highways, medical services, educational opportunities, entertainment, shopping and so on were very basic when I arrived and now these services and amenities compare favorably to those found in any city in the world.

The lifestyle has changed in that traditional patterns, just like *las temporadas* – the seasons – here are less pronounced. It used to be that Mérida was a virtual ghost town during Easter Week, July and August, because everyone spent that time at the beach; now this just isn't so.

The older generation finds the changes hard to accept. They don't like the aggressive driving or the fact that children don't do just what their parents order them to. They mourn the passing of established social codes that had been in place for generations. They don't appreciate diversification and feel that traditions have been corrupted. Yet, they accept these things—they are very pragmatic.

How does Mérida's international community differ from those found in other popular retirement destinations of México?

I would say the Mérida group is a bit more resilient and perhaps a little younger than the average foreigner living in the other Mexican communities. Anyone who elects to move to a place they know is going to be extremely hot and humid for many months of the year has to possess certain hardiness.

The reputation tropical Yucatán has for creepy-crawlies, tells me that those who come here willingly are not exactly squeamish. On the whole, this crowd is adventurous. They enjoy new cuisine and trips to archaeological sites, but they also strongly support the city's symphony and other artistic attractions.

The beach people tend to be more laid back. They do come into Mérida for shopping and special events, but really they prefer their sandy seashore, the roar of the afternoon surf and the sunset gatherings that provide an opportunity to socialize and report on the daily happenings.

Both new beach and city residents', foreign and non-Yucatecan Mexican, passion for restoring older homes is amazing, yet most of the design and décor of these restorations is understated and often funky.

Yucatán's foreign residents are generous when they learn of specific needs in the community. Many worthy projects have been instigated and are heavily sponsored by them. In general, *los gringos* (everyone who is non-Latino is called by this moniker) are well thought of, and the locals enjoy getting to know them. However, a little more initiative by the newcomers could reap even greater benefits both on an individual basis and for the collective unit.

It's vital to remember that the majority of Mérida's local population does not have the financial resources necessary to fully enjoy all that our city offers. Many families are stressed beyond belief by the burdens placed upon them. Alarmingly low income, inadequate housing, poor roads, substandard schools, careless medical attention, abusive police and gang influence are realities in our city's poorer neighborhoods. There are definitely "two Méridas".

Chapter 18

IN POPULAR CITIES SUCH AS San Miguel de Allende, I see a more affluent crowd of newcomers. The homes are very chic. In San Miguel there is great solidarity with the local community. Many resident foreigners have seen their initial good intentions morph into philanthropic careers. I have spent a fair bit of time in San Miguel and the surrounding towns, and I must say I enjoy central México immensely. It has such history and charm, not to mention the superb shopping.

Indeed many colonial cities, beach communities on both the Pacific and Atlantic and metropolises like Mexico City and Guadalajara all have thriving, growing communities of intrepid world citizens. There's not too much interest in rocking chair retirement.

To those who are considering this international lifestyle, I would suggest a trip to a variety of destinations before moving to México with the family cat.

Rent first, and if you do find your magic place, be sure to investigate thoroughly before you buy! While Mérida and other cities in México have excellent realtors, there are always those who will dump an unsuitable property on trusting foreigners. Buyer beware!

Are you considering purchasing off the Internet, sight unseen? Maybe you should think again! I strongly recommend a scouting trip where you can personally check out the homes you're considering. Besides the building itself, take a close look at the neighborhood. Will you be happy there?

When you are ready to buy you'll need legal services and it is absolutely mandatory to choose a lawyer who is also a *Notario*—which doesn't mean Notary Public. Those who aspire to this higher professional standing must have a law degree before taking the special courses required to become a Notario.

After passing rigorous exams and a three year internship, they must wait until a place is available. Only a set number of Notario positions (license numbers) are allowed per state. Usually numbers only become available when a Notario passes away, so it can be a long wait. The Notarios' actions are heavily monitored and their level of ethics and professionalism is high. Only a Notario can legally complete a real estate contract in México.

Mexicans from other parts of the country are moving to Mérida at a faster pace than even the foreigners are. Is Mérida in danger of becoming a mini México, D.F.? Not likely. The city is socially well-established, and its economy is very diverse. Yet it will continue to be influenced—in many instances, improved upon—by those who are coming to live here, especially in areas where the newcomers congregate in large numbers. A good example of the positive influence of outside groups is to be seen in the downtown area.

El centro – downtown – had fallen on hard times; there were blocks and blocks of abandoned buildings, shuttered businesses, and no money was being invested to improve the situation. The new residents have transformed the center of town.

I once overheard two Yucatecan women talking about a letter to the editor that had been printed in one of the daily papers. It made reference to the fact that many downtown landmarks are no longer owned by native Meridanos. One of the two said, "Well I personally don't care if Martians are buying the buildings; all I want is to see these showpieces returned to their former beauty."

This has indeed occurred. Mérida has a splendid centro and is a lovely place to live.

It is everyone's responsibility to keep it this way. We need to support initiatives that aim to strengthen the traditions, conserve the environment and improve our quality of life. We should not endorse the schemes of developers and overly ambitious authorities to sully our city with mega-projects that line their pockets and impoverish our already severely strained resources. Modernization needs to be responsible and we must be careful of surpassing our city's capacity for growth and change.

A good way for newcomers to support the community is to buy locally. The small markets stock many of the fruits, vegetables, spices and staples you will use. The drugstores are competitively priced and the bakeries have delicious offerings. Of course it is necessary to shop at the big box stores for some items, but your patronage of the small ones will be appreciated by your neighbors.

In January of 2010, as our college was poised to celebrate its 20th anniversary, we were thoughtful. Wonderful experiences shared space in our memory along with hurtful disappointments.

In the first part of that year our college fell victim to what appears to have been a random act of violence. A Molotov cocktail was thrown at the door of our 56th Street entrance. Fortunately, no one got hurt and half an hour later one burned computer along with blackened walls were the only evidence of what had occurred.

We were absolutely shocked. Things like this just don't happen in quiet, tranquil Mérida. We'd had no experience with violence—not even our cars had ever been vandalized. The police were very professional and supportive. Our friends, as usual were there for us 100%. We were grateful for everyone's concern, but it took some time to get over the fright.

Nonetheless, we don't allow our thoughts to remain negative for long. Setbacks are a fact of life…anywhere. You have to pick up and move on.

A new chapter is opening up before our astonished eyes. Jorge and I have retired from the directorship of the college. Although we will always be involved in some capacity, the two of us are now free to go where the wind takes us. Yet one thing is a given, Mérida will always be home plate.

For me, writing will continue to be an important focus. I felt gratified when all the copies of my first book sold out, and I received repeated requests for a second edition.

The book you are holding in your hands, *MAGIC MADE IN MEXICO* is the updated version of *Tomando Agua de Pozo – A Guide for the Neophyte Yucatecan.*

I've been asked if the content of this book is also applicable to other parts of the country.

Absolutely. Many residents from other places have written to tell me how similar the living experience for foreigners in Yucatán seems to be with that in their adopted Mexican cities, so this book has been written for newcomers to México in general, rather than just those coming to Yucatán.

Back in 1976 I could not have imagined the direction my life would take. I had little idea of the joys and sorrows that awaited

Jorge and me as we built on our dreams. We just plugged away, every day…day after day. We took some risks and were not afraid to break with tradition when we needed to. We have tried to be respectful of both our backgrounds and to build a life that has merit. I often say that one of the things I love most about living in México is the fact that never a day goes by when I am not surprised!

Sometimes, I am surprised in a touching way, like the day I attended the symphony and observed a group of elementary school children with their teacher. They were not from an elite school and were enthralled with this new experience. One little fellow in particular could hardly contain his excitement. The teacher seemed to be a sweet woman who patiently explained that the children must be on their best behavior and should not touch anything because they could inadvertently cause damage.

Once inside, the little fellow was really taken by the plaster cherubs that decorated their balcony. I could see he wanted to touch them so-o-o-o-o badly, but he didn't.

At that point, a distinguished man appeared, and looking right at the children he explained he was the conductor; it was he who would help the musicians play together and produce the wonderful music.

The boy's attention remained on the cherubs. The teacher took his wee hand in her own and gently stroked the cherub with it. The little guy looked at her for reassurance, and she nodded towards the stage where the orchestra had begun to play. The look on his face was close to rapture.

Occasionally I am totally surprised by the surreal appearance of a totally unexpected sight—like the time I saw an elephant perched on the back of a flatbed truck that was roaring down the highway towards the beach. I later realized there was a circus in town, but can you just picture how odd this looked?

I've seen such gorgeous sunrises and sunsets too. I can remember entire days that stretched out between the two. The evenings in Mérida are languid and sultry; since my first weeks in Mérida I have enjoyed them so much.

But what is it that makes life here so pleasing? To me, it's all about the people.

They are so complex and confusing and nurturing and nay-saying and cultured and crass and frustrating and fabulous! Some can act too pompously to be believed, while others are very genuine.

They all share one very Mexican trait—if they count you among their loved ones, they are generous to a fault and would quite literally do anything to make you happy. Once at a party I admired a woman's earrings, and she promptly removed them.

"Un recuerdo" – A remembrance of me – she whispered as she pressed the jewelry into my hands.

The Rosado family at Jorge's 65th birthday party in 2009

My friends are my extended family and I feel blessed to have them in my life.

My many years in this beautiful corner of the world have been very good, and I look forward to a lot more.

México is such a special place. Let the magic come inside...

In México the international community is very close

THE ALPHABET

or

Adapting to life in México: A to Z

MÉXICO HAS BEEN MY HOME since 1976. And yes, a lot of water has flowed under the bridge. All those years ago, I found the cultural stream was pretty difficult to navigate. It looked as though everyone else just sailed along while I continually floundered from one faux pas to another.

Take social greetings as a first example. Initially this seemed absolutely spontaneous, and I went over-the-top in extending affection to all. After a little more detailed observation, I began to suspect a concise code of conduct was being followed, and it was going right over my head. Very puzzling...I desperately wanted to fit in, but I needed more information. Without a guide the learning curve loomed large indeed. If I'd had some instruction, I would have been much less uptight and enjoyed my new discoveries more.

The following pages of this book will address cultural adaptation in México from A to Z. You'll read practical anecdotes about the "why, what, when and how" that will hopefully help to make your life easier. "Why" do women and men sit separately at social functions? "What" keeps people from wearing shorts in this hot climate? "How" can you communicate when your Spanish is not fluent? "Why" do legal processes take so long?

The wonder of a new country is part of its charm, but feeling constantly overwhelmed is exhausting. I don't pretend to have all the answers, but at some point since 1976 I probably faced the same issues you are facing now or will face once you decide to move to México.

Finally, THE ALPHABET gives you something to ponder. I remember how I used to have many vague questions and doubts that I couldn't put into words. I have tried to articulate some of them with the hope that my efforts will clarify things for you.

Sidewalk Pleasures

Living in the land of *Buenos Dias*, I unconsciously alter my pace
To hop over the long strings of balloon toys pulled by toddling children,
And see them turn to delight in the tinkling bells that roll in the wheels
And in the glitter of the neon paint as it catches the lights of the plaza.

The *marquesita* man turns up his flame and splashes batter on the grill,
Extra dough tails spilling onto the ground to feed the dog waiting nearby.
Eight people crowd into the back of a pick-up truck. Grandmother sits
In the plastic chair, baby on her lap, all ready to bask in the breeze of the ride.

—Marianne Kehoe

Marianne is a former Chicago resident who has taken to life in México like a duck takes to water.

This next part of *MAGIC MADE IN MEXICO* features quotations and vignettes written by some of México's full time foreign residents.

"Nothing worth the effort ever comes easy."

There's a lot to cope with, but if you persevere and keep your sense of humor you'll discover that adapting to this new life is full of excitement and deeply satisfying.

A is for... ATTITUDE
What's yours?

ARE YOU VIEWING THINGS differently than they really are? Are you obsessing? Are you discouraged? Are you questioning yourself all the time?

Adapting to life in any new place is all about attitude, and México is no different. Most of us come to live here with high hopes for a fresh start and new experiences. We are positive and we're very enthusiastic. It's all exciting and stimulating—for a time.

Then, for some of us, the differences become very overpowering and culture shock can set in; it becomes difficult to stay optimistic. Everyday events seem like huge obstacles. For example: the tradesmen don't show up as they said they would, or their work is sloppy. The new friend you met doesn't call back, or if she does you discover that some of her opinions are, quite frankly, just short of weird. The heat and humidity are a lot more intense than you believed they would be, etc., etc., etc. What do you do about this?

A few months after I arrived in México, I felt plagued with uncertainty. I missed everything I left behind, and the options

I had here did not excite me. I despaired that my dismal mood would never get better…but finally I met a person who made the difference. I made a friend!

Like me, Susan had recently moved to Mérida, and to make matters more challenging she didn't even speak Spanish. Her geologist husband worked on an offshore oil platform and spent more time out of town than he did with her. Nonetheless, this woman did not mope around all day. She joined a gym and learned some crafts. When Charlie had time off they spent wonderful times together. And most importantly, she had the ability to laugh at herself.

I remember how we met. She was in the photography shop (in those days film had to be sent to Mexico City for developing). She wanted some of her prints enlarged, so she turned to the dictionary. She wanted to say, "I'd like these blown up please." What she in fact managed to utter—with a British accent—was, *"Por favor, detonar las fotos."* She had asked to have the pictures "detonated".

Both she and the clerk wore very disturbed expressions as they tried to figure out the messages going back and forth. At this point I offered to translate, and when Susan realized what she'd asked for, delighted peals of laughter filled the small store. "I'm so muddled. Let's go and have tea," she said.

I began to emulate her positive attitude and my quality of life improved greatly.

I knew that my recently-developed, fill-up-the-day activities would not be satisfying in the long term, but I didn't worry about that too much. I have always believed that the future takes care of itself; it's getting through the meanwhile that can be challenging. No one expects that every day will be perfect. Utopia is not a place on any map. Yet if culture shock really sets in, it can be daunting. When faced with this in any degree you need to understand what's happening and work through it. It's important to keep busy and be proactive. Even participation in somewhat inane activities is better than sitting around and allowing your spirits to deteriorate by the day. To dispel malaise you need to feel a sense of accomplishment.

Let's use the scenario of the tradesmen. First of all, you must realize that these men come from a completely different background than you do. The ones who haven't been exposed to foreigners before will probably not understand what it is you want or why on earth you want it, but once they get a glimmer they'll most likely do their best to provide it for you.

Do you show your crew that you appreciate their work? Do you take meticulous interest in what is being done for you and encourage the workers? Try to learn the basic Spanish vocabulary necessary to compliment their efforts and to explain what you need. A little extra money, paid directly to them when a detail is well-done, providing a hot meal sometimes and a safe work environment always, will go a long way towards making them feel more disposed to pleasing you. Have cool drinking water and a bathroom (with a shower if possible) – accessible to them. Challenge them to take pride in what they're creating for you. If you can manage this you'll get the quality you want. You'll be purging negativity and in turn will contribute towards dispelling some of your own unhappy attitudes.

I know one woman who wanted some rather complicated tile work done in her kitchen. As she tried to explain (with the aid of a drawing) the maestro had an unhappy look on his face and was heard to mumble, *"¿Quién sabe?"* – I don't know about this.

Finally she folded up the paper, threw it in the trash and said to him, "What am I doing? You're the expert. You do what you think will look best." A few hours later, she noticed the paper had been retrieved and was tacked up on the wall. A week later she had a faithful replica of her design. The workers beamed when she bought *cochinita pibil* – a popular and famous Yucatán dish – for all to share at lunch time and beamed even more when she presented both of them with a little bonus.

Forming new friendships takes time; the instant varieties usually have short life spans. Take a while getting to know people. Meet them in neutral places like a mall, a coffee shop, a city plaza or an open-to-the-public art show; watch how they react to your views. You don't want to be judgmental; diversity is a good thing and acceptance of those with different viewpoints can add a new dimension to your social circle, but you want to see your acquaintances responding in kind. It's a two-way street.

Rebecca in her custom tiled kitchen

When I first meet new people, I don't just focus on how they interact with me; I watch how they treat others—the waiters, the car parkers, the shopkeepers, etc. When I see respect extended to all I become quite interested in the budding relationship.

It's important to take each day as an entity on its own. If you have confusing or negative experiences don't get too upset. Don't be afraid the next day or week will be as bad or worse. Lick your wounds and move on. You have undertaken a huge change in your life and will certainly take some wrong turns as you find your place here.

Although the key is to keep busy, it is also good to look at your experiences with an eye towards the future. Take advantage of new opportunities. Mérida, like many cities in México has a very rich cultural life. Even if you've never done so before, visit a village, go to the concerts, the symphony, try new cuisines, take a class or join some of the volunteer groups. Don't be hesitant to be a part of things just because you have never participated in such an activity in the past or because you are not sure you'll really enjoy it very much. Give it a try and then form opinions about it. Be as upfront and open as you can be. Ask questions. Most people enjoy being asked for their opinions and advice.

Adapting to a new home in a new country does not happen overnight. There will be times when you'll wonder what you were thinking when you made the decision to move to México! But with a sense of humor and a positive attitude, finding your niche will be an amazing adventure in itself.

Smile...you could be on camera!

Many international women have asked me. "Why do Yucatecan ladies always take a good picture?" I hadn't ever thought about that before but once it was pointed out I realized that this is true. It seems that even if intoxicated they always manage to look composed. So here are a few bullets from this *Yucateca's* personal arsenal...

- Be aware that at most social gatherings, your picture could be taken at any moment, so pose...even when you're in the background. You do not want to look at the digital camera's lens as if begging the photographer not to take your picture. Smile because he's going to take that photograph regardless.
- Always sit up straight and suck in that stomach, no matter if you weigh 90 lbs or 400 lbs.
- I repeat...smile like you are having the time of your life.
- Don't be afraid to ask the photographer to hold for ten seconds – *¡Esperate un momento!* – while you smooth your hair and ensure there is nothing between your teeth. They won't mind and this will give you a few seconds to compose yourself!

—Maggie Rosado

Maggie is one of the dynamic, young, bicultural women who are changing the way this society views the role of women. I am proud to say she's my daughter.

B is for ... BEHAVIOR
What is acceptable here?

Y OUR DRESS AND YOUR DEMEANOR will shape the locals' opinion of you. How can you strike the right balance?

When I first came to live in Mérida, I wanted to blend in, but everything about me screamed: D-I-F-F-E-R-E-N-T! Thirty-plus years later, my bicultural daughter tells me, "Mom, I'm sorry, but you look like someone who just stepped off the plane!" Not much can be done about it I'm afraid. I look the way I look, and I am who I am, and hey, there's nothing wrong with that!

Nonetheless, I have adopted behaviors that are accepted here, and I fit in better for having done so. This is not to say you must abandon your personal style in a desperate effort to be accepted, but sometimes it is necessary to modify a few things. Mexicans are very conscious of personal appearances, and their first appraisal of a new person usually involves a quick scan of how they dress and comport themselves.

In a hot climate personal hygiene is very important. Yucatecans bathe several times daily; they find it very offensive to be anywhere near a person who is sweaty or has any body odor at all. And yes, all those showers do interrupt the day, but the locals find this to be a good thing.

Traditional Yucatecan women do not leave the house in big loose skirts and stretched out T-shirts with flat sandals—especially not cracked leather Birkenstocks or neon colored Crocs! It is doubtful they even own such attire. Yucatecan women wear bras…always. All but the ultra-conservative will wear shorts and tank tops at home or at the beach or maybe to the corner store, but never to town or anywhere else where they'll be seen. Middle-aged women dress in loosely tailored clothing made of cool fabrics and always carry a fan. They stay out of the sun and may even carry a parasol.

On dress and formal occasions they put a great deal of effort into their appearance and enjoy wearing their beautiful jewelry. Young women often dress very flamboyantly, but once they have children, many change their personal style somewhat. I was not culturally sensitive when I first came to live in México. I cringe a bit at how I dressed, and it was no wonder my mother-in-law undertook a full scale campaign to change me! But this isn't the answer either, you have to hold your own and be authentic. It is more an issue of making compromises here and there.

On dress occasions, traditional Yucatecan men wear white guayaberas, long pants and closed shoes. They only wear suits to weddings and other very formal events. For casual get-togethers, they will sometimes wear Bermuda shorts and a T-shirt with sandals or runners, but many still feel most appropriately dressed in a short-sleeved cotton shirt with khaki trousers and closed shoes. Sleeveless T-shirts and running shorts are only worn at home, to the beach or in the company of immediate family.

Observing a group of Mexicans in a social situation we see that the women laugh and carry on; they can be very animated but they don't throw themselves all over the place. They take up little space; they don't slouch or lounge about—they are contained. Women don't banter back and forth with men unless they are family members or very, very well-known friends. The men are much more boisterous in their own company. When women are present they watch their language and are attentive to their partners. Discretion is very important.

At most gatherings, the women congregate together. They have little to say to the men, even their husbands, until it's time to serve food. Then they fill a plate, take it to their husbands and make sure the husband's needs are met. "Is this enough; do you need anything else, cariño?" This behavior doesn't usually sit well with women and some men from other countries; it appears sexist and subservient. This is not the intention nor is it the reality.

Traditionally, men and women have very different lives; a social occasion is an opportunity for both genders to get together with those whom they have the most in common. Although many women now work outside the home, they still feel that the really important part of their lives centers around the home and the family. The other women share this opinion, and they want to spend their time together—of course, they also enjoy telling tales about all the women who aren't there!

The men talk about "stuff"—politics, sports, and entertainment, and they too like to talk about other men they know who aren't present. It is said that *chisme* – gossip – is an art form in México.

So how should you, a newcomer, behave? If you have a partner and go to a gathering together, should you separate at the entrance and stand uncomfortably in one enclave or the other? No…by all means stand together and go with the flow.

Someone will drift by, and you'll find yourselves carried along. If it is one of the sit-down-at-long-tables affairs, look for an empty spot, ask if it is available and settle in. People will come to you... or they won't (depending on the crowd). Relax and take things as they come. If there is dancing, a woman does not usually go out on the floor with anyone other than her husband, but that too is changing.

When I was first living here, I didn't know this and would actually say to men at my table, "Let's dance!" I soon sensed I was acting too forward...again.

I started to observe how the locals interacted and tried to be attuned to what was going on. I made fewer mistakes, and eventually I found "my style" – a blend of my naturally open personality and my adopted acquiescent one. It took time, but I figured it out, so will you.

If you do inadvertently say or do something that is offensive you'll know it right away. There will be a sudden silence and everyone will look down or look away. I used to live in horror of this happening to me...and it did—more than once! But you'll live through it. If you're lucky, you'll have a savior—as I did.

One hot—very hot!—summer night Jorge and I were invited to a wedding, and I wore a dress that had spaghetti straps instead of sleeves. There was a jacket that went with the dress, but it was just too hot to contemplate wearing it. At the Mass, I did not notice anyone giving me a second look; there were plenty of women less-clad than I was. When time came for Communion, I went to the altar, and to my great surprise the priest (who was very old and traditional) began haranguing me in a thunderously loud voice, asking how I dared come to the altar of the Lord in such brazen apparel! I was absolutely paralyzed; he was treating me as though I were Jezebel! I could not move from that spot!

I then felt two small, strong hands on my shoulders, moving me back to my pew. An older lady named Maricela saw my distress, and she quickly took charge. I will never forget her act of kindness—bravery really—in depriving that grouchy priest of his sport. What did I learn? Since that day I carry a shawl or jacket with me to Mass, and no matter what the temperature I put it on before I approach the Communion rail!

If you realize that you have inadvertently committed a social gaffe...apologize if necessary and then just forget it. Be as thoughtful as you can and you'll be fine!

Social interaction between men and women is more formal in México

Becoming a Child Again

Five-year-old Dayra walked into our school not knowing a word of English. On the first day, when her teacher opened *Where the Wild Things Are,* Dayra moved as close to the book as possible to see the pictures. She listened to the teacher's words—a strange language. She didn't understand most of what she heard, yet she was filled with a sense of wonder and curiosity.

Over time Dayra listened to more stories, and in a few months she understood most of the words. Today, a year later, Dayra understands everything she hears in English.

At our school, Habla, observing five-year-olds to eighty-five-year olds, I've realized that learning a language is about becoming a child again. Letting go, listening, and being open to a new culture and new ideas. When we learn a language we begin to see the world through fresh eyes. No matter what our age, we look and listen again, with wonder.

—Kurt Wootton

Kurt Wootton is the co-founder and director of Habla: The Center for Language and Culture in Mérida, Yucatán, México. Online at: www.habla.org

C is for...COMMUNICATION
How to be effective when your language is very limited and how you can easily improve your Spanish.

I AM A VERY VERBAL PERSON and have always have been. I had some Spanish skills when I came to live in Mérida, as I'd previously lived in Peru. When I first attempted to learn Spanish in that Andean country, I used to say that I felt like I was fresh off the farm and spoke with the awkwardness of someone much less sophisticated than I believed I was. In reality I was very green in every way, and my lack of proficiency with words was the least of my issues.

Nonetheless, it was awfully frustrating not to be able to understand much of the conversation going on around me and to be incapable of saying all I wanted to say. "*¡Más despacio, por favor!*" – Please speak more slowly! – was my mantra. And I made really abominable mistakes!

The verb conjugations and tenses were absolutely incomprehensible at first, so I decided not to bother with them. I needed to communicate my needs right away...not six months later.

Soon enough, even though my sentences were very grammatically incorrect, I could hold semi-understandable conversations. My statements went sort of like this:

"Tomorrow, I to want you to take I the market; we to buy groceries."

"You to have baby pretty, big eyes and hair curly much he to have."

"I to like to dance you with but I no to know to dance."

Yes, it was pretty Neanderthal, but I was persistent, I was observant, and I listened. Soon I was hearing and understanding the correct usages, and I improved a bit each day.

If you are to become a part of this community, I feel it is absolutely essential to learn enough Spanish to carry on polite conversation. You must be able to, at a minimum:

- Use salutations and titles, e.g., *Señor, Señorita, Señora, Doctor,* etc.
- Enquire about your neighbors' health, family and well-being.
- Know the numbers, days of the week and the months of the year.
- Understand familial and professional titles, e.g., *Don* or *Doña, Licenciado(a), Professor(ora), Maestro(a),* etc.
- Name the parts of the body and everyday places you go to.
- Use general nouns and pronouns.
- Memorize basic verbs.
- Ditto with standard phrases.
- Manage a working vocabulary.
- Try to learn the correct pronunciation of Spanish. Mexicans will nearly always forgive your faux pas, but

if you mispronounce the words your Spanish may be incomprehensible to them.

Six weeks of consistent effort should get you to this point. Beyond that, extended vocabulary, verb conjugations, tenses and so on are up to you but I recommend continuous learning. It shows respect and doesn't take the effort you'd think. With just twenty minutes of study a day—this means every day—you'll be surprised how much you have picked up in a relatively short time. Language learning is a matter of repetition and practice; it's not rocket science.

Couples who don't speak Spanish have an additional challenge, as they don't try to speak Spanish except when it is absolutely necessary. If you are in this situation, one thing that might help you to learn the minimums is to try to speak Spanish with one another at least a half-hour a day. Also, if you have help in your home – a person who cleans, a housekeeper, cook or gardener – both of you should try to converse with them in Spanish every day that they are at your house.

So the big question is...how does a person go about learning Spanish, especially "after a certain age?"

To start with, I recommend six weeks of classes. Your sessions should be 2–3 hours and you should attend 3–4 times a week

If you don't like the group approach, find a good tutor who specializes in teaching beginners. Some other good exercises for improving your Spanish. are:

- Listening to music in Spanish, particularly slow ballads.
- Watching the local TV stations. Telenovelas are especially easy to follow.

- Reading the Spanish-language newspapers and using your dictionary to look up words you don't understand.
- Think about how young children learn to speak. They listen to their elders, and they repeat the same words and phrases over and over again until no one corrects them anymore! If you stop your daily reinforcement, you'll forget and have to re-learn what you just spent so much time learning.

Mexicans are very flattered when a newcomer takes the trouble to learn Spanish. They will notice your improvement and when they correct you it will be from kindness. They are most forgiving of mistakes. If they laugh, you must keep in mind that what you said was probably pretty funny. Try to figure out what it was, and you'll giggle too!

A man I know tells the greatest story about another English-speaking resident. This fellow went to the market to buy a pound of beef liver; he wanted the slices to be very thin. The butcher gave him a quizzical look and proceeded to cut the liver—very slowly and deliberately—in rather thick slabs. The gentleman got really excited and said in Spanish, "*¡No, no, más despacio!*" The butcher looked at him and resumed cutting the same thickness but still more slowly and more carefully. "*¡No, no...más despacio!*" At this point, the butcher gave up, but seeing my bilingual friend several stalls over he asked him to help.

As you can imagine, the customer had mixed up his Spanish words. Instead of asking the butcher to cut the liver in thin slices, he was asking for it to be cut slowly; it's easy to confuse the words: *delgado* – thin – and *despacio* – slow or slowly! Once his error was straightened out, he quickly got his thinly-sliced liver.

One Sunday my fun-loving friend Joanne went with her family to a popular restaurant. They were in high spirits and having a great day. All the tables had filled up and the lone waiter ran back and forth to the kitchen trying to keep up with the orders. The group tried to help by deciding on what they'd all have to eat before the frantic server got over to the table.

Once he did find his way to them, he appreciated their consideration, but as he walked away to place the order, Joanne remembered they'd forgotten to order garlic bread. Knowing it might be some time before the waiter returned, she decided to call out to him while he was still within earshot. She wanted to say, "Please wait, we'd like garlic bread too." What she actually said was, "*¡Oye! por favor, pendejo!*"

Pendejo is a very insulting epitaph in Spanish, but it is pronounced quite similarly to the words for garlic bread – *pan de ajo* – so instead of asking for a food item, Joanne had sworn at and insulted the waiter! Needless to say, the service for the remainder of the meal was not good at all!

Even after more than thirty-five years, there are some words in Spanish that I avoid using altogether. The word for comb – *peine* – and the word for penis – *pene* – are dangerously similar! One windy day, I asked a shopkeeper (male) if he had a "comb" for sale, but as you can guess, I didn't get the pronunciation quite right!

Some words don't sound too bad at all when translated from Spanish to English, but for Mexicans they are highly offensive: *estupido* – stupid – is about as insulting a name as you can call someone. *Embarazada* is a word almost every native English speaker misuses…once! Most of us have actually said, "*Estoy embarazada*." meaning to say we feel embarrassed, when in reality, we're telling people we're pregnant! I could fill pages with the mistakes I've made…and you will too, but don't let it bother you. These are just two examples of what are called "false friends" when learning Spanish. There are many, many more!

Sometimes, though, it is not the neophyte making the mistakes. Many businesses that cater to English-speakers have advertising, signs and, of course, menus that fall victim to bad translation. A popular restaurant wanted to advertise the fact that take-out service was available. They had a sign that read, "Food to take off". To me, this conjured up visions of food atop a little airplane, zooming down a runway!

I once saw a hotel brochure that featured Spanish text in black with the English translation underneath, written in red letters. At the end of the Spanish version, was written, "*Para nuestro personal, será un placer servirle*"– and in red, "Our friendly staff will be pleased to service you." Good Grief!

Menus are wonderful places to find loony language. I once saw, *Sesos Fritos* – Sautéed Brains – translated as "Fried Minds"!

On still other occasions, the names of some products and establishments sound really humorous to our ears. One example of this is something we see advertised everywhere: "Bimbo" bread or the sandwich spread called, "Goober"! There is a gift shop in Mérida called, "Tittys". And of course, the snack item called, "hot nuts" has some pretty wild connotations.

Restaurant names can be charming in a very comical sense, like, *La Langosta Féliz* – The Happy Lobster. I don't know how happy a lobster could be in a seafood restaurant! And what about the ocean-side café in Campeche called, *El Viagra* – no translation needed, but I wonder how they add the secret ingredient to the soup?

Yet words are only words; incorrect translation is funny, but when real misinterpretation occurs it is a much more serious issue.

Not knowing the language is a major hurdle, but the bigger issue is not understanding the subtlety of using the language—then using it incorrectly—and wondering why you see the reactions that come forth.

Most Mexicans avoid conflict at any cost. They do not like back-and-forth discussions. They feel threatened when their opinions are disputed, and they are incensed by aggressive arguing. I usually find myself agreeing 100% to avoid fighting with the person I'm talking with. It is very important to learn how to use your limited language effectively.

I've come to realize that it is not wise to say things like, "I think that's wrong."

Instead, try saying "¿*Será possible?*" – "Is that possible?"

You'll elicit a very long explanation, but you'll glean the gist of what the person is really concerned about.

When speaking Spanish, I usually try to couch my opinions as a rhetorical question rather than making a direct statement. "Could it be true what the paper says about...?"

By doing this I quickly learn how the person feels about the issue and how strong that opinion is. I can then decide whether or not I should go there!

Of course, there are times when it's necessary to communicate displeasure...like when the neighbor's dog just won't stop barking! Rather than yelling, "That XXX %@/&% dog is driving me nuts!" Try saying, "My wife/husband has such a terrible headache today, and the dog's barking is causing her/him great pain – *mucho dolor*. Could you possibly calm the dog down?" This subterfuge may seem silly, but it usually works.

There are many ways to immerse yourself in México's Spanish-speaking community. Everything you do and everywhere you go will present opportunities to learn more. It can become tiring—exhausting in fact! When this happens take a break, but get back out there as soon as you can.

Above all, don't be shy. Speak up! Remember that you're not the only one who makes mistakes that are puzzling to you and uproariously funny to others; don't forget, Spanish speakers commit plenty of errors in English.

Another benefit of language learning is what it does for your brain. Countless studies show that people who learn a new skill later in life are better equipped to deal with aging. We never get to the point where there's nothing to learn or improve upon. With consistent effort, you will be surprised how quickly Spanish becomes your new best friend.

and
C is for...CUISINE
The best in the country?

It is said that in all of México the very best cuisines are to be found in the states of Puebla, Oaxaca and Yucatán. I have been to Puebla and Oaxaca, and I must say that their reputation is well-deserved; but in my opinion—albeit jaded and biased—the Yucatecan is superior in taste, variety, and presentation.

Nearly all of the varied cuisines of México are, like the Mexicans themselves, *mestizos* – "fusion" cuisines of indigenous, Spanish or other "foreign" cuisines. However, only the Yucatecan recipes still use the original ingredients and original methods of cooking, substituting only pork and chicken—both imported foods—for the original meats that were used.

I could say much to describe Yucatecan cuisine, but I could never say it as well as my friend, Loretta Scott-Miller who has written the classic text, *A Yucatán Kitchen*, on the subject. With her permission, I quote:

> "The regional cuisine of México's Yucatán peninsula is a unique blend of Mayan, Mediterranean and Caribbean flavors.
>
> Over the years, thousands of Lebanese immigrants added another culinary element to the mix, but it is the indigenous Mayan base that sets the cuisine apart from mainland Mexican cooking...
>
> "Bite into a crispy *panucho* or glide your fork into a tender *brazo* and you will experience a culinary connection with an ancient culture that has endured 3,000 years. From its complex *tamales* wrapped in banana leaves, to its pit-roasted meats basted with *achiote*, it is a cuisine as rich in history as it is in flavor.
>
> "Geographic isolation played a big part in the region's development. Even in pre-Hispanic days, geography forced the indigenous Maya to look outward, gathering influences from the Caribbean, the Gulf and eventually the Atlantic rather than from the interior of México.
>
> "The region's first trading partners were Cubans and Caribbean Islanders. Later, during the Colonial era, trade expanded to the U.S. port of New Orleans, six hundred miles due north of Mérida, and then to Europe.
>
> "At one point in the 19th century, the Yucatán declared itself a sovereign state and broke ties with México. The Caribbean region of the Yucatán

peninsula continued to lag behind and didn't become a state—Quintana Roo—until the 1970s, about the time Cancún was developed as a world-class resort destination.

"Separation from México and early foreign contacts had a profound influence on the Yucatán's culture and cuisine. The Spanish colonial imprint is strongest of course, but French, Lebanese, North American, and Caribbean flavors, ingredients and techniques are also evident.

"It is necessary to make a preliminary differentiation between the Mayan cuisine of two different periods: the pre-Hispanic Maya and the Maya from Spanish colonial times. Both used corn as their basic ingredient, but they differed in their use of other ingredients and cooking procedures.

"The ancient Maya cooked their food either by burying it—cooking it over hot coals—or roasting it. They didn't fry their food or cook it on a griddle. The "bread" that was baked was, of course, made of corn. The thinnest "bread"—formed with two layers that were pressed together—was called *sucuc uah*; when it became hard it was called *chuchul uah* and when it was even harder and moldy it was called *totoch uah*. When it was mixed with black beans it was called *pich* or *muxub*; when it was mixed with chile and beans it was called *papak tsul* and the "bread" made of new corn was called *chepe*. The tortilla, as we know it today, was made popular when the Spaniards conquered the region, although even the tortilla is a "fusion" food.

"The popular drink in ancient times was *keyem* or *pozole* known as *atole* in most of México. Another was *kah* which was prepared with cocoa and corn, allspice, annatto and other spices; it could be served cold or hot.

"Ancient Maya ate wild turkey, deer, rabbits and other wild fowl, such as pigeons, turtle doves and duck. They weren't used to eating fish or seafood, because although they lived near the coastline they didn't have efficient ways to transport these highly perishable products. In spite of this, some fish dishes, like *tikin xik* and grilled manta ray were popular among the Maya. However, it is a fact that the consumption of fish by the Maya was more due to Spanish influence than a genuine interest in the practice.

"The Maya and their descendants were very fond of a broad variety of root and leafy vegetables: *chaya*, *makulam*, tender and tasty pumpkins, *chayotes*, *jícamas*, and *camotes*. Some dishes were made with deer meat, called *pibil ceh*, and turkey, *pibil kuts*—both were cooked by wrapping the seasoned meats with banana leaves and baking them in pits lined with hot coals. Also, the *chachakuahes*, "tamales" filled with deer or turkey meat in a pumpkin seed sauce and spiced with annatto and *onsikil* or *pipian* are still prepared today.

"Throughout the centuries some recipes used in cooking have prevailed; for example, the use of *kol*, corn gravy used to drench different foods.

"The *onsikil* or *pipian* is a distinct Yucatecan food that has been enjoyed for centuries; it is very representative of Yucatecan cuisine and a valuable symbol of our cooking heritage. The Spaniards found it exquisite and adopted it as a regular entrée.

"The Maya had no pork before the Spaniards arrived. The *cochinita pibil* and the *lechon al horno* are mestizo dishes: they combine the use of achiote, the plantain leaf (banana) and pork (Spanish) with the cooking underground (Mayan).

"The meat that was eaten by the Maya was looked upon suspiciously by the Spaniards and was replaced by pork, by *gallina de Castilla* – stewing hen – beef, fish and seafood. Different stories narrate the way the Maya used to prepare meals for the Spanish rulers. They would garnish their dishes elaborately, disguising the fact that these were made with "meat from a suspicious origin". The Spaniards said these foods "tempted the body just as Eve got the better of Adam".

"The substitution of ingredients and the adding of others transformed the ancient Maya cuisine into a combined Maya-Hispanic way of cooking which eventually became a new diverse mestizo cuisine, or as it is also called, Yucatecan cuisine.

"It has been said that genuine Yucatecan cuisine is that which was created by the Maya and the Spaniards. It remained practically unaltered in the 17th, 18th and early part of the 19th centuries.

"Apparently, it was at the end of the 19th century when it began to evolve profoundly, giving Yucatecan cuisine a distinctly different face.

"One specific mestizo dish that has remained unaltered throughout the centuries is the *puchero*. Puchero owes its name to the pot in which it is prepared; that is the Spaniard *olla podrida* or *cazuela Espanola* (Spanish stewpot). This stew is eaten in many Spanish-American countries. Basically, it consists of three meats (beef, pork, and chicken) stewed together with vegetables. The garnishes that accompany the meal are: minced radish and cilantro in *naranja agria* (sour orange) juice and lime juice, both of which add zest to this quite plain dish.

"The cochinita pibil has been very representative of Yucatecan cuisine for many centuries, even though, as previously pointed out, the Maya did not have pork. The cochinita pibil adopts different elements from the Mayan and Spanish cuisines. From the first it takes achiote, a Mayan spice, and the way of cooking food in underground pits. From the Spanish influence came the use of pork which prevails to this day.

"The cochinita pibil is often associated with parties and celebrations. Pigs were only sacrificed when there was a special occasion; this made pork the meat of choice for celebrations, which are frequent throughout the year. For "everyday food" it was more common to use poultry or a different type of meat that could be salted and would last longer. Pork does not keep well in hot climates, so it had to be used as soon as the animal was butchered. In Yucatán, the "warm taste" of pork and the "full sensation" it produces made it the meat of choice for special celebrations.

"Some very well-known mestizo Yucatecan dishes are distinguished by regions or associated with special days: the *relleno blanco*, the *relleno negro*, the *papazules* and *escabeche de Valladolid* all come from the eastern part of the state. The *escabeche rojo* is made with roast turkey, spiced with achiote and Castilla pepper and is especially popular for night-time feasts. In Yucatán, it customary to eat this on Christmas Eve.

"Other traditional dishes are the *salpimentado* and, of course, the many varieties of tamales; *mukbipollo* is a special type of *tamal* eaten on the Days of the Dead.

"Creole food from the Caribbean, especially Cuba, has also influenced Yucatecan cuisine. One such dish is *mondongo*, both *kabic* and *ajiaco* styles. *Bacalao*, or salted codfish is also a part of many Creole-Yucatecan recipes; the most popular is prepared *a la vizcaina*. The *albóndigas* are meatballs served in a broth with noodles; this dish also has Caribbean roots.

"*Frijol con puerco* or pork with beans, the way it is eaten today is not the way it was written-up in the recipe books of the 19th century, and it doesn't even show up in some of the first decades of the 20th century. This very popular dish was introduced by the Basque immigrants and is prepared by cooking pork in black beans. The garnishes of chopped white onion, radishes, cilantro, mint and chile; a tomato sauce and lime wedges complete the meal.

"A similar case can be seen with the *potajes* that don't appear in the recipe books of the 19th century. Potaje is a Spanish word that means a stew of various different ingredients. Originally potaje was not meant to be a complete meal but was considered a side dish or soup. However, the fact that it is filling on its own has elevated its status to entrée.

"Through the centuries and with the arrival of different ethnic groups in Yucatán, other foods were incorporated into the Yucatecan cook's repertoire.

"Notable among these new settlers were the Lebanese. Many Yucatecan dishes have roots in this mid-eastern country: *kibi*, *tabule* and so on.

"*Queso relleno* is a traditional Yucatecan dish with a Dutch component. A Gouda cheese is carved out from inside, and stuffed with ground meat, as is done with turkeys in the very traditional relleno blanco and relleno negro. Queso relleno is a great example of the introduction of a foreign ingredient, such as the Dutch cheese, that is submitted to the local procedures, resulting in a splendid new dish..."

Loretta's book, *A Yucatán Kitchen: Recipes from Mexico's Mundo Maya*, is available from Pelican Publishing in Gretna, Louisiana and through Amazon.com and other outlets in the United States.

I would advise all neophyte Yucatecans or Mexicans to learn about the unique cuisine of the Yucatán and other parts of

México too and to try as many of the dishes as possible. There are institutes where you can take classes, and also you'll find that your friends in México will happily share their recipes and knowledge. If you haven't already become familiar with the food from México, you're in for a totally marvelous culinary experience!

D is for...DRIVING
Are you up to it? How can you develop the nerves of steel you need?

S OMEONE ONCE SAID TO ME, "Mexicans are the most considerate, kind people...until they get behind the wheel of a vehicle! Then, it's like Dr. Jekyll and Mr. Hyde!" This is true. From what I've seen, drivers in all of México seem to take personal offense if anyone is ahead of them. They need to pass and get in front, no matter how perilous this may be. It's as though they'd rather pile into you than let you emerge from your driveway, slip into a parking spot or change lanes. Why? I wish I had an answer, but I can only speculate that it has something to do with suppressed rage.

My friend Theresa has suggested that the erratic driving is perhaps due to the fact that few people take actual driving lessons. They learn from their parents, older siblings or from their friends. They also pick up all these people's bad habits, and the problem compounds. They know how to operate a vehicle, but they don't know—or care about—the rules of the road. I'm sure you've noticed people driving with small children on their laps...talking on cell phones…singing along with ear-splitting decibel levels of *salsa*, *norteño* or *banda* music…or simply acting oblivious to the other cars, including yours, that are on the road. They'll cut in front of you, block your vision at a busy intersection or disdainfully ignore your polite gestures that indicate you need to change lanes.

This same friend says it is sheer folly to drive "if you've lost your nerve". You do indeed need nerves of steel to navigate the roads of México. What to do if you don't have them? Can you learn to drive à la mexicana?

If you do need to take to the streets, first be absolutely familiar with your car and how it will respond to your sudden moves. Practice in a less congested area to get the feel of the wheel. At all times be sure you know where you're going. Be certain of what lane you should be in and watch out for anyone coming your way. His blinking signal light cannot be trusted…expect the unexpected!

Next, hold your ground. If you let another car force you into a different lane, you might never get back. Keep your speed up; whatever the other cars are doing, you have to match them, or you'll likely cause a pile-up.

Finally, do not let your attention wander. Driving requires constant vigilance. You never know when a motorcycle will speed up on your right, a pedestrian will wander across the road or a giant bus will tailgate your rear!

While driving, you will also have some unexpected "cultural moments". My Uncle Douglas, a friendly but very proper elderly gentleman, used to spend his winters in Yucatán. We went many places together in my little yellow Beetle. One day he, my small son and I were driving through a coastal town, and the horn became stuck. It blared away as I frantically searched for the right fuse to pull and stop the racket. All Uncle Douglas could say was, "Oh, I'm so embarrassed!"

"It can't be helped!" I shot back at him, and with that said, I found the right fuse, pulled it out and there was blessed silence.

There were a lot of people staring at us. I gave a weak smile and he repeated, "Oh, I'm so embarrassed!"

"It's over now. What's the problem?" I asked.

He looked at me woefully and said, "All those people look at you, they look at the boy, they look at me and they think, *Silly old man!*"

At once I understood his chagrin, so I winked at him and said, "This is México, Uncle Doug; they're thinking, *lucky old man!*" He let out a huge guffaw, and we headed for home.

What if you commit a traffic violation and get stopped? What if you are set up? Know the law—it's very simple. You can obtain a copy of *el Ley del Transito* – The Rules of the Road – at a police station or where the driver's license tests are given. Study it from cover to cover! Contrary to what you may have heard, it is not a good move to try to bribe the officer. Even if he drops hints and says he can "help" you...don't go that route.

If an infraction has been committed the officer is supposed to give you a ticket, so it is important to establish right away what you've done. If you have in fact been wrong, insist on being given your ticket. It won't be expensive, and you'll avoid any possible problems. If the policeman really wants money and threatens to have your car towed away or keep your license, call his bluff. In Yucatán, for him to order your car towed away, he has to write up a report. It's doubtful he will do this if he's not justified because he'll be answerable to what he's written down.

Mind you, this practice varies in every state—and sometimes municipality. In some, the license is taken and then returned when you pay the fine, in others just a ticket is issued, so as I've said, you need to understand the law of your area or of any you'll be driving through—in México.

Following is some common-sense information that will help you to feel secure while driving; it will also keep you safe if you run into problems:

- It is important not to drive anywhere without a charged cell phone.
- You should program your insurance agent's number into your cell phone contact list because if you get in trouble anywhere in México, he or she really will help you.
- What should you do if you're in an accident and worse yet, someone is injured? Contrary to what you hear, you should not flee the scene.
- Stop, stay calm. Call your agent first! He will dispatch an adjuster (usually English-speaking) posthaste. The adjuster will then handle everything for you and explain what's going on—step by step.
- Stay inside the car and quickly gather up all the valuables you may have there, especially documents like the car registration, insurance papers, etc.
- If you are alone, get on your cell phone again and ask a friend to come and help you, especially if it looks as though you will be detained—hopefully Spanish speaking in this case—for either medical or legal reasons.
- If you're being detained, give all your valuables and important documents to the person who comes to your aid. If you are hurt, it is even more urgent that you get someone you trust on the scene as quickly as possible.
- Don't speak, don't sign ANYTHING and stay put until the adjuster arrives.

I hope the preceding has not made you decide to never get behind the wheel! Really, it isn't all scary bad news. Many drivers and police officers are very kind. I have been lost countless times and when I've rolled down my window to ask the person in the car next to me how to get to "such and such a place", quite often, they smile and say, "Follow me; I'll take you there!"

Once my car stalled in the rain, and a young fellow got off his motorcycle, and, all by himself, pushed my old VW to the side of the road! "I'll call your husband for you, if you like," he said.

Another time when my car wouldn't start, two patrolmen came to my aid. I had a trunk full of groceries and my two small children with me. They called for a tow truck, then loaded the shopping, the kids and me into their vehicle and delivered us home.

The Mexican government is just as helpful to drivers on the highways in México as are its citizens, and you will be pleasantly surprised should you experience car difficulties. There is a cadre of mechanics called *los Ángeles Verdes* – the Green Angels – who patrol the federal highways in green trucks to assist motorists who have a breakdown or other sort of calamity. If they cannot resolve the problem, they will call for backup. And, believe it or not, this service is completely **free**. The only thing that might be charged for is the gasoline furnished to those who inadvertantly run dry.

If you do develop those nerves of steel, you'll enjoy the independence and convenience that driving allows you.

You'll find yourself on roads leading to wonderful places and you'll have enchanting days. You will be pleased with yourself!

I am very blessed

This is a new chapter in my life, and I am very blessed to be able to live my dream!

No more below freezing temperatures, creaky bones or dead batteries...only beautiful sunny days and the sound of the waves on the beach. It means I'm able to take the time to "smell the roses" and to appreciate God's handiwork.

It is a part of my need for "life-long learning"; when I open my eyes each morning, I wonder, "What will today bring?"

Living here is about developing a level of sensitivity at being a guest in a foreign country and accepting how things are and not trying to change them to what "I want or had" because I want to be here with the good and not so good.

—Sharon Helgason

Sharon is a retired RN from Winnipeg, Canada. She is very active in helping the local community in Chicxulub, Yucatán, where she now lives.

E is for...ENTITLEMENT
Where you come from, you've always felt a sense of entitlement; you've known your rights and responsibilities as a citizen. Why would moving to México alter that?

I N THE COUNTRIES OF OUR BIRTH or at least in the countries where we lived prior to our move to México, most of us felt a sense of entitlement. We knew what our rights were, and we knew what we could expect from the government in terms of legal record-keeping, documentation and authorization. In fact, we probably never even thought too much about this…it was always "just there".

When I lived in Canada I do not recall ever having to worry about my documentation. My parents gave me a copy of my birth certificate when I moved away from the family home. My driver's license came in the mail when I passed the test. My employer handled my medical coverage. The tax form arrived in the mail. I filled it out, paid and that was the end of it. My academic credentials also came by mail when I had finished my education. The right to vote, to have a passport, a bank account, credit cards, etc., etc., were all taken for granted.

Once we move to this country, we quickly realize that most of us have been blissfully unaware of one of our most basic human necessities—belonging to a society and having an identity.

Many years ago, I began a bureaucratic process that became on-going! Starting in 1976 with the application for my residence document right up to the day I was finally granted Mexican citizenship in 2004. I'm sure I spent thousands of hours going from one office to another…getting photocopies, having affidavits notarized, getting pictures taken—on a white background, with no makeup, no hair covering the forehead and no earrings— waiting in lines, being interviewed, returning the next day, and the next, and the next. It was a true test of patience.

Paying a light bill, contracting with the cable TV company, having city water connected, paying taxes, banking…all these *tramites* – steps in the legal process – can take an unbelievable amount of time and energy.

Getting a phone installed took us four years! Since then the efficiency has improved, but it is still a far cry from what most neophyte residents are used to.

What can you do? How can you keep your stress level down? To start with you must realize that no amount of fuming, yelling or demanding will speed things up; in fact you'll only worsen the situation. Don't be mistaken by thinking that if the general public—perhaps following your lead—would simply speak up, things would improve. The bureaucracy and public service sector do not operate as you're used to. The fact is many of the public servants truly believe they are doing you a favor by even looking at you.

There has been some progress made in terms of transparency, but many citizens still resort to *la mordida* – a bribe – to speed things up. It may not be right but it's "the way it is". However, la mordida is not an option open to foreigners in México. You must simply accept these snail-paced processes as a fact of life.

It is important to see the even bigger picture…to appreciate how rights and privileges can be so different for one person or another. In the more developed nations we are accustomed to pretty fair treatment. This is a right we have as citizens. We feel comfortable going almost anywhere, and we don't feel out-of-place in too many situations.

In México, most of the citizens are very democratic but there are some very prejudiced people. They talk about their poorer compatriots in a very ridiculing way and make them feel inferior with the glances and gestures that are all too easy to interpret. If you witness this behavior, I think the most effective response is to understatedly defend the offended person and plainly show you are not in agreement with the speaker's offensive behavior.

One example of this would be when you're standing in line and the clerk asks you what you want, completely ignoring the poorly dressed woman standing in front of you. You could say, "The lady is ahead of me, please take care of her first."

Many of the poor have very rudimentary reading skills—if they can read at all. Among the indigenous people high levels of illiteracy are still found. And while literacy is the norm in México, "functional" illiteracy is common.

When the functional or completely illiterate have a document issued for them, they often don't notice a missing accent mark, a dropped letter or a misspelled name, and in México this can be tragic, as any miniscule error on an official document renders it invalid, and it must be reissued.

Often, the person is made to believe it is absolutely all their fault, and they must endure a harangue from the clerk or civil servant. This is why some do not comply with civil registry regulations requiring the filing of birth dates, deaths, marriages, legal land title registration, etc. Besides the fact that it costs money, which they may not have, they don't want to face the possible humiliation. This has dire consequences later on because without proper documents, a child cannot go to school, have access to health care, etc. It becomes a vicious circle.

Entitlement is not universal in México, in most cases it is an accident of birth. Those of us who have material comforts and social acceptance—to a large degree based on how we look—should do what we can to promote justice and equality. We can best accomplish this by example. We need to be aware of our blessings, be pleasant and treat people fairly. We can do this in small but effective ways, and our efforts will be noticed.

If we accept the way it is when it comes to waiting in line like everyone else, we show solidarity. If we help those in need by giving our time or money to charitable organizations, we show commitment. If we smile and treat everyone with courtesy, we show respect. Our small contributions will add up and we will make a difference!

F is for...FAMILY
Numero Uno in this culture

L A FAMILIA CONJURES UP ALL KINDS OF images in México. We imagine weddings, baptisms, Quince Años parties, First Communions, Sunday lunches, Christmas and many other holidays—all celebrated by a diverse group of people who belong steadfastly to one entity: the family.

In stereotypical Mexican families, *Mamá* is the central figure, and her life is dedicated to her family's well-being. No detail escapes her attention! She gives unlimited love and affection. She worries about everything. Did they all get up on time? Did they eat? Did they eat enough? Do they have clean clothing? Is the clothing properly starched and ironed? Are they in good health—absolutely no sniffles? Who is accompanying the younger ones? Are they totally safe? Is the homework done—neatly? Is her husband *tranquilo* – calm and happy? All this is very important.

Mamá shops and cooks huge meals; she oversees the cleaning, the laundry and the garden. She usually prepares an especially elaborate feast on Sundays, and the whole extended family comes—this is absolutely mandatory. She takes great pride in the fact that her family would be lost without her! Here lies the problem; they **are** lost without her!

It's called *mamitis* – dependence on Mamá – and many Mexican mamás subtly—or not so subtly—encourage it, something unknown in our northern culture. Younger Mexican women are trying to break the cycle, but it is deeply embedded in the culture.

When the boys marry, they are used to being waited on hand and foot and expect their new wives to do likewise. When that doesn't happen, they go crying to Mamá, who of course steps in.

The girls are also used to pampering and have little experience running a household and caring for a new husband…or themselves. They too go crying to Mamá, who of course steps in.

It usually doesn't take too much time for the Mamá to be given a new role, *la Abuela* (*Chichi* in Yucatán) – the grandmother – and this is when her pampering reaches new heights. The grandchildren are everything to her.

If Mamá passes away, the whole family often falls apart. If they are lucky there's an eldest daughter or an aunt who will assume the role of matriarch. But if there is not another strong female to take Mamá's place; the family may never recover. Without her to guide and cosset them, they have no discipline. I've seen this happen in my neighborhood, and it's very sad.

And where does Papá fit into the picture? His role is the same as his wife's, but his turf is the business. He must put bread on the table, and he takes this very seriously. If he has partners, they are usually other male family members—these are the people he can trust. Even many of the huge companies in México are family businesses.

Papá's behavior mirrors his wife's. No detail escapes his attention, and he also supervises his children's education and future employment. If he has his own business, he expects his sons and sometimes his daughters to succeed him. Otherwise, he has a life quite independent from his family.

He has his *compadres* and an elaborate network of business contacts and cronies. He quite likely has coffee at midmorning and a beer—or two or more—with them before going home for late lunch, the day's main meal. Nevertheless, he too must live up to Mamá's expectations, and is never absent at Sunday lunch or other important family celebrations.

Even politics in México is a family affair. One sees sons and then grandsons taking the political offices originally held by the patriarch of the family. Union leadership, security for life in the bureaucracy, a teaching post, a doctor's practice...these roles are usually inherited by a son or other family member.

Land and all personal wealth are bequeathed to the family; there is very little endowment to the arts, educational institutions or charitable organizations in México. However, this is beginning to change a little, and some wealthy Mexicans have made substantial bequests to philanthropic organizations.

The fact that not all family members get along does not seriously affect the bond. There can be a lot of acrimony, but when there is trouble it is the family that comes first. The bond is ironclad and gives tremendous security to all members. If you fall on hard times, your family will help out...if you need a leg up, you'll go to a family member who's in a position to help...if you get into to trouble of any kind your family will rally 'round you.

Economic necessity has caused many Mexicans to migrate to big cities or even to other countries. Their greatest sadness is to not be with their big extended families. Every chance they get they make long journeys back home to their *pueblos* or *ranchos* – hometowns or villages – to be with *la familia*.

The Mexicans living abroad particularly like to be at home for *la Fiesta del Pueblo* – the annual town celebration. This is usually held on the feast day of *el Santo Patrón* – the patron saint of the town. During these festivities there are Masses, processions, novenas; a small fair/carnival is set up and often there is a bullfight—not a "real" bullfight—as they use small bulls, and the—usually drunken—"matadors" just taunt the bull. Quite often the bull gets out and runs amuck until he can be corralled again. The bull is not killed during the "bull fight" but afterwards he is butchered, and a traditional dish, *Choco Lomo,* is prepared.

Mexicans who live away from their families also long to be on hand to honor their loved ones during *los Días de Todos Santos.*

In most parts of México, All Saints' Day on November 1st is also called *el Día de los Angelitos* – The Day of the Little Angels – when dead, un-baptized children are specially remembered. All Souls' Day on November 2nd is called *el Día de los Muertos* – The Day of the Dead – and commemorates all the departed faithful. These days are generally referred to as *Los Finados* or *Todos Santos.*

In some states, like Yucatán, October 31st is the dead children's day and November 1st is All Saints' Day – *el Día de Todos Santos.* November 2nd is the Day of the Dead making Todos Santos three days instead of two.

During the days of *Todos Santos,* entire families go en masse to the *campo santo* – the graveyard – to accompany their departed loved ones for a night…or several nights.

Special foods are prepared, and of course there is much reminiscing…Mexicans love to remember the good old days… and the not-so-good ones too. The same stories are told and re-told. I believe this is how they stay connected to their past, to their roots, to what is most important in their lives.

Although the roles of various family members have been modified somewhat in today's increasingly faster-paced society, the structure has remained basically intact. The family is the backbone of the entire country, and it must be protected at all cost. It is the nation's greatest natural resource.

Insight from a México lover

What strikes me about living in México is that celebrating is a national pastime, enjoyed by all regardless of age or economic status.

Mature adults as well as youth can work hard all day, return home at 8...enjoy a little *pan dulce* and hot chocolate. Then after freshening up they might go out at 10 to dance and party until the wee hours. Whew!

Religious celebrations have many forms. Some are somber processions with the faithful bringing their favorite saint's image to a place of worship. Others take place in neighborhoods where all are invited. Mariachis sing, traditional *horchata and tamales* are served...and don't forget the fireworks!

Celebrations can be simple family gatherings with lots of food, singing and dancing. Others are all out street parties with disco music starting late...complete with smoke and lights. Large or small, public or private, the people know how to celebrate.

And to this I say, *¡Viva México!*

—Nancy Walters

Nancy, originally from the state of Oregon, has also lived in San Miguel de Allende where she owned a night club called La Princesa...and this is how she's lovingly known. She is definitely una princesa.

G is for...GIFTING
There are so many celebrations and holidays in México...to gift or not to gift...this is the question!

WHEN I FIRST ARRIVED IN MÉRIDA, I was amazed and totally confused by the number of holidays that are celebrated with presents and/or major festivities. It seemed there was always a party being planned. The annual cycle begins with:

Fin de Año and *Año Nuevo* – New Year's Eve & New Year's Day are celebrated at the country clubs, at all the main restaurants, bars and hotels and with street parties all over the city, although it is mostly celebrated *en familia* in México. Life-sized "dolls", representing the old year are stuffed with firecrackers and batting, doused with kerosene, and torched at midnight. Talk about ritual cleansing!

El Día de los Reyes – Three Kings Day, January 6th – is more celebrated in some parts of México than Christmas Day. In most traditional communities and families—the custom is to gather together, give presents (something no longer customary for Mexican families in many areas of México) and eat the *rosca de reyes* – a sweet bread that has little dolls hidden inside. If your piece has a doll, you are supposed to host a party on the day of *la Candelaria*, February 2nd.

January 6th is also the anniversary of the foundation of Mérida and there is a large celebration in the Main Plaza.

This is followed by the *el Día de la Amistad y San Valentín* – Valentines Day, February 14th – a lovely day in México that honors friendships of every kind; it is not just for sweethearts.

Not long afterward comes *Carnaval* – a five-day festival preceding Lent, with parades, costumes, and much beer drinking – known to those from the U.S.A. as Mardi Gras.

After the dry spell of Lent comes the most popular two-week vacation period of the year: *Semana Santa* – Holy Week, the week before Easter – and *Semana de Gloria* or *Semana de Pascua* – Easter Week, the week after Easter. All the schools are closed, so this is when many Mexican families travel and see the country. The resorts are full, and many multi-generational groups also take advantage of this long stretch to visit their relatives who live far away.

El Día del Niño – Children's Day, April 30th – is a very festive day, especially for elementary school-aged kids; the teachers always go all-out with sweets and small gifts for their young pupils.

El Día de las Madres – Mothers' Day, May 10th – honors all women—future mothers, our own mothers, grandmothers, friends' mothers. It is extremely important to mark this occasion with the appropriate visiting and gifting. Although not a federal holiday, many, if not most, businesses are closed this day, at least for the afternoon, when mothers get taken to dinner. It is probably the most important of all the traditional but not official holidays in México.

El Día del Maestro - Teachers Day, May 15th – often extends into a week of celebration for the educational sector.

El Día del Padre – Fathers' Day, the third Sunday in June – honors all the papás. Fathers expect to be feted and visited on their special day, but not to the same degree as the mothers do.

In mid-September, shortly after school has begun, it is time to celebrate *el Día de la Independencia* – Independence Day. In every town and city throughout the country, the historic *el Grito* – call for freedom – is re-enacted just before midnight on September 15th in the main squares all over México. On the 16th, all businesses, offices and schools are closed.

Halloween – October 31st – is an imported festivity but it has grown in popularity to the point where it has become almost as celebrated as the traditional feast days honoring departed loved ones just following, but not with the same devotion and affection.

Todos Santos – All Saints & All Souls Days – which follow on November 1st and 2nd are very important occasions for the families to remember their ancestors and enjoy special meals and outings, as described earlier.

On the 12th of December the entire nation pays its respects to *la Patrona de México* – the patron saint of the country, *nuestra Señora de Guadalupe* – Our Lady of Guadalupe. La Señora is not just a religious icon; she is the personification of the country's identity. She is "The Heart of México".

Noche Buena y Navidad – Christmas Eve & Christmas Day – are extremely popular holidays in México; this is when the entire extended family gets together, as they do in many parts of the world. There are gifts, Christmas Eve midnight dinners and parties that last until the sun comes up.

Additionally, there is a whole array of special days: Day of the Secretary, Day of the Doctors, Mailman's Day, Day of the Students, Day of the Family, Day of the Compadres…etc., etc., etc. Every imaginable group of individuals has its recognized day and it is celebrated with a party amongst themselves and their families.

Besides birthdays, a lot of people also commemorate their Saint's Day. There is a particular day of the year when each saint in the Christian calendar is recognized. A person's *día de santo* is the feast day of the saint who they are named after. All the Lucías in México are honored on the *Día de Santa Lucía*, December 13th. All the Jorges celebrate the *Día de San Jorge* on April 23rd, etc., etc.

There are many days of special note, national and traditional holidays – for example *el Aniversario de la Constitución* – Constitution Day – *el Natilicio de Benito Juárez* – Benito Juárez' birthday – and *el Día del Trabajo* – Labor Day. There may be a holiday on these days, if not in the workplace, possibly in the schools, although the ones I have named are actually *días feriados obligitorios* – legal holidays – when all banks, government offices, schools, and most businesses are closed.

And finally, there are all the assorted celebrations such as birthdays, weddings, anniversaries, First Holy Communions, baptisms, graduations, dinner parties and….

You may ask, "What day of the year is not a specially remembered day?"

Really, there are none! Every day of the year is special to one group or another. You will probably be invited to some of these celebrations, so how do you know if you should bring a gift? If it is expected, what should you bring? For the answer to this question, I usually ask myself three questions:

How well do I know the person who is being feted?
How long has it been since I last gave the person a gift?
Do I want to give them something?

If two of the answers to these questions indicate the correctness of taking a present, I do so. Often, it isn't a big gift, it's just food, flowers or a bottle of wine.

As if all the celebrations did not entail enough gift-giving, there are also special circumstances that spontaneously generate the offering of a token of appreciation. Mexicans are very generous and they love to give out *recuerdos* – small mementoes.

This has happened to me many times; usually it has been at a social gathering, but once it occurred when I was with a group of my students. I admired a young woman's T-shirt, "What an unusually pretty top!" I told her. The next week, I found a little parcel on my desk and when I opened it, there was the same T-shirt (but in my size) and a little note from the student, *un recuerdito* – a small memento.

One thing I notice about gifting among my Mexican friends and family: when spontaneously offered, the present is not usually elaborate but it is always very thoughtful. I have friends who must store away ideas for when the occasion presents itself. Once my friend Rosalba gave me a CD that contained an obscure, but favorite, song of mine. She remembered a conversation that had taken place about six months earlier when I had talked about that song, "I found this the other day and I thought of you!"

When I do not know a person very well but am invited to an event they are hosting, I usually elect to send or carry flowers (to a woman); to a man, I take a bottle of wine in a gift bag.

If I'm invited to a party where I know the hostess—or the host—I take something I've made. If I have time, I like to bake a dessert. I know that friends always appreciate the fact that I've gone to the effort of preparing something especially for them.

Mind you, it will be a bit of a shock when you see how most of your Mexican friends respond to receiving presents—from anyone, not just you. Actually I should say how they do **not** respond! In the USA and Canada, people always make a big deal of showing appreciation for their gifts. They usually open them right up, exclaim over them and thank the givers over and over again.

In México, it is most people's custom to accept the gift, mumble a quick *gracias*, then squirrel it away and say nothing more. The gifts will get opened after the party is over. You will not see this happen. Many times, your friend won't even let you know if your gift was to his or her liking! To those from north-of-the-border, this seems very rude and it is difficult for us to see such behavior in any other light. Nonetheless it is important to try and understand your friends' perspective, so bear with me.

For most Mexicans it is paramount to appear *sencillo* – humble. They feel that if they open your beautifully wrapped gift in front of everyone, they risk making you feel awkward, and they might also put the other guests in an uncomfortable position because their present was not as splendid. As for acknowledging the gift afterwards, they won't do this either, because they don't want to be *presumido* – to presume any more from the relationship you share because you gave them a gift.

This happens even with wedding gifts. There is very rarely a thank you card or even verbal thanks. It does seem like bad manners, especially in a country where people are so effusive, but this is an important part of the culture. I must say that young people do not follow this constrictive custom as much as their parents do.

If you cannot get your head around this, I would advise you to just chalk it up as one of México's many cultural mysteries… but remember it!

If you have employees, even very part-time domestic help—a gift is expected on their special days. Often times, this is a cash gift. At Christmas time, it is actually the law to give the equivalent of approximately two weeks' wages to all of those who perform any service for you. It is called *el aguinaldo*, and must be paid in cash by December 20th. Again, do not expect the recipient to gush with gratitude because this will not likely happen.

This gifting usually extends to everyone who does anything for you: the mailman, the water delivery person, the garbage pick-up people, the gardener, and especially anyone who works in your house. It may seem excessive and expensive by our standards, but lesser-privileged families look forward to this bonus with great anticipation. They usually use the money to provide a Christmas celebration for the family and gifts for their children. Without aguinaldo, they would never be able to afford the additional expense and provide themselves with this pleasure.

In México, gifting is always appropriate but you do want to be careful not to over-do it. What you give one year will be sort of expected the next!

Give from the heart and your thoughtfulness will show that you care.

Gifts are always appreciated...
but not in the way you may be accustomed to

Perfections and Imperfections

I moved to Mérida 7 years ago, and I love it because of its perfections and in spite of its imperfections. One of those perfections/imperfections is the climate.

When I lived in Canada I had to always figure out how to stay warm. In Yucatán, when the temperature hits 40 C, and the mosquitoes start to reproduce, I know I'm not in chilly Canada any more. I've adapted...I now: (a) use cream mosquito repellant as body lotion, (b) put my **red** wine in the fridge, (c) put my **lipstick** in the fridge so it won't melt.

Ladies, this is a great way to cool down your hot lips!

—**Juanita Zak**

Juanita was born in México, lived most of her life abroad and is now happily...HOME!

H is for...HEAT

How to live with it. Why is a siesta so important? Your health and general well-being are dependent on how well you handle this hot, humid climate.

I F YOU ARE IN THE PROCESS of buying or renovating a home in Yucatán, or nearly any low altitude or beach area in México, it's very important to look for a layout that works with the climate.

You want to have as many northern windows as possible because this is the direction the cooler breezes come from— from the ocean if it is a beach town. You will also need to have cross ventilation and the higher the ceilings are, the cooler the rooms will be. Avoid southern and western exposures as the hot afternoon sun pouring in will render the rooms uninhabitable during several hours of each day...and maybe the night. Put awnings over your windows and keep the doors open to allow for the free flow of air. If you have enough space to dig even a small pool, do so!

Planting big shade trees and installing water accents will also strengthen your home's defense against the awesome Mexican sun!

Ceiling fans are a must, and most folks air-condition at least their bedrooms if they can possibly afford to. The newer style "mini-split" room air conditioners, rather than central air-conditioning (which is very expensive to operate), seem like God's gift to México!

In low altitude and beach areas, the climate can be grouped into "four seasons":

November through March: Very pleasant with a mix of warm weather and a few quite cool days; some rain. In parts of México, this fine weather can extend into May and early June. In most of México this is the very dry season.

April and May in southeastern México are very hot but not too humid; there's almost no rain, but north of Mexico City these two months are usually temperate and dry.

June through August in Yucatán is hot and very humid every day with frequent tropical rainstorms. But in other low altitude and beach areas it's late June through October that is the hottest.

September and October are unbearably humid but not quite as hot in southeastern México; however, this is peak hurricane season.

On very hot and humid days I can feel the heavy air all around me when I get up in the morning. Emerging from my bedroom and padding out to the kitchen, the first beads of sweat start to form on my upper lip and on my forehead. By the time I've set up the coffee maker, I am feeling moisture trickling down my neck and back. And by the time I take the first sip of coffee perspiration is as heavy as after a workout—a vigorous one! But that is yet to come.

I do my morning walk, and when I return home it's sometimes actually possible to wring my clothes out. I know I really need a shower; while under the spray, all is well, but when I turn off the water sweating begins immediately; it's like being in a sauna. I cannot dry off, so I need to go and stand directly under the ceiling fan for a while.

Eventually I must get dressed, though, and if I don't need to leave the house, all will be fine. I put on some loose cotton clothing, so it's not too hard to live with the heat—in fact, I find it quite pleasant...now that I've had over thirty years to acclimatize. However, if I need to go out and especially if I have to dress up, I'm in for a huge challenge.

Makeup runs down my face as I'm putting it on, and my hair wilts before I can spray it in place. Each item of clothing sticks to my body; it is impossible to look "put together". I feel like the Wicked Witch of the West in the "Wizard of Oz" when she cries, "I'm mel-t-t-t-t-t-ting!"

Walking just a few blocks leaves me wilted, and dehydration can set in quickly. In order to stay healthy, it is necessary to drink several liters of water a day (in addition to regular liquids such as coffee, tea, juices and soft drinks). Although alcoholic beverages are "wet", they actually accelerate dehydration. Water cleanses and keeps the system from losing too many electrolytes. Energy drinks purport to do an improved job but I believe good old-fashioned H_2O is the best thing in this climate. If you sweat heavily, something that makes you lose those electrolytes even more quickly, you may be wise to drink the fairly new sugar and sweetener-free electrolytic rehydrating drinks, now available at pharmacies and many other places.

Staying out of the sun is also a wise move. You can always spot the tourists. They're the ones trudging along on the sunny side of the street, while all the Mexicans are the ones walking on the shady side. Using an umbrella, parasol, a cap or hat will also help to keep the body temperature from climbing too high.

The Mexicans are also the ones who are conserving their energy. They are not fast-walking or running along and no native-son or daughter would dream of exercising except in the early morning or in the evening. To do so would be to court disaster.

I have heard some visitors rather smugly remark that they "can take it", and maybe they can for a couple of weeks, but in order to live here for any length of time, it's necessary to follow the lead of people who have been born here.

Non-residents of Mérida and much of México are also prone to scoff at the siesta. Do they think Yucatecans lie down during the heat of the day because they're lazy? Absolutely not, they do so because they know they need to!

I always rest for at least two hours. I don't necessarily sleep, but I always take the time for my siesta, and I don't go half-way either! I take off my clothes, put on my nightgown and get right into the bed or stretch out in my hammock. About 5 p.m. it's time to restart the day. I shower again, and I'm all set to put in several more hours of work, watering the garden or doing other odd jobs around the house...and I'll still have lots energy for socializing in the evening.

Partly because of the heat, the timing of social events in Yucatán and most of México is very different than it is in the northern countries.

Five in the afternoon is a popular hour for Canadians and Americans to begin a party or even have dinner. My husband and I are sometimes invited to parties that start at five. We can never get there by that time; to do so would upset the whole day because we consider it still too hot to be dressed for an evening out, and if it's a weekday, we're back at work; 5 p.m. to 8 p.m. is the time we use for finishing up the day's tasks.

When Mexican friends are included it would not be a bad idea to reconsider the time of your get-together. The absolute earliest a party ever gets going in most of México is 8 p.m.; dinner is rarely served before 10 p.m. and the parties go on into the wee hours or even until dawn for the younger crowd.

It is important to remember this if you don't want to have spoiled dinners and end up feeling resentful. I often hear foreign residents comment about their Mexican friends, "They are very nice but they can never arrive on time!"

This appears to be bad manners, but it is not viewed this way by the locals. To them, it is the contrary. They consider it strange to expect guests to arrive early and upset their day. A comparable example would be if you had a friend who was an early riser and she expected you to be at her house by 6 a.m. for a breakfast party!

If you are inviting a mix of foreign and local friends to a party, you can accommodate both groups by saying there will be a "happy hour" or cocktails beginning at 7 p.m., but be sure people realize that they don't **have** to show up at that time. Yes, this does make for a very l-o-n-g evening, but this too is customary here!

Almost every afternoon, Mérida is "saved" by the refreshing breezes that blow in from the Gulf of México. I have always loved the evenings and nights in this city. They are sultry and sensuous, and there are the heady aromas of night-blooming flowers in the air. Once the sun goes down, Meridanos love to get dressed up and go to the parks and plazas or have a light meal at an outdoor café. They actually stay up quite late, enjoying the cooler temperatures while strolling along the avenues and visiting with their friends.

One thing from the "outside world" that the Yucatecans have embraced fully is air-conditioning. They love AC—and the colder it is set, the better! It is appreciated on very hot days, although you should try and refrain from frequently going in and out of air-conditioned rooms. Who knows why, but doing so seems to encourage sore throats and colds.

We do not have a fully air-conditioned home but there are mini-splits in the bedrooms; they allow our family to get a break from the constant heat and heavy humidity. We sleep well knowing we can cool down whenever we need to. This helps to keep us from getting too uncomfortable and cranky because of the heat. It is expensive to run air conditioners but we prefer to scrimp elsewhere in order to allow ourselves this comfort.

To manage the heat, mimic the locals:

- Make the daily siesta a part of your life.
- Exercise in the early morning or late in the evening.
- Stay out of the noonday sun.
- Wear a hat, or carry an umbrella or parasol to protect yourself from the direct rays.
- Drink plenty of water.
- Do your socializing in the evenings.

Mexicans have learned to handle this extreme climate and you can save yourself a lot of grief by following their example.

and
H is for...HISTORY

My husband Jorge is well travelled, and he enjoys learning about other cultures. Yet México is truly Jorge's country, Yucatán is his state and Mérida is his city.

Over the years he has helped me to understand the social structure and introduced me to a completely new way of life. At first, I felt utterly confused and uncomprehending of nearly everything. There was such a long period of time to learn about, and over the centuries there have been so many upheavals, twists and turns. Many cultures, languages and diverse ethnic groups have contributed to the story of the nation's past.

Jorge is drawn to México as any native son is to the country of his birth. But what is it about the place that has attracted so many others? The climate can be unforgiving, the social customs are confusing and the day-to-day challenges are never ending. Why are foreigners so captivated?

To learn about the fascinating history of this country, read the section following THE ALPHABET titled OUR COUNTRY – OUR STATE – OUR CITY.

Perhaps there's more to insects than meets the eye?

They abound in Yucatán. I'm reminded of the sky-darkening plague of locusts that stripped the leaves from my lime tree and the lines of leaf-cutter ants eating away at my hibiscus. I need to forever forget the swarms of roaches I saw boiling out of a broached septic tank—tarantulas and scorpions have also made cameo appearances. But wait…

There is color in motion in my small garden. Butterflies, moths and iridescent dragonflies dash and hover.

A huge dark moth that the Maya call *x'majana* enters my house every few weeks. The significance of its appearance varies according to the person telling the story. Some say it means bad luck, others say it presages the arrival of guests; some even say it foretells death.

A few weeks ago in the U.S.A. my beloved sister and her faithful dog both passed away. A short time later I returned to México. One morning two beautiful black butterflies, different from each other, landed on my white tile floor. They fluttered weakly and died peacefully before my eyes. I can't say what that meant but I felt blessed.

—Maryetta Ackenbom

Maryetta, a former U.S. Consul, retired and lives in Mérida. She is also an accomplished writer.

I is for...INSECTS

In México there must be every bug known to man. From nearly microscopic ants to great huge tarantulas, you're likely to see them all.

WHAT WILL TURN EVEN THE MOST stalwart neophyte into a quivering mass of jelly are the insects. At first they just about drove me to insanity. I've had so many "close encounters", and I've heard tales of so many more; a lot of them involve the ugliest critters on the face of the earth—cockroaches—Ugh!

The very worst time was when I was expecting my son. A fellow Canadian in Mérida invited me to her home; I was most excited and accepted happily. We sat in her living room, drank tea and chatted about our western Canadian homelands. After several cups my pregnant belly was full and I needed the bathroom. I asked where it was and she indicated a door to the left. There I went, closed myself in and nearly passed out! There were hundreds of cockroaches in there, literally hundreds, maybe thousands! I ran out, slammed the door and my compatriot asked what was wrong? "There...are...ah...some bugs...in...the bathroom," I stammered.

She looked at me like I was truly a shrinking violet and opened the door to see for herself, "Oh my God!!!" she screamed and ran off looking for "the spray"...while I was left alone, still desperately needing to find a toilet.

She could think of nothing else but the infestation of her home and rightly so. I wandered through her house until I found another bathroom and then I went back to wait in the living room. She eventually reappeared—visibly shaken!

The next morning she called and explained that a plumber had been working in that bathroom and hadn't properly sealed up when he was through. This was like opening the Pearly Gates for all the roaches down in the septic system. I went back to her house many times and there was never even a trace of the previous incident, but nonetheless, I made sure not to drink anything...I was not going near that bathroom again!

Ants are not nearly as repulsive but they are certainly just as annoying. They come in all sizes and colors and their penchant for spilled sugar, a crumb of bread, a sliver of meat or any other trace amounts of organic material is astounding. During the rainy season, it is all I can do to keep them out of sight. I try not to think about the fact that they are still lurking in many nooks and crannies inside my house and out!

There are the ones with wings that crawl all over my white walls at night and on occasion drop down on my head from the ceiling! Another nocturnal variety march in single file, straight from their nests to my prettiest plants and can clean off all the flowers and leaves in a single night. Ants bite—many bite hard—

and you sure don't want them around you, but sometimes there's not much to be done about them, as they are just too numerous.

In Mérida, mosquitoes are very plentiful as well and can be dangerous because certain strains transmit dengue fever and other diseases. Fortunately, the city sprays and the numbers are greatly reduced from what they used to be. The relief of having fewer mosquitoes does come at a price though; I'm really not at all sure how safe that spray is, but what can you do?

Many types of beetles and other crawlies abound and a few scary bugs like scorpions and tarantulas are native to Yucatán. I don't see them too often and one advantage is that they're large and easy to spot. They also move rather slowly, so it's not too hard to smack them. Being bitten by these bugs is not very pleasant but it's not too serious either; their bites are actually comparable to being stung by a wasp. Unless you are allergic, a dose of Benedryl™ will calm the discomfort.

So what can you do to keep the "home invasions" to a minimum? I do not hire fumigators and rarely use commercial sprays; I feel if they are lethal to the bugs, they can't be very good for humans or pets either. If I'm going to be outside at night and there are a lot of mosquitoes, sometimes I give in and spray a little repellent around my ankles, but I don't let it get on my hands or near my face. A light application seems to be enough to keep the biting at bay.

However, this seems to do no good when it comes to my "public enemy number one" – cockroaches – for them, I buy "roach motels". These are little black plastic discs with small openings around the sides. There is some kind of toxic substance inside and the cockroaches carry it back into their lairs and then die off. I place these strategically throughout the whole house.

I have designed my storage space to be as open as possible. Roaches love closed-in dark spaces; if everything is exposed to the light and air they won't nest there.

With ants there is little to be done except to "wipe them out" with a wet cloth wherever they appear. I also watch for where their colonies are...you can see them marching one-behind-the-other into tiny holes they drill in the walls or between the tiles. When I find an opening I stop it up with a thick paste I make from powdered detergent and water...this works for a while but new entrances will be seen sooner or later, and I have to repeat the process.

I am also careful to check my shoes and shake out my clothing before I put it on, because sometimes bugs will be in the folds or deep in the toes of footwear. Putting screens on the windows and making sure that doors close tightly helps to keep the bugs outside where they belong.

In this climate insects are a fact of life and you will never completely eradicate them...control is the best you can hope for. I have learned to tolerate insects up to a point and I am grateful for small mercies...at least most of them are not very **big**!

You'll see insects everywhere, even as fountain sculptures like this one in Chapultepec Park in Mexico City

Fun, Stimulation, Food and Love.

Gosh, is this the right order???

Fun is our fuel. Fun in laughing at all the things you can't understand - drivers??? Fun in meeting new friends and hearing and learning new things - Spanish is fun?

Stimulation - Expect the Unexpected! Open your mind and explore and appreciate all that is so unlike what we knew as normal. Learn about ancient civilizations on our doorstep. How many Spanish verbs?

Food - the avocado is indigenous to México - Guacamole Heaven! Chiles that delight your taste buds and presentation - my mind's eye is filled with color and my mouth is watering. There's a dish called a *Gringa* or a sandal - uhm?

As for Love - the crowning joy of deep and thoughtful feelings for *"mi esposo"*, *"mi amor"*. *"Oye, Oye"*, this is a beautiful country with beautiful people who may have so much less materially than we have. However, they give bountiful amounts of love and kindness.

Could it be that this Virgo is a secret romantic?

Time to go have a cup of coffee and hang out the wash!

—Janice Knight

Janice and her husband George visited Yucatán for years... when they retired; these two archaeology buffs found their home just steps away from Mérida's Museum of Anthropology – perfect!

J is for...JOURNAL
Writing is a great way to keep track of your feelings as you settle in to this new life.

I HAVE KEPT A JOURNAL for most of my years in México. I don't write in it every day, but whenever I want to or need to I find it is a tremendous help. If I'm trying to solve a problem, I often go back and read about a previous time in my life when I had a similar issue to face. I am reminded how I felt then and what I did about it.

I am especially careful to keep track of the funny things that happen. Oh, there have been so many! I think a sense of humor is vital, and if you can use it to work something out, so much the better!

One day, I was driving in the rain and the streets were flooded. My little VW bug lost its brakes, and I was not able to stop. So seeing there was nothing coming my way, I turned right down a one-way street. I was not going in the right direction and who was lying in wait...just out of sight? A cop, naturally!

He had a gleam in his eye and anticipation of a nice mordida no doubt filling his mind.

In Spanish, he told me I was going the wrong way, and I would have to pay a substantial fine and have my car towed away unless I let him "help" me. I pretended not to understand a word.

"*Yo…centro…correcto?…*Me…downtown…right?" I asked in my most exaggerated English-accented Spanglish.

"*No, no, no Señorita,*" he replied and again repeated his threats and his offer to "assist" me.

I smiled broadly and repeated, "*Yo…centro…correcto?*"

We went through this dialogue a few more times until eventually, using hand signals, he told me to turn around. He posed like a pointer and indicated the way towards town; "*¡Centro!*" he cried.

"*¡Muchas gracias!*" I chimed as I drove off, having neither paid mordida nor gotten a ticket! And you know what? I have used this strategy quite a few times since; it always makes me chuckle.

Sometimes the joke is on me and a valuable lesson can be learned. The day that I celebrated my twentieth anniversary living in Mérida, I was walking through the Plaza Grande and as usual, I was accosted by a hammock vendor who urged me to buy his wares. I wanted him to get the message, once and for all, that I was never going to buy one of his *turista* products. I told him, "I've been walking through this plaza for twenty years; you always ask me to buy a hammock; I've never done so, and I never will!"

With a twinkle in his eye, he said, "*Señorita, ¿quíen sabe?* Maybe one day you will!" I was humbled by his response and I decided he was right.

Now when I hear, "*¿Hamaca Señorita?*"

I smile and say, "*M-m-m-m ¿quién sabe?*"

From time to time in my journal, I jot down the price I pay for everyday items and am astounded to see how prices have doubled, tripled or even quadrupled...everything has gotten so expensive!

I write down what the weather is like—1988 was the coldest winter I've ever spent here...2003 was the hottest summer—and sometimes I record what our family ate for dinner.

I like to write about parties we attended, special family occasions, and yes, I record conflicts we've had. As I say, by no means do I make daily entries; although if there is a crisis, I sometimes do so for its duration.

After more than thirty-five years of sharing a busy life with Jorge I find that we have both forgotten a lot of the details. Some of them seem to be completely gone! Certainly I can remember how I felt at different periods of my life more clearly than I remember what actually transpired.

When someone brings up a past event, it's useful to be able to go back through my journals to see if there's some sort of mention. Often I find the forgotten details on some tattered page. The mundane and the marvelous experiences in our personal and professional lives are all there to read about.

As a mother I like to record what is going on in my children's lives. Often it is very practical—a few months ago, my daughter had swollen glands and asked if she'd ever had the mumps? Looking through the old journals, I was able to assure her she'd indeed had them.

It's interesting to note how my son and daughter react to situations, each in their own way. It's incredible to realize that their behavior as young adults is not much different than it was when they were little guys. Their basic personalities have changed very little over the past decades. What does this tell me about myself? Am I still the same person I was when I moved to México?

Yes and no...I have the same personality but my life experiences have honed my priorities, my attitude, my skills, my coping mechanisms and my empathy towards others. Looking back through my journals, I can read about the definitive events that helped me make the compromises I needed to make, and those that reinforced my personal convictions.

Many of the newcomers I've met over the years have been very frustrated and impatient with the progress of their adaptation and the options they have open to them.

Sometimes in my journals I've been able to find mention of a similar episode that I went through. When I recount my experience they realize that obviously I survived, and seeing what I have done since coming to México helps them feel that they too will probably make it through whatever it is they're facing.

The record of how I have felt and what I've done helps me on a daily basis. Maybe keeping a journal could do the same for you.

Keeping a journal can help you with
your adjustment to living in México

You know you have lived in Mérida a while when:

- You ask your host..."Appointed time or Mexican time?" (which is "-ish" time, i.e., 5-ish)
- The shopping cart guys at Costco and other supermarkets know which car is your car. They remember where you parked when you don't.
- You actually shop and buy stuff at the Houston Airport.
- You look forward to eating "Mérida Chinese food".
- A trip back to the homeland always includes a call for mail pickup and delivery.
- You've added a few Mayan words to your vocabulary.
   And finally...
- You understand that *fiesta de traje* means bring something...not "wear a suit".

—Ellyne Basto

Ellyne, who hails from New York, and her husband Chucho from Mérida, moved to his home town several years ago. They own and operate a very popular B & B, Cascadas de Mérida. Online at: www.cascadasdemerida.com

K is for...KISSING
Lots of this goes on! When will a hug, a pat, a handshake or a nod suffice?

When I moved to México, one of the first things I noticed was all the kissing! I could see it all around me. Where I come from in Canada, I was used to observing mothers and fathers kiss their small children at every opportunity. Little ones need a kiss hello, a kiss bye-bye; they need a kiss to say, "Well done!" and one when their feelings are hurt. They need "I love you." kisses and quick little ones that say, "Be careful out there!" But what about big, hulking, almost-grown boys? Do they need this array of kisses from Mommy and Daddy?

In México they certainly seem to. I've seen gruff-looking men who meet on the street give each other resounding kisses and hugs and then one will tousle the other's hair and say, "*¿Cómo estás hijo?*" – How are you son? *Hijo* – son – is used in a friendly, non-literal manner throughout México. Any and every male, particularly the young ones, seems to be called *mi hijo* – my son, pronounced MEE'hoh – by nearly everyone, even women and relatives little older than him.

Afterwards, father and son often lope off together, arms around one another's shoulders. Mexican men are not at all shy about showing affection. The same young man, upon meeting his mother will probably get double the hugs and kisses and also get asked, "*¿Ya comiste?*" – Have you eaten?

However, if the men are not shy, the women can be totally uninhibited when it comes to showing their feelings.

Women usually "kiss on first meeting" but not always.

Those who are related or are good friends go through a whole ritual. Their greetings include many kisses, stroking the cheeks, embracing the shoulders and full contact hugs followed by a kind of prolonged rocking back and forth—while still clenched in one another's arms. Mothers and daughters, sisters, cousins, school and family friends, *comadres* – the women's version of *compadre* – neighbors, grandmothers and aunts all seem to get this full treatment in certain situations.

But on other occasions, the women will approach each other; turn their cheeks, purse up their lips and air-kiss near one another's ears, pull away, and smile tightly. I could not for the life of me figure out when the different styles were appropriate and when not.

Sometimes I would come across a woman I knew well and give the full, effusive greeting...only to feel her firmly pull away.

I started really watching for the subtle signals. It isn't easy to figure out, even after having observed the rituals, literally hundreds of times. But for what it's worth, here's what I've concluded:

Men and women who are related usually exchange an air kiss when meeting. If the man and woman are *compadres,* or long-time family friends, there will be a kiss on the cheek and a sort of quick-hug. Physical greetings between men and women are usually quite conservative.

In social situations when women and men do not know one another and a kiss is not appropriate, I see they look at one another and either shake hands or nod in one another's direction and say, "*Mucho gusto*" – Pleased to meet you.

Still, I've observed there are some women who do not follow this generalization. They approach men with full contact hugs or a resounding kisses on the cheek. I see men who look very flustered and ill-at-ease. It is especially embarrassing for non-Mexican men.

What can they do at such awkward moments? Returning the greeting is not the right thing. It is best for them to step back, disengage from the clutch, smile and say, "*Mucho gusto*." Then turn and greet the next person, in the correct way. For the rest of the event, they should try to stay away from the enthusiastic lady. Hopefully she'll get the message and not be so inappropriate the next time. It will be a further deterrent if an accompanying wife or girlfriend gives the woman, "the look"—you know, the one that says, "Stay away!"

There are occasions when your reputation precedes an actual encounter. I was once introduced to a man who, upon hearing my name, "pounced" on me with a kiss, "*¡Qué gusto!*" – What a pleasure! – he exclaimed. I was quite taken aback until I realized he was "a friend of a friend", and we had both heard a lot about one another but never actually met before.

Two men who are related, often cup one of their hands on the nape of each other's neck or on the shoulder and with the other arm, they clench the opposite shoulder; they lean over one another and commence to pat each other on the back—quite forcefully sometimes—this is called *el abrazo*.

Professional colleagues, teachers and students, doctors and their patients, my employees and I all kiss from time to time but not always. Usually this occurs on holidays or at other festive times.

It's hard to know when, where, who, and how to kiss...if you can't see what you should do, it's probably best to wait and see what the other one does and follow suit.

There were other related-to-kissing activities that used to floor me, namely the asking of personal questions and the use of very descriptive nicknames. Where I come from in Canada, to enquire about a relative stranger's livelihood, how much money they paid for an article or their opinion about other mutual acquaintances, would be considered extremely rude. But in México this is not the case at all. It shows that the other person is interested in getting to know you—when it comes to the gathering of information, there is no wasting of time on formality.

Calling one another *Gordo(a)* – Fatty – *Flaco(a)* – Skinny – *Chivo(a)* – Goat – and so on...was something I thought was very strange and unkind, but that's just not so...nor is it meant to be. Political correctness—if it even exists —does not carry the same connotation in México as it does in the U.S. and Canada.

I remember the first time someone called me *Gorda*. I burst into tears. "They hate me!" I told Jorge. "Why else would they call me such an awful name?"

I was not easily convinced when he told me this was an endearment...and to tell the truth, it is one cultural hurdle I've yet to sail over.

Still, whether you feel at ease or not, extending greetings is absolutely mandatory. In this culture one of the very rudest things a person can do is to enter a room full of people and fail to acknowledge every single person in there. And by every single person, I include the old auntie asleep in her wheel chair and the newborn infant cradled in his mother's arms. You never go directly to the person you need to speak with and ignore the others. At minimum, a nod in each person's direction and a mumbled, *"Buenos días"* is expected.

Yes, it's pretty hard to figure out all this how-to-greet and when-to-and-when-not-to-kiss business, and it's hard to get used to the contrasting verbal familiarity that Mexicans fall into... while still addressing each other as *Usted* – the respectful or formal way of saying "you".

It certainly does add a dimension to social interaction that's missing in other cultures. I was quite overwhelmed during my early years in Mérida. The most daunting circumstance was when I'd arrive at a party or get-together of some kind and I'd see the others, making the rounds, kissing everyone on the cheek and calling one another by their nicknames.

To this day, I still don't know some people's "real" names. I didn't want to kiss all those people, and I certainly didn't want to call anybody *Gorda*! But I plunged in anyway; it was easier than standing awkwardly aside, offering a little wave and a tentative smile.

The best course of action is to observe the others and do as they do. After all, a little extra affection and attention—offered or accepted—is never an altogether bad thing. Go with the flow and it will become second nature to you!

Every day is like Saturday afternoon

The love of my life was my eighth grade boyfriend, Roger. Alas, we were separated from each other through no fault of our own. I married and divorced, raising my daughter as a single parent. My life in the U.S. was fulfilling, but I longed to retire to a place of tranquility, with gentle, carefree people and a sultry tropical climate. Yearning for a time and place where I could immerse myself in a culture different from my own...I dreamed of México.

A dream forgotten was to share my years with someone just like Roger. When he found me again, after 42 years, I knew I was right not to have accepted anyone but him. In one of our first conversations he told me of his dream of retiring...in México.

And so we did. Now my days are filled with good friends, balmy breezes and a México that nurtures creativity and adventure.

—Rainie Baillie

Rainie is a psychologist and relationships counselor, and a writer. The experience and insight gained during her 40 year career is the inspiration for her soon-to-be-released book Win at Love. *She and her husband Roger live in Mérida.*

L is for...LOVE
Is it all you need?

MOST OF THE WOMEN AND MEN I know who have come from other countries to live in México have done it for love.

Sometimes the love object is another person, sometimes it is a lifestyle, sometimes it's the weather, sometimes it's the culture, sometimes it's the music, sometimes it's the food and sometimes it is just the land itself. The Beatles popularized a song with lyrics that claimed, "All you need is love". Is it really?

I know a Canadian woman who planned everything she ever did; when we first met she was a young university graduate and was "going places".

Then, she met a Mérida man (in a bar of all places...in Canada, she never went to bars) and fell so completely "in love" that no one could help her see her way clear. She tried to make a life with the man, and many years of tortuous battles and passionate reconciliations followed until finally she was free of her obsession with him. She is now living quietly in her home town, sadder but wiser.

I know an American man who was so enamored with Mérida after his first visit to the city that he returned time and time again. Whenever he could he partied, soaked up the sun and eventually retired here. After a few years he was much less enchanted. For him, the heat, the insects, the humidity and the lifestyle were just too exhausting on a full time basis. He sold his lovingly refurbished colonial house and returned to his former home…happy for having had the experience but content to stay "back home" from then on.

I know another man from the U.S.A. who seemed to be one of the happiest, most well-adjusted people I knew. He loved his Mexican wife and child and got on well with his in-laws. After many years living in Mérida he returned to his native city alone, in order to attend a family wedding. There he met an old flame and did the embers ever ignite! He ended up leaving his Mexican family and moving in with the woman.

He said later that his attraction to her was so strong because he never had to figure anything out…it just "was". He said he never realized how tired he had become of always needing to sit back and analyze his every move.

He had never wanted to offend anyone, so he was overly cautious, and he burned out on adapting to the culture. He never returned to live in México, but eventually he reconciled with his wife and they now live in the United States. He says, though, that he's very careful to ensure that she has opportunities to speak her language, practice her faith and have the lifestyle she wants in their home. He knows that when one lives in a foreign culture, a refuge is necessary from time to time.

I know a beautiful Cuban woman who came to México when she was very young. By a circuitous set of circumstances she met an older man from the city and they married. He wanted her to be his "everything" and for a time she was quite pleased with her place in his life, but then she began to feel "hemmed-in".

The man did not want her to grow as a person; he didn't want her to have her own identity; he wanted her to be his alone. She separated from him, but the children they had together kept her bound to Mérida. Eventually he came to understand her needs and she came into her own. It took a long time but they both made compromises and have now seen their children marry and start their own families. They are content with the life they chose.

Finally, there is a Canadian woman who met her "true love" and completely and utterly turned her life around in order to be with him. She was also very enamored with the generous, hospitable people she met and she reveled in the music, sights, and sounds that were all around her in México. Then serious doubts set in and she questioned the wisdom of her decision. She went through many trying times and "butted her head against many brick walls" until she realized that life is what you make of it. Little by little, she found her way and is now extremely happy. That woman (no surprise here)...is me!

A love relationship often begins with stars in the eyes and butterflies in the tummy. If the spell is broken, can we ever find the good judgment needed to go forward and ultimately be even happier than when the stars were at their brightest and *las mariposas* were soaring away with our appetites?

Strive for balance. As an import into this culture you need to be cognizant of the facts. As amazing as the initial situation appears to be, periods of dissatisfaction will definitely come along. Hopefully, contentment and peace will replace the initial giddiness.

For those of us who have lived a significant length of time in a place other than where we were born, these ups and downs are a constant in our lives. But does this behavior mean that the passionate love we started out with was just an illusion? During the periods of disenchantment or when our dreams are dashed, do we need to feel as though our love was misplaced?

Sadly, this is sometimes the case. If the difficult times are far outnumbering the good, it may be best to cut your losses and move on. Some of us are just not meant to be transplants. As avant-garde as her life was, Frida Kahlo said, "There is no greater luck in the world than to die in the house where you were born."

Some people are simply like this.

But when the good times outnumber the not-so-good, and when you can see maturation in your attitude, you need to get to work and go beyond the infatuation stage. You need to realize that all the back-and-forth, the ups-and-downs and the shock of discovering you were out-of-line in your original assessments are simply part and parcel of the forging of your new life. You need to keep sight of what initially attracted you to México and build on that foundation. When the melancholy sets in, you need to accept it and work through it. Above all, it is important to remember that you started with love. It may not be all you need, but I truly believe it is the primary ingredient for building a life of substance in another country.

M is for...MÉXICO
How and why it makes us happy

D ID YOU PICK UP THIS BOOK hoping to get some answers to a few nagging questions?

Now that you're halfway through the alphabet, maybe you are still not too clear about one of the really **big** mysteries:

Why is it that you want to live in México?

A few of your friends and family members have probably tried to tactfully tell you that México isn't safe; the people are too different; the language is hard to learn; the infrastructure is lacking; the political situation is unstable; there has been violence and, "Hey...what are you thinking? Have you gone nuts?"

Some of you no doubt have some very solid comebacks:

- It is warm all year 'round.
- My pension check goes much further.
- Health care is extremely reasonable.
- I can afford to have help in the house.

- I am far away from the pressures of my family.
- In México I am free to do as I please.

Perhaps you can feel ownership of a few of these justifications, but there's also something totally intangible. When pressed for further details you probably shrug and say you really can't explain what "it" is, but you feel drawn to México, you sense that this is where you belong.

If you are reading these lines and nodding your head up and down, you are one of the many who has become enchanted by the MAGIC MADE IN MÉXICO.

But wait…if you start telling the cynics that you've been struck by some kind of Mexican magic, they'll be even more worried about you!

In an attempt to be more specific, I conclude that we are attracted to México because of the people. If magic is involved, they are the sorcerers! In this country it isn't uncommon for a stranger to drop what he or she is doing, get in their car and lead you back home when you've become lost.

Do people in other countries show such tolerance of those who don't speak the language?

Isn't it amazing how people want to include you in their family and social events every day, even when you can't be a very active participant?

Where else in the world do you get the impression that your happiness matters?

Most Mexicans are generous and friendly. There is the arrogant social climbing class whose heads have grown too big for their brains, but you can choose to stay away from them. However, if you do engage them in conversation, you'll find that even they are interesting and will accept you as you are. No one here is out to change you…freedom reigns!

Such acceptance from others encourages us to accept ourselves just as we are. There doesn't seem to be a huge pressure to conform. Some new residents have told me they have rediscovered their passion for life. After we've been here for awhile, we see that our true selves are more upfront, instead of hiding in the back. México's less frantic pace allows us to enjoy life more fully.

My case is not unique but it is probably somewhat different from the usual one. When I moved to México, I was very young, too young to make a sensible decision, and once I had committed to a man I truly loved and had married him, I knew it would be extremely difficult to extricate myself. But that was a moot point because I didn't want to. I wanted to adapt and be happy living in México. I knew this was a special place.

I saw happy, well adjusted people all around me, and if I wanted to be like them, I would need to make some changes in my attitude; it wasn't up to the whole country to make adjustments for me.

Once I began to look for ways to be happy, they came to me in spades. First of all, I needed to look after my physical environment. I am a nester; I need cozy, well-balanced, harmonious surroundings. I had an almost-empty house; I possessed very little money and had only a vague idea what I wanted. On one of our grocery shopping forays, my mother-in-law showed me where the artisan market was located. She didn't think I'd want to buy anything there, but I sure did! Soon I found myself scouring the place for baskets, pottery, fabric and unfinished furniture. I sewed and sanded; planted and painted; I soon had a very eclectically decorated home that pleased me, pleased Jorge, and…we breathed a sigh of contentment.

I knew that I needed to share my life with more people, so I went looking for them. When you're in a new place, you must often be the one to approach people who interest you. They won't all be beating a path to your door. Some of my first friends are still my good friends. When we met, I didn't know what we had in common, but I listened to them and I soon found out. It's true, I have encountered some difficult people, but nothing ventured, nothing gained.

Which brings me to my next observation: it's vital to be open to new activities and life styles. I had never considered crafts as an income source, but one of my first friends in Mérida taught me that making decorative items and baking could provide me with a tidy sum while I waited for the "dream job" to become available. That was a long time coming, so it's a good thing I found alternative ways to make money. How else would I have bought all the handcrafts that I needed to decorate our home?

If opportunities are not immediately coming your way, don't wish away your time, waiting for something to happen. Make it happen by showing up. Be mindful of what you're doing and enjoy the expected and unexpected perks that come along… when they come along.

Be humble. This is not a matter of downplaying your strengths and merits; these should be celebrated. But appropriate gratitude must also be there. My good friend Rainie says, "We have been given gifts, but we develop skills."

I believe we need to give thanks and share them. To me, that is a big part of humility.

After I had lived here for some years, Mérida became much more diverse—more entertainment venues opened. We had a symphony, theaters and foreign films. My experience with this sort of thing had been extremely limited up to that point, but I tried everything and liked it. As a result, I now enjoy new cultural interests.

Little by little, ways to help others came my way. At first I felt apprehensive. What if the people didn't understand my Spanish? What if I inadvertently offended someone? Over the years, I have been involved in many worthy causes and I have definitely received far more than I've given out.

Respect is the attribute Mexicans cherish above all else. I discovered that if I treated people with good manners and kindness, I would almost always be treated this way in return. I learned to take the time to notice needs, and I offered what I could. This was usually no big deal at all. It is not the extraordinary things we do for others that are noticed and remembered; what counts are the everyday kindnesses and how we make others feel.

These are my personal ten commandments. I suspect they are the same ones being followed by happy people all over the world. I know they work here.

- You must want to be happy.
- You have to be flexible.
- Look for potential opportunities.
- Be open-minded.
- Stay in the moment.
- Practice humility.
- Consider new ideas.
- Embrace change.
- Be generous.
- Be respectful.

Having said all of the preceding, there is one fact left to address. There are also a slew of very bad people living in México, as there is nearly everywhere. There are corrupt politicians; cops on the take; shady contractors; careless doctors; condescending social paragons; abusive merchants; drug dealers, thieves and other criminal types...the list goes on and on. I think that they are more visible in México because **everything** is more visible in México. Life is right on the surface. What you see is usually exactly how it is.

Maybe this is the answer to why we want to move to México? In a place where life is displayed openly and obviously, it's easier to be ourselves...and we stand a good chance of living happily ever after.

You'll always be surprised

Hamish and the Vet

Early one morning while we were across México from our home in Mérida, our cell phone rang. Carolina, our Maya housekeeper had found Hamish, our old Border Collie and best friend, unmoving and lying in a pool of vomit. Unable to return, we told Carolina to call an unknown, but recommended, veterinarian.

Later, Carolina reported that the vet had hurried over, transported Hamish in his air-conditioned animal ambulance to the clinic, placed him on an IV and took blood samples and X-rays. The lab results would be available in a few hours. That evening, the vet called his report to us. Carolina visited the clinic twice a day for several days until Hamish was released and then brought him home in a taxi and stayed with him until we could get back.

A few hours after we returned, the vet was in our kitchen explaining Hamish's condition and treatments. Hamish, who didn't much care for vets, weakly walked into the kitchen, rested his chin on the man's leg and closed his eyes.

The most eloquent "thank you" I have ever witnessed.

—**Bob Jack**

Bob and his wife K are landlubbers again after living for years on their boat "Rima". He is now writing a book about the sailing/ cruising lifestyle. His adventures are not for the faint-hearted!

N is for...NETWORK
It's vital to form one.

W HEN I FIRST CAME TO LIVE IN MÉXICO, one of the
biggest hurdles I faced was my lack of a network. I did not
know people to whom I could go for information, and I needed
to know so much: where to shop, the name of a good doctor,
how to clean away that crusty hard water residue I'd never seen
before, how to keep the bugs from reaching pandemic levels and
so on. My husband tried to help, as did his family, but they were
not from my culture; they did not know my needs. It was very
frustrating, since I wasn't able to find other women who knew
where I was coming from.

This is not the usual experience nowadays. There is such a
large international community in México that finding foreign
residents who have been here longer to show you the ropes is
not difficult, and there are wonderful sites on the Internet that
give you all information you need.

- Rolly Brook's *My Life in Mexico* at rollybrook.com is an
  insightful great read.

- For truly soulful musing, check out "Felipe" on his blog, *The Zapata Tales* at tzuru4.blogspot.com, where you'll discover a whole string of pearls that will set your heart to dreaming.
- If you want to understand the socio-political scene in México, Richard Grabman's *The Mex Files* at mexfiles. net is the best there is.

Many foreign residents live in México year-round, and an even greater number spend a good portion of the winter in México, so you will meet English-speakers in grocery stores, at the immigration office, at the International Women's Club and the International Men's Club, at the English Language Library and a host of other places in your community.

However, not everyone you come in contact with will be helpful; neither will you warm up to everyone. But little by little, you'll make acquaintances and build your personal circle of good friends. You will probably be surprised by the variety of people you meet…from every walk of life. I always say that living in Mérida has afforded me an opportunity to get to know people I never would have met if I'd stayed in Canada. I have friends from every geographic region of the U.S.A. and Canada; I have good friends from different European countries. I have many friends from all over México and even one friend in Mérida who is from Hong Kong! Each of them offers something unique, and I am grateful to have them in my life.

Some people try to adapt so completely to this new environment that they almost divorce themselves from their compatriots. They are so anxious to be a part of the México scene that they reject their former one. They have good reasons I suppose, but I've found that is a very difficult road to travel.

We're all products of our upbringing, and not many of us can ever separate ourselves completely. We need to embrace this culture...certainly! Yet, nearly everyone needs to have contact with other friends who are like theirself, because with these friends they don't need to explain everything they do. They know what your needs are because they have the same ones.

I know a woman who came to live in Mérida about twenty years ago. She moved into a very typical area, quickly got to know her neighbors and began to live her life à la mexicana. She studied Spanish with zeal; shopped in the market exclusively; learned to prepare regional cuisine; sent her children to a public school close by her house and made many contacts at the nearby church.

I met her at a city function and recognized her as an American. She is blue-eyed, a natural platinum blonde and there is no mistaking Midwest carriage when you see it. I addressed her in English. She very quickly answered me in Spanish and told me she was very happy in her new life and had no need to speak English. *OK with me*, I thought, but we'd see how long this lasted. I saw her again about six months later, and although we spoke only in Spanish, she had a lot of questions for me about where she could get American products and so on.

The third time I ran into her was on the beach. We chatted—in English—and then sat to have a drink in the shade, and she blurted out, "This is so-o-o-o nice; I needed to speak English!"

"Of course," I said, "and I admire how well you've learned Spanish."

She went on to say that she wanted to make friends in the international community, but didn't think she could keep her old language and customs if she was going to fully embrace the new life she wanted to live. I went out-on-a-limb and, as gently as I could, told her that I believe we all have an infinite capacity for a variety of experiences and acquaintances.

Since that time, she has made many friends from many different cultures, and her life has balance and depth. Her commitment to respecting the Mexican culture remains strong, but so does her attachment to her foreign-born friends.

The more diversity we allow into our lives, the richer each component becomes. I don't believe we can cut off our roots, not even while we are putting down new ones.

On the other side of the coin are those who move to México and really have no interest in learning the language or anything about the culture. They want the lifestyle they left behind and will do whatever it takes to achieve this. They are critical of the way everything is done in this country, and to them, nothing is as good as it is "back home". Despite their complaining, most of them want or need to be here for a variety of reasons. Even when this is the case, they still have to find a way to be happy...or at least keep their misery to themselves. Those who are negative and spend a lot of energy complaining will find they make few interesting friends. Only other lonely souls will be attracted to them, and that's hardly going to be conducive to a satisfying life!

There were very few non-Yucatecans living in Mérida during the first half of the time I've resided here. In more recent years, many Mexicans from other parts of México and foreigners from many countries have moved to the city. A lot of them are recently retired and very active physically and mentally. Many of them have bought old houses and are lovingly restoring them to their former splendor. They want to be involved in the community and are willing to give of their time, their energy and resources. These people are a boon to the city in every way. Their enthusiasm brings new vigor to tired old neighborhoods and their creative ideas spark new enterprises.

Not all of them are completely adapted to this culture, and they have issues but they certainly make a great effort to overcome them. Not all will stay indefinitely, but a substantial number will do so. I really like these people and am happy to be getting to know them.

If you haven't done so already, go out and meet some new friends and build your network. This will help you to sort your way through the pitfalls all neophytes face and with them, you can enjoy all that this wonderful place has to offer.

Mérida, late afternoon

Mérida, late afternoon, we are driving home from a siesta hour grocery shop. In front of our car is a motor cycle with passenger. We see the back of the passenger, a substantial woman wearing a vibrant yellow shirt and electric magenta Capri pants. She is carrying a coffee table. One end of the table is sitting on her thigh, and her arm, stretched out, is holding the other end in place.

Trudy turns to me and says:

"I know I've been in México too long when I look at that woman on the motor cycle and think...*I wonder where she got that coffee table?*"

—Lorna-Gail Dalin

LG is no doubt one of Mérida's most humorous residents, her quick wit delights us all.

Be Ready for the Unexpected

Take nothing for granted... Rejoice in the "Ah-ah-ah-ah" moments

—Debi Kuhn

Debi and her husband Tom have found their place in the sun... Debi writes a blog, Debi in Mérida.

O is for...OFF CENTER
How you may often feel, especially when your decision to live in México is questioned.

WHAT MAKES A PERSON DECIDE to move to another country? To pull apart their life, sell many of their possessions, give away a lot more and pack the little remaining into suitcases or boxes and take it along? How does one decide what to sell, what to give away and what to bring with them?

I have a copper wall hanging that I bought in Chile almost forty years ago. It isn't particularly beautiful or exceptional in any way, but I like it very much. It reminds me of my first travels and the independence of my youth. I remember vividly how I took it down from the living room wall of my west-end Vancouver apartment, made a drawing of how all the parts hooked together, then dismantled it and wrapped it carefully to bring with me to México. I left behind all kinds of practical items and sentimental ones...but this came with me.

Within a few days of my arrival I pulled the pieces from the bottom of the suitcase, reassembled the fish and set it in place on a wall in my new home in Mérida. People would come into the house, see it and ask, "What's that…is it from Canada?"

I'd go through the explanation of where it came from and would be asked, "Why did you bring it here?"

When my mother visited the first time, she asked, "Why did you carry that all the way here?"

The friend who was with me when I bought it, exclaimed, "You brought the Chilean fish to Yucatán; why didn't you bring your Robert Bateman prints?"

Maybe the copper Chilean wall hanging is an allegory of my life and the decisions I've made…different, not always understood but uniquely mine. Just as I'm questioned about the fact that it's been with me all these years, I am asked about the choices I've made. In the early years when this would happen, it would upset my fragile equilibrium.

Adjusting to all the newness is challenging enough without having to deal with people who constantly query your sanity.

I myself was often unsure about what I'd done and having to explain myself was difficult. Needless to say, I didn't like being caught off guard or losing my center, but as the years went by it took me less effort to find myself again. Really, being asked hard questions has made me revalidate myself over and over again.

Here are a few commentaries I hear all the time, followed by tactful retorts:

> Many newly arrived couples say, "Our married children and grandchildren brutally ask, "Don't you care about your family anymore?"
>
> Smile and say, "Of course we care about our family and we still want to spend time with you but we want this too."

The question, "What will you do if you become ill?" is a common one.

Maybe the person thinks there's no health care in México, so set them straight. "If I become ill, I can go to an excellent doctor at a modern medical centre right here." Then give them the link to the local hospital's website and tell them if they have a good look, it will be clear that the medical facilities in México are excellent and they needn't worry.

When former neighbors ask, "Is this a good idea at your age; don't you think you should be around familiar places and people?"

Just say, "I believe change is healthy at any age; if I only wanted to be around the familiar places and people all the time, I would not have left. I hope you'll visit and see our new home."

My banker, real estate agent and accountant all say, "You need a support system!"

Reassure them, "I have a support system—a new one—and it is becoming firmly established."

And finally, there's this response that usually stops further enquiry, "Thank you very much. You're kind to worry about me and your concern makes my new life easier."

Books about México abound; some of the very best have been written by elderly México-lovers, like Ethel Stockton, who between 2002 and her death at ninety-four in 2010 wrote, *Old is a Four Letter Word* and three sequels, *Old Fashioned, Old is Better* and *Not Too Old,* (and a fifth, to be published soon). Or

Harriet Doer, whose *Stones for Ibarra*—written when she was eighty—became a best seller and a movie, starring Glen Close.

From what I have seen, those who decide to blaze new trails for themselves are often considered to be malcontents. They're not easy to understand, and they need a lot of determination to withstand the criticism. This determination is what we have in common…the part about being malcontents is a misconception.

Many of the men and women I met in México during my early years "did it for love". They met their life partners here and gave up their old lives to be with that person. Many took this decision impulsively, and some of those impulsive decisions did not stand the test of time. Yet most of those who are still here have rich and rewarding lives, beyond anything they envisioned all those years ago.

My friends and acquaintances who have moved to México later in life are an interesting group. Many are children of the 1960s whose early idealism was put on hold during the years of building a career, raising children and becoming financially secure. Then when their children were grown, they retired and life could once again be whatever they wanted it to be. The old wanderlust set back in, and they set their sights further afield. They somehow ended up south of the border and have full, creative lifestyles; why would that make them unhappy?

One person in my family was very against me living away from Canada; he hounded me and hounded me. Finally, I made two lists: "Why I should live in México" and "Why I shouldn't live in México". We went over it together and he finally admitted that his negativity was mostly based on his fear of losing me. This is often the crux of the matter…we need to reassure our loved ones that we will stay in touch…and do so!

Sometimes a certain smugness can set in; this is not desirable. Neither is it a good idea to try and convince others to follow our lead. We have made choices that are not for everyone. We need to concentrate on enjoying them.

The naysayers don't need to be appeased, but our loved ones need to be shown that we have not gone off our rocker. They worry about us and their concerns need to be addressed. The best way to do this is by example. Be happy and enjoy your new life. Have a sense of humor and be generous. Invite your family and friends from back home to visit and show them your world...warts and all!

This just about sums it up for me. We are questioned, we are challenged, we do hit bumps in the road (figuratively and literally) but life is what we make of it.

Even though the uncomfortable questions initially threw me off; they have helped me to keep my core intact, and I'm richer for having addressed them.

The Yucatán is a sanctuary

Choosing to live in the Yucatán instead of anywhere else in the world has proved to be one of the best life decisions for my husband and me. We are filled with gratitude.

In México, dogs are used for guarding families, homes or businesses. Many locals are fearful when they see a dog and his owner walking along. Some of them seem to melt into the side of a building, hurry past the dog or even cross the street.

Buddy Love, our blonde mix of lab, golden retriever and south-of-the-border collie, trots proudly beside us as we stroll down the sidewalks. I greet everyone that we approach and quickly say, *"¡No muerde; no muerde! Está muy feliz porque vive en Mérida...Yo tambien!"* – He doesn't bite. He is very happy because he lives in Mérida! Me too! Buddy stops, wags his fluffy plume of a tail and looks upward with dark chocolate eyes. He smiles graciously.

Consistently people relax, return his smile, and respond with, *"Muy bonito"* – Very nice. If they ask what his name is, I respond, *"En inglés es Buddy, en español es Amigo!"* – In English, it's Buddy, in Spanish that means Friend!" Then people begin asking questions about me.

Our engagement in many conversations with the local people is prompted by our dog, our tail wagging ambassador in México!

—Cherie Pittillo

Cherie and her husband Greenwood are happily living and loving life in Mérida. Their combined artistic talents and generous spirits enrich the city.

P is for...PEOPLE
How to meet them:

THIS BOOK HAS A LOT TO SAY ABOUT how you can find friends who will understand your way of thinking, and how you can form networks with those like yourself who have come to México in search of a new lifestyle and new challenges. But what about the people who are from this country? Since they seem to be very interesting, you must be curious about them; like me, you sense that they have a wealth of knowledge to share.

Watching them, we conclude they are spontaneous and generous because we see this all around us, even though every day we may encounter hot-tempered drivers, surly store clerks and inefficient bureaucrats. The parks and plazas are full of loving parents, playful children, affectionate couples and serene older folk.

So what makes these people tick?

What brings them joy?

What truly upsets them?

How can we meet local citizens who will become our friends?

How can we progress past the polite nods, move forward to kisses on the cheek and finally receive those effusive hugs that good friends exchange?

Where can we find these people?

Your neighborhood is a good place to begin. When you move in, by all means be friendly! If you have restored your home, you know the neighbors are probably curious to see what changes you've made; why not invite them over to see? If your project was exceptionally dusty or noisy, you could also use this occasion as an opportunity to thank them for the patience they showed while the work was being carried out. They will probably have lots of stories to share about the history of your home and those who lived there before you.

Ask their advice about what you still need to finish on the house and how to find essential items. Is there a good painter nearby? Where is the closest bakery? What plants will grow well in the garden? If you show interest in their opinions, they'll be flattered and open to getting to know you better.

Most Mexicans are not distrustful people but they are cautious. They don't usually rush into relationships without careful assessment. They are accustomed to their families; these are usually large and diverse, so they provide most of the required companionship. They also have their school friends and friends-of-the-family to fill the small void the family unit fails to satisfy. Yet, I've found they are as curious about me as I am about them; they really want to know what I think. They are also very interested in learning about the country of my birth and they enjoy hearing stories about my childhood and the life I led prior to moving to México. It might be a nice touch for you to make a small album of photos of the family, friends and home you left behind. After all, "a picture paints a thousand words".

Friends of friends have also become my good friends. When I go to a social event, I make a point of speaking to everyone I come in contact with, offering at least a *"Buenas noches"* and a smile. Mexicans do not often approach someone they don't know, so it's important to make the first move and show you want to be part of the party. But don't be too forward; usually a well-placed compliment will elicit interest among the group.

"Isn't this a beautiful place; have you been here before?" or...

"I really like the dress you're wearing; did you buy it in Mérida?" or even...

"How do you manage to look so fresh in this heat?"

What if you don't know enough Spanish to say any of the above? Well...you can learn; Spanish is really not a difficult language. During my first years in México, if I knew I'd be going to a particular place, I would try to think of what people might say to me and how I would answer back. I used to create dialogues in my head and then practice saying them out loud when I was in the bathroom with the water running and the door closed. My version of singing in the shower! Of course most times, no one would say any of the things I'd imagined them saying, but it was all good practice.

After attending a number of parties and meeting new people, I knew that I would be asked about where I come from, if I enjoyed living in Mérida, etc. I often got frustrated with that often-repeated "Q & A" session, so I learned how to ask some questions of my own. When I was asked where I come from, I'd say, "I'm from Canada; have you ever been there?"

"When did you go there?"

"Which part?"

"What did you like best?"

To the question about whether or not I like living here, I'd say, "Oh, very much. Are you a native of Mérida?"

"Have you ever lived elsewhere?"

"What do you like best about your city?"

Often times, I'd learn as much about my new acquaintances as they would about me. Over the years, other sources of great enjoyment have been the casual encounters I have with everyday people. When I'm out walking or shopping, I greet people—I've noticed they always do—"*Buenos días*," I say as I pass by.

I try to be friendly. In this way, I've had many small but memorable experiences.

Once when I was driving through a town, I felt absolutely parched, so I went in search of a drink. I spied a stack of watermelons and decided I'd buy one to take home. I approached the vendor and told him how good his watermelons looked and then checked them all out. Finally I selected the one I wanted. He must have sensed my need for liquid and asked, "Wouldn't you like to have a slice now?" From another melon, he cut off a big juicy piece and gave it to me...it was warmed from the sun and so sweet! I went on my way again but often, when I feel thirsty, I remember that incident and I crave watermelon!

Don't be shy and don't be afraid your Spanish will come out incorrectly. If you show you're open to friendship and interested in their culture, Mexicans will respond to you. They are characteristically curious about people from other places. Before you know it, you'll have a diverse group of new people in your life.

Q is for...QUALITY
Life here serves this up in spades

H OW DO WE DEFINE QUALITY OF LIFE? It must mean different things to different people, but by and large we could agree that it is a collection of enjoyable and worthwhile pastimes that bring us pleasure.

I watch television programs and read magazine articles that depict how little time many north-of-the-border families spend together. Everyone is busy—all the time!—and often each family member has interests that the rest of the family doesn't even know about. How has this happened north of the border, and why isn't it the general norm in México?

I would theorize that economics has a lot to do with it. Many families in the north have at least two full time salaries contributing to the bank account. Add this to the fact that credit is widely available and the temptation to spend, spend, spend is hard to resist. It becomes a vicious circle...more money is needed to pay for "the stuff", so parents and older children work longer hours to do so (or at least to make payments on the credit cards). This results in less time spent together as a family.

Revolving credit can be a great boon to both the people and the economy, **but**…what worries many thoughtful Mexicans is the recent trend towards unreasonably high-interest credit cards and other types of revolving credit, even including home mortgages.

This is something that can trap people, particularly those who do not have a lot of disposable income and do not fully understand the responsibilities attached to these financial obligations. They could potentially find themselves in a situation not unlike that of the peons who could never escape their debts to the "company store" on the old haciendas.

Because at least three quarters of the country's population live in some degree of poverty; they cannot go out and spend a lot of money. They simply don't have it. So they stay home and enjoy inexpensive leisure activities with their extended families. Everyone brings something and a good time is had by all.

Many Mexicans are musical, and even if they lack talent they still enjoy singing and strumming on the off-key guitar. Most women are accomplished cooks, and I would venture to say that the meals they make for a fiesta like *chilaquiles, enchiladas*, salads, pilafs and pasta dishes could not be had in a restaurant for many times the cost of what they spend in the preparation. A lot of men and women are very creative and they manage to fashion all kinds of decorations, accessories and toys out of practically nothing. I received a handbag once that had been made with candy wrappers and glue and believe me, it looked very "exclusive". A lot of satisfaction is derived from this excellent reusing of what many would simply throw in the trash. In turn, this contributes to the further contentment with the life style.

Because many of México's citizens use public transportation and have to think twice about spending those precious pesos...they walk a lot. Sometimes an older sibling or parent will accompany the children and this too provides opportunities for lots of great conversations.

Even families that do have means are often happiest when in the company of their relatives and old friends—people they've always known.

When foreign residents in México witness this phenomenon they are often seized with a desire to belong. They emulate their neighbors' behavior and soon have formed a circle of good friends they can share their days and evenings with.

Most of the time the currency exchange rate between the dollar and the peso is favorable for those on dollar incomes, and this allows more financial freedom. Couple this with the fact that many of the services and commodities cost much less than comparable ones outside the country and it just keeps getting better and better.

Finally, in México, we can "grow younger"...in our thinking and in our actions. There is just so much to fill the senses. There are markets to shop in, ruins to explore, new foods to taste, new music to listen to, beaches to walk along and yes, languages to learn. Exposure to all of this will indeed make you look and feel more youthful and energetic.

A woman I met recently told me that she did not realize the potential she had. "Before moving to México, I never had time to even think about what I wanted to do. I just put one foot in front of the other—day after day. I was not present in the moment by any means, and everyone I knew was in the same boat."

She unexpectedly found what she'd been missing in her life when she visited a mutual friend's house in Mérida. She said, "During my time at my friend's house, she invited me to attend the symphony one evening, and asked me to go with her to a card group that she had just joined, which would meet the next day. There would be breakfast with friends on one midweek morning, and at the end of what used to be the work week, we'd be having lunch with another group. She read at least a book a week and had all kinds of new opinions and things to converse about. I decided I too wanted that way of life...and now I have it!"

She told me she completely changed her way of thinking, and upon her return to her home town in the U.S.A. she immediately set a date for her move and began to sell her belongings. Her children wondered if indeed a move was what she needed.

After seeing her determination, they decided a move was in order...but not to México; she belonged on the funny farm. None of this deterred her, and she has not looked back. She says, "Sometimes I wake up in a cold sweat from a reoccurring nightmare. In this awful dream, I never moved here!"

Not everyone makes such a hasty decision. Plenty of people spend months, even years, carrying out a phased move. I happen to agree that this is much more prudent. Yet all the same, my heart jumps for joy at spontaneity.

Now...what's your story?

¡Viva México!

Little girl, where are they taking you?

My husband Paul, our daughter Paula, and I were walking home from downtown one afternoon. We were in a hurry for some reason...who knows why. I guess I was pulling Paula along; she was lagging because she was so small.

A very lovely young Mexican lady and her child caught up with us and the lady stopped us. She asked Paula, "Little girl where are they taking you?"

At this time Paula didn't speak any Spanish. She looked at me and asked, "Mommie what did she say?"

Then we had a nice chat with the lady. She was very kind and just wanted to be sure Paula was safe...If we only had more people like that looking out for our children...

—Juanita Geraghty

We call Juanita "the steel magnolia". She lives right downtown and enjoys her forays in to the warrens of stores. Anything you're looking for, she can find it!

R is for...RESPECT
The importance of this cannot be stressed enough.

DESPITE ALL THE SOCIAL CHANGES of the past few years, respect still retains highest priority status. For traditional Mexicans, it is very important to not publicly offend, criticize or be scornful of another person's choices or lifestyle. In most families, Mamá is cherished and Papá is listened to with full attention. Children do not talk back cheekily to their parents or grandparents, and elders are revered. Teachers are obeyed. Younger siblings are taken care of, neighbors' idiosyncrasies are tolerated and passers-by are greeted in the streets: *"Buenos días"* or *"Buenas tardes"* is always murmured as one walks by.

When a person comes into a room, they greet everyone there, often with kisses and endearments. If two people are speaking and another person comes into the room, the conversation stops, and the newcomer is acknowledged. If someone is having a party and you bring an extra person—or persons!—without notifying your host, the extras are welcomed as though they were at the top of the guest list.

On the other hand, if respect is not shown, the absence is palpable.

In most places in North America or Europe, showing this over-the-top courtesy is not common, so newcomers to Mérida may not think to extend it. Because some Yucatecans do not have a lot of experience with the social mores of other countries, they can easily be offended if the pleasantries are not forthcoming. It is difficult to know what exactly should be done, but the basic rule of thumb is that no one should be left alone in a crowd. If you are in a group, be sure everyone is greeted and introduced to everyone else present. If someone new comes into the room— even if they are, in fact, interrupting—they should be made to feel welcome. Inclusion is very important.

As guests in this country, we need to take a back seat sometimes. Mexicans do not really appreciate our opinions of all that's wrong here. We need to be very sensitive of what we say when native-born people are within earshot. I was at a party once and there was a group of foreign men loudly discussing the merits of the local supermarket.

"Why don't 'they' have a properly equipped hardware section?" one fellow asked the others.

"I know what you mean, I was looking for 1¼ inch screws the other day, but do you think I could find them?" answered his buddy.

They continued to criticize the way the store was stocked, how poorly it was run, and then went on to complain how "hardly anyone speaks English".

My Yucatecan husband was not amused, and when we got into the car, he exploded, "Who do those guys think they are? To start with, most people who shop at that store don't ever have a need for 1¼ inch screws; they have workmen who buy them…

at a hardware store! Secondly, we are on the metric system here, and thirdly, we speak Spanish in 'this' country!"

I don't think the men had any idea that they were being offensive, but Jorge would have nothing to do with them after that—not ever!

Neither are Mexicans at all interested in hearing about how products, services, schools, government, etc., "...are better run back home". I've known women who claim that even Jello™ is, "...not as good" here! This sort of statement shows a lack of respect that is highly offensive to Mexicans.

I've had it pointed out to me that Mexicans themselves will often comment about inadequacies they encounter, but that's different...it's OK to berate your own culture and way of doing things, but no one likes to hear outsiders do so. This is how we feel about our families. We can badmouth them all we want and do so very vocally, but if anyone else does...watch out! It is best to keep our opinions to ourselves when we are in the presence of Mexican friends and acquaintances, but sometimes it can't be avoided.

How can we state what we feel without coming across as rude? Let's go back to the case of the fellow who needed 1¼ inch screws. Instead of criticizing the store—which was interpreted as a badmouthing the whole culture!—it would be better to ask, "Hey, I tried to buy 1¼ inch screws the other day; the store I went to didn't have them...where can I go?"

This may sound like taking things too seriously, but the sensitivity is there, and you have to work around it.

I've heard newcomers speak hotly and loudly about so many situations and circumstances they don't understand and often they preface their complaint with, "What's the matter with these people/this country/this government?"

Once I attended a concert that was quite late getting started... an English voice beside me exclaimed, "Why can't anything here ever start on time?"

All the Yucatecans in the vicinity had very offended looks on their faces; I was most uncomfortable, and the English-speaker was poised to continue with his commentary....

"Remember, lots of people here understand English; be careful what you say!" I whispered to him. To his credit, he kept quiet after that.

It's also a good idea to refrain from speaking English loudly in public. Try not to call out (at full volume) when you see a friend down the isle of the grocery store. Neither should you laugh uproariously because those around will not understand the joke and could conclude you're laughing at them. Most Mexicans are not used to boisterous North American ways and after all, we are guests in their country.

Once in a while, you will probably encounter a Mexican with very strong opinions about your home country. I have had this experience and usually cut the comments off by saying, "Let's not confuse the politics with the people!"

This usually softens the attack, but if it doesn't, I continue, "As a foreigner here, I am not permitted to make political statements; I don't want to create controversy, so let's talk about something else."

The bottom line is that as transplants in México, we have to adjust our yardstick to the expectations here and avoid making direct criticisms of everything that is not satisfactory to us. We need to respect people and be sensitive to their needs. We need to be tolerant of what we encounter and save our evaluations until we are in the privacy of our own homes.

This isn't always easy, but if you can manage to adopt this behavior, you will be considered *muy educado* – very well mannered. People will warm up to you and treat you with the same respect you've shown them.

and

R...is also for Retirement
What's it like to be RETIRED?

I wanted to include information about retirement in this book, but as I'm new to it, I'm not much of an authority. I started researching and came across this article by Dr. Brown on the YahooGroup, MazInfo. He expressed himself so well that I contacted him for permission to include his piece. He most graciously agreed, and as I don't believe I could possibly add anything more, here you have:

Coping with retirement

I would like to put a slightly different spin on the "retirement question." Some is general; for me it is personal. It all is therapy to help me cope with a challenge I clearly did not anticipate. Maybe it can help others to cope too.

An individual or a couple can probably "successfully" retire in Podunk, MI or on the French Riviera...and he or she or they can be equally miserable in either place.

Many retirement communities and publications list activities available to this growing percentage of the population. They are well-meaning but they matter not, if you have no interest in what they present.

Regardless of size, location, etc., every place has "things of interest".

The significant question is, "What are your interests?"

For so many years for most of us, a career or job defined how we utilized the majority of our time. The weekend (or day off) and holidays had meaning because they were usually radically different than the rest of the week. There is no such distinction in retirement...unless you make them different.

Lesson #1 (for me)

Retirement should be as well-planned as your job or career was before retirement.

While working, we too often bemoan the lack of time for fun or other pursuits. We look forward to retiring so we can indulge in these interests. However, upon retiring, when there is too much time, we fail to really develop any of these endeavors. The organization of the day/week is gone, and we no longer look forward to these "fantasy activities".

You need to know what you will do when you retire; organize it the way your "former life" was organized, and then go about doing it. Obviously, you need to retire where you can perform your desired activities.

- It is much harder to go from a 40-80 hour work week to a "0" hour work week than many of us anticipate. It is challenging to go from a position of respect—if you were good at what you did or had significant seniority—to a level of insignificance.
- It will often be a problem when you feel no longer needed. It is challenging to view yourself as old and irrelevant, attitudes that can develop in retirement.

- Health care availability, quality and cost can be very important.
- You can go to the same restaurants only so many times, walk the beach only so often and consume (safely) only so much alcohol before you realize that each evening you are coming home to yourself.
- You become your own support; and will probably be denied the daily support of peers (you know, those folks at work you couldn't wait to get away from?!?)
- You can only pretend to be having fun for so long, before it becomes apparent to all that you are NOT having fun!
- Prior Proper Planning Prevents Poor
- Performance applies to retirement as well as it did to work. Many with whom we retired are now gone from México; returned to work; divorced; sick; bored; disillusioned; headed towards alcoholism or worse!
- Most were/are wonderful people but with a common thread: the failure to plan sufficiently. I include myself in that lot.

Lesson #2 (again, for me)

- Know your partner (friend, spouse), for it is in this relationship that you will spend the most time.
- Work will no longer serve as a distraction, escape, excuse or a source of support. These needs will now need to be met by yourself and this other person.
- If the retirement decision(s) you have made do not meet the needs of both of you, retrospectively, work will seem like Heaven compared to retirement Hell.
- After many years of working, you are unlikely to magically leave work and enter Paradise with all your dreams being realized. Sadly, it seems not to work that way.

- Think about retirement, plan and schedule what you would like to do; then make it happen! It does take effort. Before, you HAD to go to work at 7:30; now, you don't HAVE to do anything, and if you didn't plan something, NOTHING is what you are likely to be doing!
- I used to know everything; now, I know a lot...about that kind of NOTHING!

—John Brown

Dr. John O. Brown, Jr. is a retired MD who, with his lovely wife Kimberly, retired to Mazatlán two years ago. John and Kimberly dived right into volunteer activities and found one need that wasn't being met...free Spanish for Fun weekly practice for foreigners to come and practice their Spanish...with native Spanish-speakers... so they formed one!

Retirement is fun in México

México is always unexpected

My husband says that "México is always unexpected", and I think that really sums it up. Living in México challenges your expectations and assumptions.

For example; we pay our utility bills in person rather than automatically or online like we did NOB (north of the border), but we have a choice between the old fashioned teller at the window and a new state of the art machine that scans the bar code imprinted on the bill and accepts our money.

What makes me smile is that often the security guard will offer to help you if you have problems and at the new modules in the malls the attendant does the scanning for you. A nice mixture of the modern and the old.

I am always slightly amused when I see a *Yucateca* dressed in a very traditional manner taking a photo with her cell phone. And the sight of a big husky man sporting a pink "Dora the Explorer" backpack as he slowly follows his toddler in the park never fails to make me smile.

—Theresa Gray

Teresa is writing a children's book and is the author of a popular blog, What do I do all day?

S is for...SETTLING IN
Becoming a Meridano, Tapatío, Chilango, Mazatleco or whatever.

THE FIRST CHALLENGE A NEWCOMER FACES is getting established. You need so many things, starting with a place to live! Next, you need to get everything that will be contained therein: appliances, cleaning products, plants, furniture, bedding and groceries...maybe a cat? The details are endless and it will take a long time to accomplish everything. There is not space here for a list of every process and product you'll need to affect or acquire. Rather, let's look at the steps you need to take and the pitfalls you should try and avoid. But before even starting, I really must stress the importance of renting a place before you buy one.

Most Americans and Canadians are conditioned to thinking that this is like "throwing money away". Believe me, it isn't! You need time to feel your way around and if you plunge right in and buy, you may find yourself the owner of what turns out to be a totally unsuitable property (aka: a millstone around your neck!).

If you have a good real estate agent, he or she will be your first source of information. As you look at properties to buy, the agent should acquaint you with the services, stores, hospitals, parks, schools, etc., available in or near to the neighborhood being shown. The agent should honestly point out the wrought iron workshop, the mechanic on the corner or other potentially irritating neighborhood features. These things are important considerations when deciding where you'll purchase your property.

If you are a person who enjoys shopping often, you may want to be close by an open neighborhood market you can walk to. If you are the once-every-two-weeks consumer, you'll want to be near or have easy access to a big supermarket. Once you have settled on a place, have signed all the paperwork and forked over a considerable sum of money, then you will be ready to start acquiring all the goods and sundries for your new home.

Watch out for the first step, it's a big one! The great majority of new homeowners in México need tradesmen to make the place habitable. It is a rare property that is 100% ready for you to move into. New homes are basically concrete shells unless they are in a newly developed subdivision, so you'll probably need to start from scratch—putting in screens, window protectors, lamp fixtures, fans, cabinets, closets, appliances, gardens…. Most of the older homes, gracious as they are, need a great amount of renovation and upgrading before you can even think of moving in.

Again, your agent will probably have suggestions about who can do this work for you, but be careful! Be very careful! I've heard absolute horror stories from naïve neophytes who have put themselves in the hands of smooth-talking, charming architects and builders and lived to rue the day they set eyes on these people. The estimates were way too low, the materials were not premium—not what you paid for—the workmanship was shoddy and the completion date was way, way too optimistic.

Often these professionals do not mean to be dishonest; they are just so anxious to get the contract and to please you that they'll offer whatever it is you want. They don't think things through and while they are promising the moon, they truly believe they'll be able to deliver it! (see U is for...UNDERESTIMATE).

Instead of taking recommendations from strangers...get networking!

You will meet other members of the international community all over town. You might want to reread N is for...NETWORK for tips on how to meet those who have recently built or bought a home in Mérida. Usually they are more than happy to talk about their experiences and pass on names.

Some of them will probably let you see their places, and you can judge the workmanship for yourself. With broadband Internet being available everywhere in México nowadays, nearly any place in México that has attracted more than just a very few foreign residents will have a local Internet forum or chat group, or if not, there are always the big ones that cover—at least they try to—all of México; one of the most popular of these is the free Mexconnect.com site. On these forums you can ask almost any question you want...and get answers quickly.

Once you have hired an architect or a builder, you cannot just let them carry on with the job; you need to be an active part of the whole process. If you aren't; you'll regret it: building materials will "disappear"; work will not be done to specifications; time will fly by and your beautiful home will not be anywhere near done. This is not to say you need to be on site 24-7, but you do need to show you are aware of every stage of progress.

If you can, you should go there every day—at different times of day—and get the workers to show you what they did yesterday and what will get done/are doing today. If it isn't happening, you need to see the foreman or architect, who either is the builder or who will contact the builder. You are perfectly within your rights to have a lazy worker or the whole crew replaced.

You need to be reasonable though; it isn't easy to work in this heat and humidity; a certain leeway is necessary. You need to be pleasant but firm with the workers and it is helpful if you speak Spanish. However, even if you don't, you soon will; there's no better immersion setting than a construction site! It won't take long for the workers to understand you and you'll quickly learn what is possible and what is not. You'll probably be very pleased with most of the work, but inattention to detail will, at times, drive you crazy. This is why it's important to be there every day; nothing too huge can go amiss in one day!

If you absolutely cannot be in town during the building or renovation, look again to your network and see if there is someone who will oversee the project for a fee.

No matter how positive, negative, long or short the building or restoration experience is for you, at some point your house will be ready for you to move into.

Without doubt, during the construction period, you will have found many things that you need, and you'll really enjoy setting up your new home. In Mérida, as in nearly all larger towns and cities in México, there are a host of places where you can have all kinds of furniture custom-made, for a reasonable price. There are usually several stores that specialize in an incredible variety of fabrics that will make curtains, bedspreads, cushions, etc. Antique dealers abound—their shops are often called *bazars*— you need to be careful, but bargains can often be found. One of my best buys was an old wardrobe in terrible-looking condition that I got for the equivalent of about $100 USD. The person who sold it to me stripped off the old varnish and re-finished the piece for an additional $50 dollars. Appliance stores are also plentiful, as are places where you can buy lighting fixtures and accent pieces. You may ask, if all these places are here, how can you find them? Again, through your network...you'll find most people are very willing to share their information.

Shopping for day-to-day provisions will not be the same as what you experienced where you lived previously. Once you learn your way around it will be better than it was back home! The variety and freshness of the produce and the selection of goods is quite astounding, but you won't find it all under one roof. Shopping trips with a long list are an experience all in themselves. If you want to have a well-stocked pantry, bar, garden and locker, you'll have to learn where these items can be bought. Again, ask around...someone will point you in the right direction.

Personally, I love the neighborhood open markets, and I do much of my shopping there. Yes, I buy meat, poultry, and fish at the market; it is a little unnerving the first time you see chickens hanging from a cross-pole and slabs of meat out in the open. As my mother-in-law advised so many years ago, I shop early in the morning, when I know there hasn't been time for any deterioration to have taken place. The meat is always fresh and very tasty. I also buy my grains, legumes, fruits and vegetables at the market. I buy fresh flowers...and sometimes I find something really unusual—like fried grasshoppers that had been brought from Oaxaca! I let that opportunity go.

For cleaning supplies, canned goods, paper products, personal care and hygiene items, I am an ardent fan of México's many large supermarkets. There were few of these during the first fifteen years I lived in México, so now I appreciate their very existence. True, I don't always find everything on my list, but I get most of it and that's good enough for me. Mérida—and most Mexican cities that have attracted many foreign residents—also have a wealth of specialty stores where you can purchase anything from natural food products to German home-style ham, French cheeses and good wines.

And we should not forget the bread! There are excellent bakeries in **all** of México, and they are responsible for many of the extra pounds on my figure!

If you cannot find an ingredient for one of your signature recipes, or you find a particular item doesn't have quite the taste or texture you're used to…live with it. It is possible to substitute many items and the results can be quite exciting.

The neophyte's first year is full of surprises—good and not-good-at-all—but day by day, you'll learn much more, and when you reach day number 365, you'll have a sense of deep satisfaction.

Or you won't!

Living in another country is not for everyone. If you feel this way, you're not alone. I have met many couples who have made me ask myself, *How did she/he ever get him/her to move here?* Sometimes, living in México is one partner's idea of Heaven and for the other, it's Hell. If this occurs, and if you can, cut your losses and move on; many have done this. If it isn't possible, then a compromise must be reached somehow.

Once again, I stress the importance of a network. You'll meet someone who can help you, someone who's been there, done that and has found a solution to the problem.

One final suggestion: get a cat. A cat is not demanding but can be very affectionate. A cat will pay for its keep by catching all kinds of bugs, lizards, snakes and...sorry...the occasional bird. Your cat will keep the mice away. If you need to be out of town for a while, your cat will understand and be quite satisfied as long as someone brings her fresh water and kibble every day. And how do you find a cat? Don't worry about that...your new cat will find you!

You will find everything you need, but you may have to search for it

Some thoughts on tipping and being charitable

Tipping for service always begs the question: In what circumstances is it expected? What is the customary amount? What is acceptable? Should it always be voluntary? Why is it sometimes added to the bill, as in some restaurants? Is it necessary?

In Latin American countries the front line personnel are often paid a very minimal wage and depend on tips as a supplement.

Your personal attitude is important. Here in México, many of us view this as a "social tax". Personally I have found the benefits to be considerable and rewarding. We affect the life of every person we interact with and often in ways we can't even imagine. Giving 10 or 50 pesos to someone in need may or may not be a significant amount to the giver but can make a world of difference to the receiver. I feel it is important to try to make a difference and there are so many ways to do that. When we bless others with unconditional kindness we are always blessed in return.

—Larry McIntosh

Larry, a former high school French teacher from Canada spends his time between Mérida and Progreso. He and his spouse, Reg never dreamed they'd live permanently in México but as Larry says, "Here we are and we love it!"

T is for...TIPPING
Who should receive tips and how much?

THIS IS A LOADED TOPIC BECAUSE...just what is tipping? We know what it is where we come from, but in México it encompasses a lot more. Many people have no formal job; in order to survive—without turning to a life of crime—they take "work" that many of us consider totally pointless. I used to be very irritated by this until I realized just what was at stake.

There are the men who park and guard cars on every street where more than six vehicles are to be found. They blow their whistles and flap their red rag at you and cry, *"'Dale, 'dale, 'dale"* They actually make it more difficult to park sometimes. But as I have learned, this is what gives them the means to support themselves and often others as well.

It is important to smile and say thank you and when you return to your car, to give them a tip. The amount I give varies. If I am on a "dangerous street", or if the "parker" has practically thrown himself in front of another car, so I can nab the spot, he gets more!

There are the "entertainers" at intersections. These young boys juggle balls, turn cartwheels, mime or sing; we had a fire-eater for a while, but mercifully, he's no longer in the city. After the performance they quickly dart from car to car for a small bit of change. I usually give them a few pesos.

There are the charity cases; these are often women with children, who ask for change as cars are stopped at a light. Sometimes they are old men, cripples and amputees. I always give to them; I have been told not to but I do so anyway…I don't give too much, but as I put the coin in their hands, I say, *"¡Qué Díos le bendiga!"* – "God bless you!" I learned to do this from my mother-in-law. I also give to organizations like the Salvation Army.

There are "charity cases" in other places too. They come to my door; I pass them on the sidewalk downtown; they circulate through the parking lots. I have gotten to know some of them over the years—they have had really hard lives.

There's one woman in particular who lives in the downtown streets of Mérida; she is deaf and definitely schizophrenic. She has a whole stash of boxes—I'm told they are filled with shredded paper—that she keeps in sight always, and she hands out pamphlets from a local store. That is her "job" and if you don't take one, she will sometimes follow you and smack you on the head with the "offering" you didn't take. When you take the paper from her, she sometimes expects a coin or two. I always give her one; it's better than getting whacked again! I also seek her out sometimes and give her a sandwich and a Coke™, as do many of us who live or work downtown.

The municipal and state governments have social programs that pretty much keep children off the streets…there is no need for them to be there. If I do see a child begging, I tell the closest policeman and ask him to have the Family Services Agency (*DIF*) investigate.

I regularly tip waiters between 15 and 20%; if the service is poor, I give 10%. Once in a while, I get a really surly waiter... he gets stiffed, although this rarely happens.

It's important to check your bill when it comes because sometimes there is a "service charge" already added on. If I see an extra figure, I ask if this is what it is, and if it is I don't usually give anything additionally. I tip hairdressers 20 to 50 pesos, depending on what I had done. I don't tip taxi drivers per se, but I will round off the amount to the nearest 10; if the fare is 35, I give 40, and so on. I give a few pesos to the person who bags my groceries, more if he or she takes it to my car and a bit more if I have a lot of heavy merchandise.

At Christmas time, tipping takes on a whole new dimension. In México, by law, all employees receive a Christmas bonus of approximately two weeks' salary.

As all these services—parking cars, bagging groceries, etc.—are considered by a lot of people to be their jobs and we are their employers in a sense, so they too hope for a mini-bonus from us. It gets a little complicated and requires a stockpile of smaller bills, so in December, I always keep a change purse easily accessible.

With so many people to tip, it can get to be expensive. What I have done is to designate an amount of money each week. I have the money in coins and put it in my change purse. I use this money as I see fit. If I have some left over at the end of the week, I carry it over to the next. Usually a special need presents itself soon enough and I don't have a surplus for long. On the other hand, if I run out of change (each of us has our limit), I don't make any more contributions until the new week starts and I try not to feel guilty about it.

One day, a friend and I were exchanging opinions about this "tipping" issue. I told him about an incident I'd had that week: I was stopped at a red light when all of a sudden a young boy jumped on top of my car and commenced to clean the windshield. I really don't like this practice. "Hey, get off my car!" I yelled at him.

He kept wiping the window. I was pretty cross and started honking the horn. He got down and silently looked at me with the most mournful, sad eyes...I was very, very upset by this. I didn't know which of us was right, but I sensed it wasn't me... what should I have done?

My friend said, "It's like a social tax, Joanna, those of us who are blessed have to pay it." He continued, "Sure it is a bother to always have people asking for something...but I'm sure glad I'm the one who is being asked and not the one having to do the asking."

That rang true for me, and I've had a different attitude ever since. That boy washing the windshield did not succeed in cleaning the glass but he was the one who cleaned up my attitude towards "tipping". I hope that "what goes around comes around".

Many of México's workers depend on tips for their family's survival

The creativity of the people is profound

I am continually amazed and entertained by the ability of the enterprising Yucatecans/Mexicans to adapt and recycle in unique and different ways. The creativity of the people is profound.

For example, the other day I saw an old flatbed pickup truck rattling down the road with a man bouncing up and down in the back on a makeshift seat. That seat was an old toilet!

Or how about the other old truck crabbing sideways down the *carretera?* The ancient vehicle was patched together with different metal and wooden pieces from different sources to make up the walls and floors of the truck. It worked fine. The back bumper looked like a section of an old railroad tie.

The eclectic look. Modern mixed with old. Chunky with streamlined. The visuals here are always interesting and fun…if just a tad odd! A colorful reflection of the people.

—Colleen Leonard

Colleen is an artist and also manages the award-winning "Hacienda Petac".

U is for...UNDERESTIMATE
This will happen a lot.

HOW MANY TIMES HAS:

"I'll be there right away!" been said? Yet several hours go by before they eventually run in breathlessly with several very good reasons why "right away" took so long.

"It will cost 2,000 pesos to fix your car," been estimated? But when you go to pick the car up, the bill is much, much higher, since the parts had to be specially ordered, or something else was discovered that needed fixing for your vehicle to run smoothly.

"Your house will be completely renovated by Christmas!" been heard? And it is April before it's ready for moving into, and in fact, the work still isn't "quite" done? There's dust everywhere, and the tile workers are still chip-chip-chipping away.

Underestimation is very frustrating, but it is a fact of life in México.

I attempt to deal with underestimation by planning well ahead and expecting the unexpected. Yet even with my cautious attitude, I often get surprises.

A couple of years ago, we remodeled our entire home. We changed rooms around and put in a pool. New wiring, plumbing, floors and windows—the works! The engineer, our contractor (in México, only degreed engineers or architects are issued contractor's or builder's licenses), told us he would need five months (not to mention many pesos) to accomplish everything on our wish list. Fortunately, friends who would be out of town kindly offered to lend us their home, and we moved into their house on April 1st.

It soon got to the point that we dreaded going "home". The first time I went to see how things were progressing, I was greeted with the sight of the *Flor de Mayo* – Frangipani tree – in a horizontal position. I asked, "What happened to my tree?"

"Oh it was in the way of the machine that will dig the hole for the pool." (The machine was a good three meters over to the left). They had cut down my tree for no good reason!

Right then and there, I decided to "expect the worst and hope for the best". But really, after the incident with the tree, things didn't ever again get out of hand. Seeing how much my plants meant to me, every evening the workers hosed off the surviving plants. Many of my orchids made it through the ordeal and the Flor de Mayo? Well, the workers snapped off a piece of it, put it in a pot and five months later returned it to the earth. Drive by our house today and you'll see my tree in all its leafy, flowery splendor. Yes, I certainly underestimated the resilience of the plants and the sensitivity of the crew.

We actually figured the home improvements would take 50% longer than the estimate and planned accordingly. But when planning a renovation project at your house, don't assume your experience will mirror ours. In other words, it will be best not to organize the housewarming until you are actually moving in!

Parties and celebrations are often planned spur-of-the-moment because no one is ever really sure the hoped-for date will pan out. Imagine your pool party, scheduled months in advance, yet on the appointed day the mysterious leakage has still not been identified! If you are going to enjoy living in México, you'll have to learn to live with this.

Underestimation can be found in other areas as well, and again, many times it is me who underestimates the people and situations. In México, people are extremely resourceful. Even in the most difficult situations they don't just throw their hands up; they get right in there and find a solution.

I remember when Hurricane Isadora hit Mérida a few years ago. The city was directly hit by the Force 5 winds—the destruction was unbelievable. More than 50,000 trees fell. Houses were destroyed; businesses had their entire façades blown off. The streets were so littered with debris that it was impossible to drive anywhere. There was no power, water or telephone service. It was like a war zone. I figured it would be weeks before we could get back to normal. But…

In just 24 hours, the roads were mostly clear; there were basic services downtown, and every day afterwards the improvement continued.

I had exchange students from other countries in home-stays on the other side of town and wasn't able to contact them for three days. When I did so, they told wonderful stories of how their host families and neighbors all pitched in to clear the streets and clean up the yards.

"They didn't have too much equipment," one of the students said, "So they gave me a carving knife and I hacked back the branches with only that!"

They were amazed at how Mérida's residents shared their provisions. Another student explained, "We had no water to bathe, so the neighbor let us clean up in his pool."

Two weeks after the disaster, the city was really taking shape again, and brigades of citizens were still working hard. It was at this point another group of foreign students arrived. They were very glad to have missed the storm and yet were dismayed at the piles of broken branches and rubbish still waiting to be carted away.

Those who had experienced the hurricane told them, "Don't complain about anything; you have no idea how hard your families have worked to be this ready for your arrival!"

Another "après-hurricane" story is from 2005, when the Mexican Caribbean was hit very hard by Hurricane Wilma; almost 60,000 tourists were evacuated from Cancún and the Riviera Maya to Mérida!

Our city is not at all equipped to handle anything of this magnitude but the citizens opened their arms wide! Schools, community centers and sports auditoriums set up shelters. The water companies donated until their supplies were gone; food wholesalers and restaurants did likewise.

The civil protection agency coordinated the distribution of all the necessary services, and the airport administration managed to get all those people on their way home within three days. At one point there were thirty-seven planes parked on the runway!

Private citizens took people in and offered what they could. Our students patrolled the streets searching for "refugees"; one of them brought a British couple to me and asked if they might use my bathroom and shower. They did so, and also shared a meal with the Food & Beverage class. It was quite something to see! I never imagined that the authorities and the citizens of Mérida would be able to handle such a catastrophe with such efficiency and kindness. Again, I underestimated.

For months after the hurricane, the City of Mérida website received letters of thanks from grateful travelers. The following year, I met a couple who came back to Mérida to visit the family who had taken them in.

This too is culturally typical of México. Those who need help nearly always have it offered...before they even think to ask.

Eagerness to please is usually at the heart of the underestimation that is rampant. As always, looking back through history will help explain why this attitude became so deeply ingrained in this culture.

México's indigenous societies were ruled by a small elite class. Then came the Colonial period, Independence and the Revolution...and very little changed.

Over the eons, the indigenous people in México learned it was best to tell the ruling class what they wanted to hear—and they did so. This mentality became firmly entrenched; it suits most citizens because they really dislike confrontation, even when they know the issue will catch up with them later. The ubiquitous attempts not to ruffle any feathers are still in place today.

To a lesser extent, so is the servile demeanor. When an elder or authority figure has an "all business" look on their face and singles out some one, the person usually asks what the boss needs by saying, *"Mande"* – Order me – or *"A sus ordenes"* – I'm at your service.

Inside his or her docile exterior, the person may be cursing but they don't show that. Mexicans are polite to the extreme.

And this is why they will optimistically tell you what they think you need to hear.

Knowing that you will run into this attitude, time and time again will help you deal with missed deadlines and so on. To be successful in México, you need to be prepared to take things in stride, and be as flexible as possible.

So much will seem strange at first, but you will quickly adapt

Rain God masks – Yucatán

International Women's Club members participating in
the Women's Walk for Health

V is for...VOLUNTEER
One of the best ways to make new friends is by volunteering.

WHEN I FIRST CAME TO LIVE IN MÉXICO in 1976, I did not make many friends until more than a year had passed; I was very lonely. I realize now that I could have volunteered my time to help needy groups and individuals. Most organizations are grateful to have help; the members will happily embrace newcomers who are willing to pitch in!

In Mérida there are organizations and clubs where non-Spanish-speakers can feel welcome and needed. Some of them are listed here:

Mérida English Language Library (MELL): "Our" library has been called "The Miracle on 53rd Street." In many ways it is that but really, there's a difference. Miracles just happen. The Mérida English Language Library has not; it has grown through the hard work of hundreds of volunteers. The organization receives no public funding. All income is from membership and donations.

MELL was founded by Elizabeth Dunkle. Upon moving to Mérida in 1994, this New York author was dismayed to find there was such a dearth of reading material. At the time, the international community was quite unfocussed; they simply lent books and magazines to one another. It was enough for most of us but not for Elizabeth!

Today, The Mérida English Language Library is an incorporated (*A.C.*) Mexican not-for-profit institution serving Yucatán's cross cultural English language needs.

Many local students and professional people have improved their language skills—and their opinion of the international community—through the library.

Similar English-language libraries are found in most of the cities that are popular with foreign retirees.

If you are new to México, look for the local English-language library and volunteer. This is one of the best ways to integrate into the community. Libraries have a whole cadre of people who work on projects, file and catalogue, answer correspondence and meet and greet visitors and members as they come in. Whatever your skill, libraries will find a job for you. Do you think you have no skills? They will help you discover a host of them.

International Women's Club (IWC): Founded in 1984, this group is open to women of all nationalities who speak English. There are approximately two hundred twenty members, although not all of them attend every meeting, and many do not live in Mérida all year 'round.

The goals are friendship, self-improvement, and service; offering women a way to associate, exchange views, and get to know the community.

The club also holds several fund-raising events throughout the year. Money from these events benefits the group's charities. Other activities are planned according to members' interests, such as retreats and excursions. Special Interest Groups and

Special Projects Groups provide a wide variety of activities and vary from year to year.

Again, most every city in México popular with foreign retirees has something similar: Red Hat Club, Women's Luncheon Group, etc., etc.

International Men's Club: This club is much newer and much less structured than the IWC. Several times a month, a social breakfast is attended by anywhere from twenty to forty men.

Often there is a speaker, and a collection for the local food bank is taken up at each meeting.

Other cities in México that are popular with retirees often have mixed groups that do the same sorts of things: Friends of Mexico, Hands Across the Border, etc., etc.

The Beach Gals: This group is not to be confused with the IWC; they are two completely separate women's associations. The loosely-structured Beach Gals group was formed in the winter of 2002–2003, to provide a venue for women who live on the coast to get together and socialize. Many of the members are strong supporters of animal rights and work towards helping the many unfortunate strays and abandoned pets.

There are many of these informal groups in México. They do a lot of good work and they have a lot of fun.

There are also numerous projects taken on by individuals that aim to support the rural villages. **The Santa Elena Sustainable Development Project** is one of these. An extended family from the area has hit on a novel way to provide an income locally, allowing them to remain in their community. The women make crafts for sale, and Abel, the head of the household, escorts tourists on walks through the countryside. He takes them to unexplored archeological sites and other places of interest, The tour is called, "Walk the Mayan Way – A Look at a Contemporary Yucatecan Village".

The Santa Elena Sustainable Economic Development Project

EducaTEyucatan supports children and teenagers in the nearby village of Cholul with their educational needs. They have a breakfast program; school supplies sponsorship and also provide college scholarship to young women.

The **Telchac Scholarship program:** The original idea behind this project was to provide fifteen students from grade school and Jr. High with all the needed items for school start up. More sponsors responded and at the last minute someone signed up for six kids – yes, **one** sponsor with **six** kids, taking the total to thirty students in the first year. Not bad!

The **Red Cross Women's Group:** In Mérida, the Red Cross is a very important social and medical resource. The Red Cross has ambulance service, and it also administers the Cancer Hospital. They also have plans to open an emergency phone line to coordinate services during natural disasters. Almost all the workers are volunteers, and there are never enough of them. If you are a retired medical worker or technician or if you know how to repair anything...you have a job waiting for you!

Purpura Plastica is an organization that encourages developement of children's self-esteem through artistic expression. Their workshops and shows attract a delighted following of international and local art enthusiasts.

Albergue de Ancianos de San Joaquín García: This residence for seniors is located on the coastal road between Progreso and Chicxulub. Founded in 1975, it is home to approximately eighty elderly residents who have no one to care for them. A retired Canadian nurse, Sharon Helgason, has been instrumental in getting the international community to help support the Home.

Sharon is a very active volunteer and also supports **The Chicxulub Food Bank & Breakfast Program:** The breakfast program provides a nutritious breakfast once a week to children from the food bank program; as well, it distributes vitamins to the children.

With so many new foreign residents in Mérida, many of the volunteer organizations are networking and planning joint fund-raising activities. These are always very enjoyable events and they are also excellent places to meet more new friends.

And in other towns and cities there are Humane Society type groups, orphanage supporting groups, hospices and many, many others worthy of your consideration.

Do you have any experience with event organization, marketing, and ticket selling? Any of the above-mentioned organizations can find a place for you!

And hey; if you can't find the exact group that fits **you,** look around and see what needs aren't being met...and start one yourself!

Working in México

When you first leave home as a young man or woman, you are filled with anticipation of what lies ahead.

When you leave "home" in your fifties, reality sets in very quickly as you ponder: "What am I doing going to a foreign country where I don't even speak the language? What will I do with my time if I am not working?"

I had heard about the Mérida English Library and when the current director retired, a friend suggested that I apply.

My first day on the job at MELL, armed with a small amount of Spanish learned in classes, I tried conversing. The helpful *Yucatecos* corrected me respectfully. My spouse, a language teacher, helped with written communications. The telephone was a major problem, as was going to a store to buy library supplies. Dictionaries are a godsend! Next mastery? Maybe Maya!

—Reg Deneau

Living at the beach and enjoying retirement is Reg's "day job". About three times a week he comes into Mérida and "moonlights" at the Library. He says his commitment to MELL gives his life great balance.

W is for...WORK
What kind of employment is available in Mérida?

FOR THOSE WHO WISH TO MOVE TO México but cannot or do not want to stop working, opportunities exist but it can be challenging to find a niche. Unemployment and under-employment are large social issues in México and it is difficult for foreigners to find remunerative jobs. As well, anyone working in México must be willing to work for much lower wages than they would expect for the same positions in North America or Europe. And, as nearly every place in the world, you have to get permission to work. Sometimes that's not too difficult in México, but sometimes it's impossible, or so difficult that you give up trying to get it. The local office of *Migración* – Immigration – can give you all the details.

Typical of all of México, here in Mérida, members of the international community have been or are currently working in or have opened business in the following fields:

- Aerobic Dance and Exercise Centers
- Agricultural Consulting
- Animal Daycare
- Announcers, radio and television (Independent)
- Antique Dealers
- Apparel manufacturing
- Architectural services
- Art Dealers
- Art Galleries
- Arts & Crafts (creating and selling)
- Automotive Repair businesses
- Retail Bakeries & Baked Goods stores
- Bars and Clubs
- Barber Shops and Beauty Salons
- Bed-and-Breakfast Inns
- Bee Production cooperatives
- Boat Rental or Leasing agencies
- Body Building & Physical Fitness studios
- Bookstores
- Child Day Care services
- Chiropractors
- Chocolate and Confectionery factories
- Choreographers (Independent)
- Civic and Social clubs
- Computer stores
- Cookie manufacturing companies
- Copy shops
- Custom Computer Programming services
- Dance centers
- Directory Publishers
- Entertainers (Independent)
- Event Planning services
- Family Clothing stores
- Film Producers (Independent)
- Fine Arts schools
- Florists
- Furniture stores
- Garden Centers
- Gift stores
- Graphic Design services

- Home Design & Consulting firms
- Horseback Riding stables (Recreational)
- Hotels
- Jewelry making & sales
- Journalists (Freelance)
- Language schools
- Management Consulting organizations
- Men's Clothing stores
- Modeling (Independent)
- Newspaper Columnists (Freelance)
- Orchestra Conductors (Independent)
- Painters, i.e., Artists (Independent)
- Performing Artists (Independent)
- Photo Journalists (Freelance)
- Photography Studios, Commercial or Portrait
- Physical Therapists
- Professional Training schools
- Property Management agencies
- Real Estate agencies
- Restaurant and Food businesses
- Retail stores
- Sailing Clubs
- Sculptors (Independent)
- Sea Kayaking (Recreational)
- Teaching (Elementary & Secondary schools, Universities)
- Toy stores
- Travel agencies
- Translating and Interpreting
- Tutoring
- Web Design
- Web Hosting services
- Wedding Consultants
- Women's Clothing stores
- Writers (Freelance)

This is quite a list, isn't it? But what is the most common job open to native English speakers?

If you answer, "Teaching the English language," you'd be right. There are many, many language schools as well as regular schools (Kindergarten through University) that like to hire native-English-speaking teachers. Depending on the type of institution, appropriate credentials may be required.

Teachers who can instruct in other languages such as French, German, and Italian are in quite high demand as well. An Internet search will provide a long list of potential employers, although it will be very difficult to secure employment without being present and available for a personal interview in México. There are also many opportunities for tutoring and teaching private classes. Again, you'll need to be on site to set these up. Getting permission from Migración to work in México definitely requires your presence.

Translators are also in demand, but the pay is not good. For some reason, the general public does not appreciate how time consuming and painstaking translations are. Usually individuals will procure contracts by leaving their cards with the large corporations, government offices, and tourism establishments. To do interpretation at special events, a good place to begin a job search is the Convention Center.

Information Technology, Communications and Publishing are areas that are saturated with young locally-trained professionals. They work well and for considerably less than their counterparts in other countries. Actors, entertainers, musicians, craftsmen, jewelers and other artists are another group that will find it challenging to find remunerative employment in México. There are some opportunities for teaching and for classical musicians, but there are many excellent local artists vying for the same few positions. This being said, the artistic community is very welcoming and those from outside México will find a wonderful, stimulating environment for learning and sharing talent.

Real estate companies are open to hiring foreigners but you often must be able to work in Spanish as well as English. Fluency in other languages would also be very advantageous. Again, an Internet search will introduce you to many companies where you could apply.

Even though there is huge competition from the local population, the tourism industry is a good source of employment, but there are certain positions that are not available to non-Mexicans such as guiding at federal archaeological sites and museums.

If you have specialized skills in ecotourism, there is work available but again, you will be excluded from working in federal ecological reserves.

Hotels and resorts hire young deejays and hosts each tourism season—this is a great, fun job for awhile, but it is extremely taxing due to long hours and a very demanding physical schedule. Many large international resort chains have websites that feature an "Employment Opportunities" section and quite often have openings for English-speaking sales positions.

Specialized English-speaking tradesmen are certainly needed in México. There is a demand for talented woodworkers, hydro specialists and building professionals. The local tradesmen are very hardworking, but many lack the attention to detail demanded by the international community.

The restaurant industry is another high volume employer but there is a lot of competition, and the pay is not what you would receive in, for example, the U.S.A.

It is by no means impossible for foreigners to have working careers in México. However, most of those who have been well compensated financially are true entrepreneurs. If you have drive, energy, some start-up capital and lots and lots of patience, you can be very successful in México.

Many enterprising individuals have come to México, launched and successfully run their businesses. There are excellent opportunities but caution must not be forgotten. If you are considering opening your own business, you'll be well advised to do a lot of research first, talk to the local community and heed their advice.

Particularly research any lawyer (be sure he is a Notario) before starting out. Many inexperienced lawyers abound, and there are some who are outright dishonest. I am not generalizing or saying that misguided legal advice is not given elsewhere. In México, most lawyers are completely honest but be sure you find one of this persuasion or your company will fold before it opens the doors.

The other person you must have to start a business in México is a Mexican accountant *Contador Público (L.C.P.)* – the equivalent of a C.P.A. in the U.S. – but in México it's nearly impossible to open and run a business without one, especially for a foreigner.

Since the permission to work or open a business cannot be handled by an out-of-country consulate or embassy, you will need to enter the country on a tourist permit. Once you have found employment, you will need to deal with visa issues.

You cannot get a working visa until you actually have a job offer. The prospective employer must submit the offer in writing along with additional documentation. Not all companies are willing to do this. Be sure to bring originals and photocopies of all your professional training degrees and diplomas, your original birth certificate and your marriage certificate, if applicable. You will need to have these documents translated into Spanish once your visa processing begins; you will also need photographs and various affidavits.

To sum it up, employment opportunities are to be found in México, but it is not a quick, painless process, and you will need an extra reserve of patience as you wade through the bureaucracy.

I have worked for most of the years I've lived in México. The work environment is different than what you're probably used to but if you keep an open attitude and learn from your colleagues, you can have a very diverse, exciting career.

Work as an English teacher is widely available in México

X...MARKS THE SPOT!

IN MY WEBSTER'S DICTIONARY, few words begin with X, but in México the names of many places do indeed. The letter does not owe its popularity to the Spanish language but rather to the indigenous ones that had a fondness for the rich *sh-sh-sh* sound, as this consonant was pronounced in 16th century Spanish and is still pronounced in the Maya, Náhuatl and Chichimeca tongues.

The two Mayan centers X'caret and Xelha are located in the southeastern state of Quintano Roo. Because of the Mayan pronunciation, the names should be said: Sh-kah-REHT and SHEHL-hah. The first time I visited both these archaeological sites, they were undeveloped and freely accessible to the public. The first featured an underground river and the other a coral reef.

Xelha can be reached by traveling south of Playa del Carmen. It is not known when the Maya founded this site, but certainly it was well established by the sixth century C.E., and it served as one of the ports for Cobá, an important inland Mayan ceremonial center.

Although the civilization had declined, there was still a small group of people living there when the explorers, Stephens and

Catherwood, visited in 1841. Today the lithographs Catherwood made of the Mayan sites continue to amaze and educate.

In the 1970s the reef habitat seemed so densely populated with colorful marine life, I felt like I was swimming through a wall of fish. When I stayed still, the "wall" would move closer and gently nibble at my salty skin. What a sensation! Local families liked to spend the day, enjoying the bright sunshine and Caribbean breeze.

In 1994, the government of Quintana Roo awarded a development concession to a progressive investment group that has turned Xelha into a water park featuring a sparkling Caribbean beach, excellent snorkeling and of course, shopping! More than seventy species of fish are still to be found in this natural aquarium but the "wall" is no longer there. I guess we all have our own interpretations of what constitutes "progress".

X'caret, located close by was also founded as a trading center and later used as a base camp for Spanish conquistadores. It too has been developed into a water park. In 1990, the privately owned—the locals call it Maya-Disney—park was opened. The biggest draws are the underground fresh water river and the opportunity to swim with dolphins.

Although Xelha and X'caret are no longer pristine, the maps belonging to outdoor-loving tourists certainly have these two destinations marked with an X.

A completely different city whose name also begins with an X is Xalapa, the capital of the State of Veracruz. The Náhuatl roots *xal-li* – sand – and *a-pan* – water place – have been combined to form the name which roughly translated means "spring in the sand". The locals pronounce their city's name Shah-LAH-pah or Hah-LAH-pah. Alexander von Humbolt visited the city in

1804 and christened it "city of flowers". Indeed the temperate climate is ideal for growing many colorful blooms.

Xalapa, with a population of about 500,000 is not the largest city in the state, that distinction goes to the port of Veracruz with more than 2,000,000 inhabitants. Nonetheless, it boasts a rich cultural life and several unique institutions:

> *La Casa Xalapa* is an impressive, one story 18th century home that houses the Museum of the City of Xalapa. In the multiple exhibition areas, some of the finest examples of art work from the entire country are to be seen.
>
> The Musical Conservatory in Xalapa is actually an annex of the *Universidad Nacional Autónoma de México (UNAM)* – the Autonomous National University of Mexico – and is considered to be the finest music school in the country.
>
> The museum and conservatory have attracted other artists of every genre, providing the city with a breath-taking array of cultural attractions and X-citing entertainment options.

In central México, we find the nation's capital, Mexico City. Xochimilco, pronounced shoh-tchee-MEEL-coh, a small village that once lay on the outskirts of the huge city has now been incorporated into the general metropolitan area. The land around the town's lake was densely populated during pre-Columbian times.

Using the lake's decomposing vegetation, the inhabitants of Xochimilco constructed fertile, floating islands – called *chinampas.* These are still farmed today. The canals that run between the chinampas are a popular tourist attraction.

The locals decorate their low-riding, flat-bottomed boats with flowers and place tables and benches down the middle. Onboard they sell hot spicy food and cool delicious drinks to the tourists who come in throngs to traverse the canals. Mariachi musicians in their own skiffs, and handcraft vendors in theirs, pull up alongside the merry boatloads. The laconic pleasure of a Sunday afternoon spent on the Xochimilco canals, in the company of good friends is very near the top of my list of favorite things.

And what do we do if the provisions run out before the ride is over? *¡No problema!* Lots of boats going by will gladly supply you with more tacos, tequila or *Dos XXs.*

Y is for...YOUTH
Is it possible to recapture?

I RECENTLY MET A MAN WHO moved to México over twelve years ago. He met a younger Mexican woman with children... and married her. He told me, "I feel as though twenty years have been taken off my age!"

Another woman I met at a party told me, "I came to México to put all the negativity behind me. I didn't really have any idea how that would happen but I rented a small house and gave myself permission to contemplate my life and what I should do about it." She concluded that she should have done this years earlier. She said she felt as though she had been reborn and went on to have a rewarding life, full of friends and interesting activities.

A handholding couple once confided that México had saved their marriage. "We got so involved with everyone else we forgot about '**us**'!"

There are many stories like this circulating in the international community. What is it about México that has this effect on people?

After much observation, I have noticed there is a common denominator. It isn't just that these individuals moved to

México—these rejuvenated people and others like them were willing to change. They stepped back, looked at their lives and took a leap of faith. They have not remained stuck in the same boxes that held them captive for years.

Change is **not** a scary thing once you immerse yourself in it. And contrary to what a lot of people think, it is not a long, laborious process. In fact, as soon as you decide to do things differently you have effected the change. It's happened. Of course, you have to maintain it.

I know another couple who came to México, lived deliriously happily for several years, then got themselves just as caught up in life here as they'd allowed to happen in the U.S.A. They had to step back and reassess their commitments.

Now you may be thinking, "I don't want to change big things about myself. I just want to feel a little more positive." I do not advocate making huge changes; neither do I feel everyone needs to. Maybe it is more a question of having true perspective.

When we feel happy and carefree, we often say, "I feel younger!" What we really mean is that we feel better, more positive and carefree. Why do we equate this with youth? Maybe it is because we can't remember feeling like this in a long time. The responsibilities of life: the marriage, the career, the home, the kids, their college fees, increasing stress, etc., etc., sometimes feel too burdensome. Instead of enjoying these parts of life, we feel sucked up and strangled. Why?

Maybe, over time, we have allowed this to happen. By moving to México, we have a second chance. We can let go a little. I don't mean we have to divorce ourselves completely, but with a little distance the stress does not seem so overwhelming, and we feel the load is lighter.

In reality, this has little to do with México and lots to do with ourselves. When my father died, my mom had a very hard time. I finally convinced her to come and spend a couple of months with us in Mérida. She looked strung out and lost when she arrived and when she returned to Canada everyone said how great she looked. She said, "In México there's always so much going on, and it's so hard to figure it all out. I got so mesmerized trying, that I forgot about my grief for long stretches of the day. I was released from the grip of depression!"

Another friend has made some changes in her life by giving to others. She said she was always interested in the Mayan culture and she wanted to visit the villages. However, she could not speak a lot of Spanish, so she hesitated to actually go. But when she became involved in a craft project she found herself helping women in the countryside. "I don't speak much Spanish but I can show the ladies what they need to do…and then too, we laugh a lot which is universal."

One of my best friends has been an English teacher for nearly forty years. She says the daily contact with her young students keeps her young, "I see the way they dress and talk. I hear their music, so how can I not be up-to-date?"

Rekindling former interests is another way that many retired foreign residents have gotten back their old passion. Since I began writing I have met many who are beginning their second careers as writers. Most say it had been an early love they had to drop, as "life" took up more and more of their time.

Same thing for painters. There is a retired doctor living here, who upon his retirement enrolled in the Fine Arts academy. He now says, "I am a painter. This is not a hobby; this is my second career."

It is easier to "re-invent" yourself when you are away from your old environment. And for those who want a lifestyle overhaul, México provides an empty canvas and a full palate of vibrant color. There is inspiration in the physical surroundings and in the people.

"I'm not in Kansas anymore!" says one of my favorite people. A fairly recent arrival to Mérida, this woman takes hold of life and hugs it close. She is willing to try anything—once—and if it suits her, she embraces it with passion.

"I love that in México I can try so many new things. If one thing doesn't grab me, I can find something else."

One friend of mine who quit a thirty year smoking habit says, "I should have come to Mérida a long time ago because as soon as I did, the stress I'd always felt just blew away and I was able to quit smoking for good."

Another recipe for feeling young is being grateful. In this country there is such need, yet the people who live here have generosity. After Hurricane Isadora, I went to a village with some of my students to distribute food, clothing and medicine that the school had collected. We arrived at a town in the southern part of the state and saw extreme flooding.

Yet up on one bit of higher land a group of kids had organized an impromptu soccer game. My students rushed over to join the fun, except for one tenderhearted young woman. She was so distressed by the damage she saw all around her that she became quite overwrought.

A little boy saw this and brought her a chair from his house to sit on. She sank down on the plastic seat and tried to give him a smile. He took a piece of cardboard from his back pocket and started fanning her. Turning to me he said, "When Mama is tired I do this for her." Hearing that, my poor student looked as though she would lose any remaining composure she had, but instead she leaned over and hugged the child.

"His little body was so strong that I knew I had to be too." She stood up, took his hand and said, "Let's go join the game!"

Sofia Loren said once, "There is a fountain of youth: it is your mind, your talents, the creativity you bring to your life and the lives of people you love. When you learn to tap this source you will truly have defeated age."

Children are wonderful partners for practicing Spanish

You'll be surprised at all the novel things you'll do in México

No two days are ever the same

Candelario came by as he often does in the afternoons to chat or help around the place. But today he came and his eyes were sparkling with mischief. In the background the ringing of a bell had alerted him and he ran down the hill shouting "*¡Tepache man. Tepache man!*"

I cried out, " Who's the Tepache man ?"

"Nada, *Nada - wait and see,*" he shouted.

He returned with two bags full of liquid which he said was pineapple juice.

"M-m-m-m-m, tastes good!" He laughed so hard that he spluttered on his straw.

The more I drank the more lightheaded I felt then I realized this is fermented pineapple juice!

Watching my face, he burst out laughing again, taunting me "You're drunk! You're drunk!"

Me...a summer afternoon drunkard!

We both laughed. I shrugged and said in English, "You little minx!"

After 6 years here in the beautiful Yucatán...no two days are ever the same.

—Valerie Pickles

Valerie, originally from England, owns and operates The Pickled Onion Restaurant in Santa Elena, Yucatán.

Z is for... ZERO – ZIP – *NADA*
The bottom line...

Each of the states in México is unique. I have visited many of them...several on multiple occasions. I appreciate different things about each and would cite all of them as perfectly suited to different types of foreign residents. Some are for urbanites and others for those who love the countryside. For some, lying on a white sandy beach all day is Heaven and others shun the sun. There are those who love to shop in local markets and those who only buy at large supermarkets. One group loves the mountains; another, the coast.

The earliest residents of Yucatán, the Maya, believed in the duality of everything in our lives:

> There could not be good without evil
> There could be no day without night
> There could be no heat without cold.

Certainly this still rings true today. The challenges of living in México can be stimulating at times and constricting at others. The people can be very colorful, and yet when they mire themselves in provincial attitudes, they can be depressingly grey and uninteresting. Living in México is particularly complex. Uncovering one layer of its mystery exposes another. Life here is a fragmented composite of the comprehensible and the mysterious: history, customs, language, facts, myths and more—many of your perceptions will be at odds with one another.

A good friend once commented, "Have you noticed that most of the people who have come to live here are kind of unusual?"

"But so are you and I," I answered.

Moving to a new place and starting a new life is not for the fainthearted; it isn't easy to adapt to another culture, particularly one of this complexity. Every day I am challenged by "something", and this has led me to conclude that:

> My most rewarding days in México have been those when I had no **A**genda...

> The **B**est of everything can be found here but often, I have to look for it...

> This **C**ulture is incredibly rich even though the recognition of and respect for it is often depressingly unrecognized.

> **D**esperate poverty coexists alongside tremendous wealth...

> **E**ducation is the most crucial factor in improving the lives of the poor...

> In México, it's all about the **F**amily—this comes before all else...

> The **G**eographical location of southeastern México places it among the areas of the world that will

experience tremendous growth in the coming decade...

Improved **H**ealth care is another vital element that is necessary to improving the lives of the impoverished social classes...

I love the **I**diosyncrasies of the Mexicans...because of them my life is anything but dull...

Just when I think I've got it all figured out...I'm thrown a curve ball...

Keeping quiet and observing is often the best course of action when faced with a confusing situation....

If I had it all to do over again, I would definitely, choose to spend my **L**ife in México...

Macho attitudes hold everyone back...

We all need a **N**etwork of friends and acquaintances to adjust to life in a new country...

Open markets are great places to learn, to shop and to meet people...

Parenting is a multi-generational responsibility in Mexican families...

Quarrels and arguments are seldom forgotten; Mexicans have l-o-n-g memories...

I've learned the true meaning of the expression "There's no **R**ight or wrong, there's just different."

I am more comfortable in the heat when I **S**low down.

Time does not have the same meaning here...

Ups and downs are taken much more stoically in México...

Color is used **V**ividly...

The **W**omen of this region are strong, but they are only just beginning to realize this...

Xylophones or marimbas are common musical instruments...

Yucatán is truly my home...

Zero, zip, *nada*...is the bottom line!

Music is part of the *MAGIC MADE IN MEXICO*

Map of México

OUR COUNTRY –
OUR STATE – OUR CITY
The History of México,
Yucatán and Mérida

ONE WAY OF DEFINING OUR PLACE HERE is to learn the history. Understanding the past helps us to be more comfortable in the present.

México prides itself on great cultural and artistic achievements but also must lament heartbreaking social, military, economic and political struggles. Through reading, we learn about and better understand the people, events and reactions that make up the history of this land. What once seemed strange—even outrageous—will slowly start to make sense. Gradually, as our perspective shifts, we'll discover the magic of this place. This is when we'll truly feel that México is our country too.

OUR COUNTRY – MÉXICO
A Short History of México

I: Pre-Columbian México

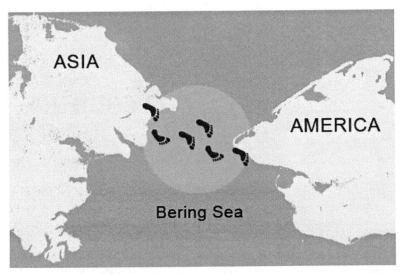

Most scholars seem to agree that the ancestors of México's indigenous people crossed the Bering Strait at least 20,000 years ago. They were nomadic hunter-gatherers who settled in México during the Archaic period—5000–1500 B.C.E.

In the Pre-Classic period—1500 B.C.E. to 300 C.E.—the first civilization to reach its peak was the Olmec. They established their cities—La Venta, San Lorenzo, Tres Zapotes and Laguna Azul—in areas known today as the states of Veracruz and Tabasco. But little is really known with much certainty about the Olmec culture.

The Mayan world is probably the best-known of the Classic Mesoamerican civilizations. By about 250 C.E., the Maya were the prominent group in present-day southern México, Guatemala, western Honduras, Belize and northern El Salvador. Many archaeologists believe that the Maya developed their highly accurate calendar and hieroglyphic writing based on the earlier achievements of the Olmec.

During most of the Mayan Classic period, Teotihuacán, north of today's Mexico City, was the dominant city in the central part of the country.

Teotihuacán was probably built by the Totonac people and was the center of a powerful culture whose influence extended over large expanses of the Mesoamerican region. It was a multi-ethnic city with distinct Zapotec, Mixtec, Maya and Nahua quarters.

In the Late-Classic period, even though Teotihuacán no longer had pre-eminence in its central Mexican homeland, frequent cultural exchange with the large Mayan centers occurred.

After the decline of Teotihuacán in the 6th century C.E., the Toltec culture dominated central México—from 750 to 1000 C.E.

Although several cultures developed in the 13th century in the central part of the country, the Aztecs were the most important of these. Actually, they never called themselves Aztecs, but rather Mexica, and the language they spoke was Náhuatl. After a long migration the Mexica tribe arrived at the valley of México in 1168 C.E.

Legend says the founding of their capital city, Tenochtitlán, occurred in a place where an eagle was found atop a cactus, devouring a serpent. This image is what would later inspire the design for the national symbol of México.

In 1492, Christopher Columbus set sail from Europe, looking for a route to the Orient. Instead, he landed on Hispaniola—the Caribbean island where the countries of Haiti and the Dominican Republic are located today—and the history of the entire planet was forever changed.

An engraving of Mérida's Cathedral in the colonial period

II: The Colonial period in México

The settlement of New Spain was an extraordinary period in history. The main protagonists were a competitive group of adventurers, and there was a constant struggle for supremacy and for favor with the Spanish monarchs.

The first lands in America to be claimed as Spanish colonies were two large Caribbean islands: Hispaniola and strategically located Cuba. In the early years of the Spanish dominance, the Governor General of Cuba, Diego Velázquez was the maximum authority for the entire territory. From Cuba, he oversaw further exploration and expansion of the colonial settlements.

In 1519 Hernán Cortés was just thirty-five years-old, and he sailed west without Velázquez' authorization. His audacious behavior would have probably resulted in his execution had he not discovered the Aztec capital, Tenochtitlán (where Mexico City is now located), and collected some of its treasures.

Cortés knew better than to return to Cuba and report to Velázquez. Instead, he sent two of his most trusted captains directly to the Spanish king. When the monarch saw the splendor of the Mexican booty—gold, silver, precious stones, exotic fabrics, dyes, spices and hardwoods—he rewarded Cortés' initiative and named him *Conquistador de México*.

By 1521 Cortés had completed the conquest of Tenochtitlán and had dispatched his officers to additional locations. Diego de Mazariegos led an expedition to Chiapas in 1528 and, in 1531, Captain Nuño de Guzmán was sent to Querétaro, Michoacán and Jalisco—which included present day states of Nayarit and Sinaloa and part of Sonora.

Cortés made certain that provisions arrived regularly from Europe: iron, gun powder, tools, cannons and other arms; as well as grape vines, cattle, horses and pigs.

Unmarried Spanish women were brought to México to become wives of the single men. Cortés thought that stable unions with European women would have a positive effect on his men. However, many of the seasoned conquistadores (including Cortés himself) kept their native concubines.

During the decades that Cortés lived in México several important schools and hospitals were founded and the colony grew quickly. Perhaps feeling threatened by his popularity and growing influence, the Spanish king ordered Cortés back to Spain where he died in 1547 at the age of sixty-three.

Viceroys were appointed to México and were charged with the sustainable development of the colony. In 1535 the first Viceroy, Antonio de Mendoza y Pacheco, traveling with iron-workers, glassmakers, carpenters and other specialized trades-men, journeyed from Spain to México. This official delegation brought looms, a printing press, silkworms, books, seed and scores of other items that were essential to the establishment of society. This group also diversified agriculture and industry in the new colony. Over a period of seventeen years, de Mendoza supervised the building of needed infrastructure throughout his dominion.

The life of the early colonial settlers was not an easy one. Great pressure was exerted by the Spanish crown to send frequent shipments of valuable goods such as: *palo de tinte* – a wood used in the manufacture of red dye – cochineal insects – prized for the scarlet dye made from their crushed bodies – hardwoods, salt, spices, textiles, tobacco and other agricultural products. Taxes that had been collected were also sent to Spain.

Many of these shipments never reached their destination due to storms and piracy. An unknown amount of the cargo fell into the hands of renegades who controlled a thriving black market.

The Catholic Church was the central focus in colonial México. All events and activities, including those of com-merce, trade and warring were done in the name of God and the Spanish crown. Evangelization was the banner under which the new authority operated—anything and everything had to be legitimized by the Church.

Apart from daily Mass and other religious rites, there were a succession of feasts throughout the year. Each patron saint was honored with religious and social celebrations—prayer and observance went hand-in-hand with food, drink, music, and dancing. The high holy days of the Church calendar were marked with special devotion. The clergy held enormous power over all social groups.

Literacy was the special province of the religious and upper classes. Only some of the elite were taught to read and write, and very few members of the lower classes had access to any education. In this way, control of communication could continue to stay in the hands of the Church leaders. The masses were taught to recite the litanies and prayers and to chant. They were instructed in Church teachings by way of religious paintings that depicted the stories from the Bible and Church history. It was an honor to be deemed talented—and saintly—enough to learn the techniques of painting, sculpture or stucco molding.

During the early years of the Spanish colonies, most pioneering females were the wives of the leaders of the Conquistador army. It must have been supremely challenging for these European ladies to live in the new territories without the social structure, the comforts or the family support they were accustomed to. Historians point out that the presence of the wives did indeed have a civilizing effect on their husbands and contributed significantly to the stability of the new society.

The Spaniards who did not have European wives set up housekeeping with local women and had families. In fact one of the Spaniards in Yucatán, Francisco Barrio, married a grand daughter of Emperor Montezuma of Tenochtitlán. This Aztec princess had come to Yucatán with Doña Beatriz de Herrera, who was the wife of Francisco de Montejo *"el Hijo"* – "the Younger". When the princess's husband died, she entered a convent along with a retinue of servants to attend her. After all, royalty was royalty.

Eventually, a complicated caste system that categorized a person's lineage evolved, and a strict social hierarchy was instituted. Rank and privilege in New Spain were largely determined by the amount of European blood coursing through one's veins. Those born in Spain, of two Spanish parents, the *peninsulares* – referring to the Iberian peninsula of Europe – held the highest status. Children born in México of two Spanish parents were called *criollos* – creoles – and held second place in the social order. Next were the various *mestizos* – mixed bloods. The children of two mestizo parents had more prestige than full-blooded indigenous, but there were many, many different categories of mestizo.

Many historians believe that not awarding full stature to the children of two Spanish citizens was the Iberian crown's greatest miscalculation. Because those who were Mexican-born could receive no status from their bloodline, they looked for their identity in the land. This engendered loyalty to México and such feelings were a large contributor to the Independence movement.

One notable exception to the strict rules of caste and gender was Sor (Sister) Juana Inés de la Cruz. A child prodigy, Juana was sent to live in Mexico City at age sixteen and came under the tutelage of the Viceroy's wife, Leonor de Carreto. Her literary accomplishments—as well as her writings on theology and science—soon made her famous throughout New Spain. Matters came to a head in 1690 when a letter was published attacking Sor Juana's focus on the sciences and suggesting that she, i.e., women, should not meddle in theology. Fortunately, powerful representatives from the Spanish court were her mentors and her work was printed in Mexico City on the first printing press of the American continent.

In 1693 Sor Juana ceased writing rather than risk Church censure. She reportedly sold her extensive library of over four thousand volumes and her musical and scientific instruments as well. Fortunately, some of her manuscripts were saved by the Viceroy's wife. After ministering to the other sisters during a cholera epidemic, she was struck down in April 1695.

By the year 1550 approximately two thousand Spanish citizens lived in Mexico City. Hospitals and schools were established. Social structure was well defined and many amenities were available to the upper class. In 1551 the first university in Mexico City was founded with all of the rights and privileges of *la Universidad de Salamanca* – the most important educational institution in Spain.

Agriculture in the fertile Valley of México thrived, and north of Mexico City mining activity was increased. Exports of silver and gold were priorities for the colony.

Keeping México and the other colonies dependent upon the motherland was a major concern of the Spanish kings. They controlled the importation of goods into New Spain through the consortium that operated the trading vessels known as *la Nao de China* – usually called Manila Galleons in English – they sailed from Cádiz, Spain to México and from Acapulco, México to Manila in the Philippines. Some of them carried silver coins that were minted in México under very strict controls. These were used as currency in all the Spanish holdings.

The ships returning from the Philippines to México carried silks, spices, metal and jewels, precious stones and pearls; those from Spain came with olive oil, porcelain, wool, building tiles, kitchenware, soap and a host of other products that could only be acquired through this trading syndicate.

Political events in Europe had profound effects on the Spanish colonies, but none was quite as far-reaching as Napoleon Bonaparte's removal of King Fernando VII from the Spanish throne and the subsequent imprisonment of the Spanish monarch in Paris in 1809. Despite resistance from the Spaniards who were loyal to Fernando, Napoleon's brother, Joseph, was installed as the Spanish king. This event was calamitous for Spain.

For approximately three hundred years, the Spanish crown had been the dominant world power. They'd endured some competition from the Dutch and Portuguese, but through astute negotiation they had held on to all their colonies, especially those in the Americas.

The liberal reforms introduced by the Spanish Constitution of Cádiz in 1812 greatly changed perspectives overseas. This document stated that that free-born colonials were to be referred to as Spanish-Americans as opposed to their former pejorative designation, creoles. Furthermore, it guaranteed the right of a free press for the residents in the colonies and revoked the requirement that all publications be approved by the old guard.

Finally the new constitution established that there would be three governing bodies: the Executive (the King *en absentia*); the Legislative (the deputies); and the Judicial (the courts). Most importantly for the Spanish-Americans, the colonies and cities could elect their own deputies.

But by 1799 Mexican-born Spaniards had begun organizing a serious insurgency movement. By no means did this receive unanimous support among Mexican society. Opinions were heavily divided between those who wanted independence and royalists who wanted the Spanish colonial rule to continue.

Finally, at midnight on September 15, 1810, with rousing encouragement from the leaders of the insurgency, the common people moved firmly forward. From the steps of the church in the town of Dolores (in central México, now called Dolores Hidalgo) a rebellious Catholic priest named Miguel Hidalgo y Costilla dramatically waved a flag bearing the image of the Virgin of Guadalupe and called on the faithful to join in the fight for liberation.

Exhausted by centuries of repression, the masses responded with cries of, *"¡Viva México! ¡Viva la Virgen de Guadalupe!"* Every year at midnight on September 15th this scene is re-enacted in every city, town and hamlet in the country and is known as *el Grito* – The Cry.

III: The Independence of México

On the night of September 15, 1810 when Father Hidalgo roused the population with his cry for independence, the movement that had been incubating for so long spread rapidly throughout the land.

Those who recognized that México had grown beyond the confines of dependence on a mother country continued to increase in number. In their minds, the colonial authorities perpetuated too many injustices: high taxes, limits on trade, a demeaning social order based on lineage, abominable treatment of the lower classes and indigenous people, a ban on citizens' right to travel freely, censorship of the press; and prohibition of ownership of private printing presses.

In 1814 Napoleon Bonaparte was defeated in Europe. Fernando VII was reinstated as King of Spain and quickly abolished the Constitution of Cádiz. Nonetheless, México resistance continued to increase steadily. A return to the former repressive system was not supported by the majority of the population of New Spain.

The colonial elite had benefited greatly from the established order and did not want to see México become a separate political entity. This group had many economic resources and many followers. They resisted these changes with every means at their disposal.

Augustín de Iturbide was a colonel in the Spanish army. In 1820 he was sent to lead the loyalist troops in battle against the insurgents led by the rebel general, Vicente Guerrero. When Iturbide was confronted by fierce resistance the very pragmatic career army officer decided to change sides. He wrote a reform manifesto called e*l Plan de Iguala* – the Iguala plan. The document stressed that independence was the principal goal; the Catholic Church would remain the only official religion; Fernando VII or one of his heirs would be the constitutional monarch and a provisional government would be appointed that would facilitate the formation of a national Congress and the writing of a Constitution.

This sounded like the best compromise possible, so one by one the rebel generals, including Guererro, sided with Iturbide's plan. Many of the loyalist officers, including the future president Antonio López de Santa Ana, also switched their allegiance. The constant fighting since 1810 had weakened the resolve of all participants.

México's independence from Spain was proclaimed on September 27, 1821. The eleven-year war of independence was over. Political independence was achieved, but the economic and social conditions remained the same. The Spanish elite, the clerics and the military strong-men retained their former privileges and the goals of emancipation and justice for all were practically forgotten. Within three months, the old elite had entrenched itself deeply into their new roles and proclaimed Iturbide Emperor of México. Iturbide's coronation was on the 21st of July 1822 with full regalia; the Catholic hierarchy even officiated in the Cathedral.

The Iturbide Empire lasted only two years. He was ousted from power, and on May 11, 1823 he left México to live with his family in exile. And so began another cycle of plots and counter-plots that embroiled the new country in one conflict after another.

Three individuals were the main protagonists during the following ninety years. Antonio López de Santa Ana was president of México at least eleven times between 1833 and 1855; Benito Juárez, ruled for fourteen years from 1855 until his death 1872 although his presidency was interrupted by the Habsburg monarchy's rule, known as the French intervention in (or occupation of) México, from 1864 to 1867; and Porfirio Díaz—who came to power in 1877 and held it until 1911.

Santa Ana formed alliances with both the Conservatives and Liberal factions of the country. He was an extremely dynamic leader who had an unusual talent for aligning himself with the right people at the right time, even if that led to insurrection within his own political party.

His personal agenda was often a strong motivator: in 1834 he altered the federal constitution because he wanted to be named Emperor. His policies caused rebellion in the northern state of *Coahuila y Téjas* – Coahuila and Texas – and for a period of two years, 1841 to 1843, the Yucatán actually declared itself an independent republic because Santa Ana's federal government had perpetuated too many injustices to be acceptable to the Yucatecos.

The Mexican-American war officially began in 1846. For many years, in ever increasing numbers, American settlers had steadily migrated westward, occupying territories that belonged to

México. President James K. Polk embraced "Manifest Destiny", the belief that the U.S. basically had a God-given right to occupy and "civilize" the whole continent. When he was elected President of the United States, he authorized the annexation of Texas—where a break-away republic under English-speaking U.S. colonists had controlled the territory since 1836.

Violent but indecisive battles raged through the coveted Mexican lands, and the Polk Administration concluded that only a complete battlefield victory would end the fighting.

On March 9, 1847 twelve thousand American soldiers landed on the beaches near Veracruz and half a year later on September 14th they entered Mexico City. The city's populace offered resistance to the occupiers, but by mid-October the U.S. Army had full control. On February 2, 1848 the Treaty of Guadalupe Hidalgo was signed and a nominal amount of money was handed over to México. More than forty percent of México's territory was surrendered to the United States of America.

Later, Ulysses S. Grant, the American president—whose own distinguished military career began as a young officer with the invasion force—said of the Mexican-American war, "I regard the war as the most unjust war ever waged by a strong nation against a weaker nation."

While the Mexican government was distracted by these dire political events in central and northern México, they nearly lost the southeastern portion of the country as well. The Yucatecan Maya, who had been subjugated since the Conquest, launched a major uprising in July 1847. This was the start of *la Guerra de Castas* – the Caste War.

Since independence from Spain, México had been shaken by conflict after conflict. The country's resources were all but depleted and the population no longer had the will to fight.

They wanted peace. In 1855, Santa Ana was forced from the presidency for the last time, and Benito Juárez became part of a provisional government under General Juan Álvarez. This was the beginning of the period known as *la Reforma*. The Reform laws curtailed the power of the Catholic Church and the military. Juárez led the liberal side, and in spite of the conservatives' initial military advantage the liberals drew support from numerous regional groups.

Facing bankruptcy and a destroyed economy, Juárez, once he became president, stopped paying the foreign debt. Spain, Great Britain and France reacted by seizing the Veracruz customs house in December 1861. Spain and Britain soon withdrew, but Emperor Napoleon III did not, and he launched the French intervention in México in 1862.

The conservative sector of the country saw this as their opportunity to take back control of the nation. They boldly approached Prince Maximilian, the brother of Emperor Franz Joséf of Austria, and he agreed to become Emperor of México in 1863. This royal house was approached because the Spanish monarchs were descendents of the Hapsburg dynasty, Maximillian was known as a good Catholic and it was assumed that he would side with the church elite and abolish the Reform laws that were considered anti-Church and anticlerical.

The Imperial couple, Maximilian and his Belgian born wife, Charlotte von Battenberg, set up their residence at Chapultepec Castle, which at that time was on the outskirts of Mexico City. Centuries earlier, this large estate had been a retreat of the Aztec emperors. They took Spanish versions of their names, Maximiliano and Carlota, in an attempt to win over the populace.

To the dismay of his conservative allies, Maximiliano wanted to uphold many of the liberal laws and policies that had been instituted by the Juárez administration. He was in favor of land reforms, religious freedom and extending the right to vote beyond the landholding class. Maximiliano admired Juárez and offered an amnesty if he would swear allegiance to the crown; the Emperor even offered him the post of Prime Minister, but Juárez refused both the office and the amnesty.

The Mexicans won an initial victory against the French at Puebla, which is commemorated annually as *Cinco de Mayo* – May 5th – but the French just bypassed Puebla and continued to advance, forcing the elected government in Mexico City to retreat north to Chihuahua, where Benito Juárez set up his government-in-exile in El Paso del Norte, now called Ciudad Juárez. There he would remain for the next two-and-one-half years.

Pressing conflicts in 1866 in Europe caused Napoleon III to withdraw his troops from México, but Maximiliano refused to return with the European forces.

On May 15, 1867 the Emperor was captured by Juárez' troops. Following a court-martial he was sentenced to death. Before his execution by firing squad, his last words were, "*¡Mexicanos!* I die for a just cause – the independence and liberty of México. May my blood be the last to flow for the good of this land. *¡Viva México!*"

Empress Carlota never recovered from the shock of her husband's death. Many believed she was driven insane by his violent end—even though her mental decline actually happened prior to his execution. She lived her remaining years as a recluse.

Benito Juárez returned to Mexico City and served as president until his death from a heart attack in 1872.

Porfirio Díaz is remembered as a ruthless but effective leader. Although he had been a dedicated follower of Benito Juárez, he had become disillusioned with the Juárez government. From 1871 to 1876, Díaz was an outspoken citizen fighting against the regime of President Juárez and his immediate successors, and during this period he also established his own powerful political machine.

It was in May 1877 that Díaz became the formally elected president of México for the first time, and from this point on the Díaz regime maintained control by whatever means necessary. He established a centralized government in Mexico City, and from there he controlled all activity in every corner of the Republic.

It was under Porfirio Díaz that México entered the modern age. Infrastructure was commissioned throughout the country, and economic prosperity took hold. During his more than thirty years as president, Díaz created a systematic and methodical regime with a strong military mindset. His first goal was to establish peace throughout México. His second goal was see the country modernize and prosper.

Some have called the period that Díaz was in power the golden age of Mexican economics. Sadly, the country did not enjoy peace for long. New political ideologies would cause still greater bloodshed.

IV: The Mexican Revolution

The Mexican Revolution, which began in 1910, came about because of many different factors. To begin with Porfirio Díaz, due to his advanced age and years in power, was losing his influence in the Mexican political arena.

Internationally charged sociological issues such as child labor and union organization played a part, as did the new, dynamic political movements like socialism in the form of the labor movements of the United States and communism in Russia. World War I also played its part. The international economic situation

Pancho Villa and Emiliano Zapata

and the lack of a middle class were other variables. Fueled by these and other national and international occurrences, power struggles between military, political and social reformers in México reached the saturation point.

The consensus is that fraud during the Mexican presidential election of 1910 was the catalyst that sparked the Mexican Revolution. The revolutionaries, led by Francisco I. Madero, had reached such a level of dissatisfaction with the Díaz government that they saw no other means of change except to force Díaz to resign.

In 1911 Madero was elected president, ending the nascent revolution, but two years later a politically conservative general, Victoriano Huerta, overthrew Madero and assassinated him in a coup d'état. This re-ignited the civil war.

Pancho Villa was one of the best known revolutionary generals. As commander of the *División del Norte* – the Northern Division – he was the de facto authority in the northern Mexican state of Chihuahua, which, given its size, mineral wealth and proximity to the United States of America, provided him with extensive resources.

U.S. president Woodrow Wilson did not trust Villa, but he decided to support him because Villa's army seemed to be the most disciplined, and Villa appeared to be the most capable of the Mexican revolutionary generals. Wilson wanted a stable regime across the border.

Villa's dominance in northern México was broken in 1915 through a series of defeats he suffered at the hands of Álvaro Obregón and Plutarco Elías Calles. The U.S. relationship completely fell apart when his troops invaded Columbus, New Mexico on March 9, 1916. After that, the American administration was determined to capture him.

Wilson sent troops into México to hunt Villa down. Although President Carranza did not want foreign armies in México, he was forced to respect an old treaty that had a provision allowing troops from either country to pursue bandits on either side of the border. But the Americans could not find him. Pancho Villa eluded the soldiers who marched under the command of General Pershing, and eventually the Americans were forced to give up.

Villa retired in 1920 and was given a large estate which he turned into a "military colony" for his former soldiers. In return for a peaceful retirement, Villa agreed to stay out of politics, but in 1923 he again began stoking the rumors of his legendary persona on both sides of the Rio Grande, something considered political by the Obregón administration—a breech of his retirement settlement. He was eventually assassinated, most likely on the orders of Obregón.

In 1910, Emiliano Zapata became the head of the *Ejército Libertador del Sur* – the Southern Liberation Army – and also fought to oust Díaz from the presidency. Zapata overthrew city after city, but as his army gained momentum, Madero asked Zapata to disarm and demobilize. Zapata responded that, if the people could not win their rights when they were armed, they would have no chance once they were unarmed and helpless.

Madero sent several generals to negotiate with Zapata, but these efforts had little success. Zapata continued to fight the central government throughout the Revolution until finally, on April 10, 1919, he was ambushed and killed. Following his death the Liberation Army of the South slowly fell apart.

One of the most important groups of supporters of the Revolution was comprised of women. Called *Adelitas* – from a popular revolutionary song, "la Adelita"– the women not only cooked and nursed the troops, but often fought alongside the men, earning them the popular name of *soldaderas* – a feminine equivalent to the Spanish word, *soldado*, meaning soldier.

Many of these women were extremely poor and uneducated, yet their bravery and sacrifice made the struggle possible to maintain. They have been immortalized in such films as "La Cucaracha" starring María Félix and in popular folk songs like "Marieta".

Finally, a "constitutional" army led by Venustiano Carranza managed to bring an end to the war, and the 1857 Constitution was radically rewritten to include many of the social premises and demands of the revolutionaries. This constitution, the Constitution of 1917, with amendments, is still the Mexican Constitution.

It is estimated that during the Revolution 900,000 died, although most died of disease and starvation rather than actual combat.

From 1924 to 1929 the conflict known as *la Guerra Cristera* – the Christian War – raged throughout the country. The issue was the same one that had plagued the country since colonial times; the competition between the Catholic Church and the secular Mexican government, with the Church leaders refusing to accept the authority of the government whenever their interests were not served.

There were particularly violent and destructive confrontations in the state of Tabasco and in central México. Churches and convents were sacked; religious art was destroyed and clergy were persecuted. A novel that impressively depicts this era is *The Power and The Glory* by Graham Green.

1934 marked the beginning of a new era. General Lázaro Cárdenas became president. History remembers Cárdenas as the Mexican president who truly ended the Revolution and brought peace to the country. He is also lauded as the politician who created a practical political formula for stability and who asserted México's rights as a nation. He was a very popular president, and his wife was beloved for her work with the disadvantaged. Cárdenas was also a supporter of avant-garde artists such as Diego Rivera and Frida Khalo.

Cárdenas decreed the end of the use of capital punishment, which is still banned in México. Russian exile Leon Trotsky was welcomed into México by Cárdenas, and although Cárdenas was not as left-wing as the socialists wished, Trotsky described Cárdenas' government as, "The only honest government in the world."

After the Spanish Civil War ended Cárdenas gave safe haven and protection to all exiles, including the Spanish president and his government-in-exile.

Central to his political ideology was the organization and incorporation of trade unions, *campesino* – poor farmer – organizations, middle-class professionals and office workers into the rank and file of the reorganized ruling party.

During Cárdenas' presidency the government expropriated and redistributed millions of acres of hacienda land to campesinos, principally in the states of Yucatán and Jalisco. The urban industrial workers gained unprecedented unionization rights and wage increases.

Agrarian reforms included turning over haciendas to local cooperatives – *ejidos* – and establishing a government bank, Banrural, to give technical and economic support to the cooperatives.

Cárdenas' efforts to negotiate with the foreign oil companies failed, so on March 18, 1938 he nationalized México's petroleum reserves and expropriated the property and equipment of the foreign oil companies in México. The announcement inspired a spontaneous six-hour parade in Mexico City; which was followed by a national fund-raising campaign to reimburse the international oil companies for the expropriated property and equipment.

The company that Cárdenas founded was Pemex – *Petróleos Mexicanos*. Despite corruption and poor management, it remains the most important source of income for the country. Seeing the need to assure the technical expertise needed to run it, Cárdenas founded The National Polytechnic Institute.

Cárdenas also nationalized the railways in 1938 and put them under a "workers' administration".

V: The Era of the PRI in México

It is impossible to write about 20th century México without reference to the Institutional Revolutionary Party – *Partido Revolucionario Institucional (PRI)*. While other political and economic organizations rose and fell, the PRI endured. It not only endured, it prospered until it encompassed absolutely every area of Mexican life.

The group that would eventually be known as the PRI was formed in 1929, just prior to the beginning of the Great Depression. Once elected, President Lázaro Cárdenas headed the National Revolutionary Party – *Partido Nacional Revolucionario (PNR)* – the political party that was to become the PRI—officially founded in 1949—making him the politician who is widely considered to be the strategic planner for one of the longest serving elected governments in the history of the world.

Most autocratic governments have been fear-based but the PRI was much more humane; it has always been favor-based. In return for turning a blind eye or convincing opposing forces, the PRI offered its faithful legions a union contract, land to build a home on, a minor political appointment or any number of other advantageous positions, etc.

In the early 1950s, a different industry boomed—tourism. The President of México from 1947 to 1952 was Miguel Alemán, who was a great supporter of tourism as a source of income for México. During his term in office new infrastructure was built, and Mérida and the Yucatan were finally connected by railroad to the central part of the country. Other areas in the country also embraced tourism during this time, and Pacific coastal towns became very popular winter vacation destinations. Acapulco in particular became a mecca for the rich and famous who built palatial residences or spent their holidays in the sumptuous new hotels.

In 1968 two events occurred that had long-lasting and very different effects in the country. The first took place at a historic plaza in Tlaltelolco, which is a very old neighborhood with a huge new housing development close to downtown Mexico City.

In the late 1960s, young people were clamoring for change and went to the streets to make their views known. The autocratic Mexican government tried to quell the discontent with little success. Even many of the universities' faculty and deans supported the students' cry for educational and social reforms. On October 2, 1968, frustrated by failed attempts to retain control, the army was ordered to open fire on the students during a rally in *la Plaza de las Tres Culturas* – the Plaza of the Three Cultures – a historic plaza in Tlaltelolco.

Pandemonium broke out, and unconfirmed thousands disappeared or were killed that day. At the time this tragedy received little international publicity because all efforts were being expended to promote the other important happening—the Mexico City Olympic Games.

The Olympic celebration did what it was intended to do; it put México on the map as a developing power in Latin America. Meanwhile, the nation was left to mourn Tlaltelolco...quietly. Only in recent years have the facts of this dark episode come to light. For many, it was the end of an era of innocence, and the beginning of the end for PRI dominance.

The recently-built Olympics sports infrastructure was utilized again in 1970 for the FIFA World Cup Soccer – *Fútbol* – Championship in Mexico City. Once again, the country took great pride in showing the world it was a leader on the international stage. The reality was quite different.

México was in serious debt, and beginning in 1976 a series of devaluations created financial instability that was to worsen continually for more than two decades. The peso had been at 12.50 against the U.S. dollar since the early 50s; it would reach 3,000 to the dollar before the three zeros were removed and a new peso was instituted in 1993. Now, in 2010, more than thirty years after the first devaluation in 1976, the peso-to-dollar exchange rate is not too different from what it was back in the 1950s.

The large middle class that existed in México in the mid-seventies would be diminished by increased taxes, lower wages and shrinking job security. One by one, families slipped below the poverty line, yet somehow they always managed to keep from falling completely off the edge. I believe that Mexicans are among the most resilient and resourceful people on earth.

The 1980s in México were similar to this period all over the world. Growth of global enterprises accelerated, and small family-owned businesses began to lose their market share. Consumers were pleased to have the national and international chains set up operations in the city, as they afforded a much wider selection of goods and competitive prices. The first shopping malls opened in the suburbs, and existing businesses were forced to improve their services. But this was a double-edged sword, since the investment was no longer supporting the traditional economic centers.

On Thursday September 19, 1985, Mexico City suffered an earthquake measuring 8.1 on the Richter scale. Eighty percent of the damage was confined to four of the city's neighborhoods that also had the highest concentration of hospitals. Nearly all the buildings that collapsed were located in a zone that included Tlaltelolco. Once again, a tragedy of unfathomable magnitude had hit the largest housing complex of the city. Terrified people, trying to escape, jumped from high windows to their death. More people became trapped in stairwells, elevators and apartments without any way to contact the outside world. Lines of fifty to a hundred men passed rubble by hand and with buckets, desperately trying to reach victims.

In the area most severely damaged by the earthquake heavy machinery could not be used at the site until five days after the earthquake, as no one wanted to cause any cave-ins that might bury survivors. There were countless acts of heroism and an amazing number were rescued up until ten days after the mega-quake. The government's slow response to the catastrophe was another step toward the fall of the PRI.

The signing of the North American Free Trade Agreement – the NAFTA treaty – was greeted with optimism that was short-lived. The promise of greater prosperity for all was completely dashed with the financial collapse of the country in the mid 1990s. 1994 to 1996 was a challenging time to live in México; foreclosed mortgages, repossessed cars and bankrupt businesses were commonplace. Eventually a U.S.A. led financial aid program helped the country to get back on its feet, and an austere economic policy was instituted, causing widespread social unrest.

On January 1, 1994 in the impoverished state of Chiapas, "Zapatista" rebel forces occupied the city of San Cristóbal de las Casas. The group was led by the charismatic Subcomandante Marcos. The Subcommandante always wears a balaclava, but his eyes can be seen; they are green, and that, along with his height and build, clearly shows that he is not from a local indigenous group. When asked what his group wants, Subcomandante Marcos explained, "We want the same rights and opportunities as the rest of the Mexicans."

The government committed many errors in the handling of this recent sad episode in our history but eventually much-needed reforms and rights were granted to the indigenous people in that area and some form of order was reestablished.

One of México's greatest challenges is to determine how indigenous people can be a part of a modern economy and provide opportunities for their young people, without the loss of traditional values and customs.

Many believe that the answer to this is sustainable economic development. If the indigenous populations are able to make a decent living in their traditional communities, they will not have to migrate to large cities or even to other countries. If they stay in their villages they have a much better chance of preserving their lifestyle. However, others believe that the traditional lifestyle preserves traditions that are completely contrary to the constitutional rights of the Mexican people, so it's a conundrum.

A tragic blow occurred on March 23rd, 1984. Luís Donaldo Colosio, the PRI presidential candidate was gunned down in Tijuana during a campaign appearance. The perpetrator claims he acted alone but evidence exists that makes many suspect that there were other politicians were involved.

The financial and social unrest during the final five years of the 20th century were instrumental in the PRI's fall from power. This political party and its forerunner, the PNR, had held the presidency for over seventy years.

VI: The Twenty-first century in México

The year 2000 saw unprecedented changes in the political arena. The National Action Party – *Partido de Acción Nacional (PAN)* – won the federal elections in July and by December a

Mexico City's zócalo

charismatic new president was invested. The country had great hopes that democracy would grow.

In June of 2002 secret security files were released. Many of them dealt with the disappearance of hundreds of political activists and university students in the 1960s and 1970s.

President Fox said his government was not afraid to pursue prosecutions and the country held its breath. After all these years would justice be served? Later that year former President Luís Echeverría was questioned about massacres of student protesters in 1968 and 1971 but exonerated of wrongdoing. Three army officers were charged with first-degree murder over the killings of 134 leftists in the 1970s. It looked as though the whole investigation was tied up neatly with a bow.

The first decade of the twenty-first century has been lamented by many. It seems as though classic opportunities were lost, one after the other.

Although the inquiry continued into President Luís Echeverría's involvement in the massacre of leftists, the judge refused to order the arrest of the former president. It was business as usual in the political arena. The high hopes for change began to erode and the historic opening that the citizens had hoped for completely evaporated.

Political tension was high in 2005 as the Party of the Democratic Revolution – *Partido de la Revolución Democrática (PRD)* – candidate, Andrés Manuel López Obrador and Felipe Calderón, the PAN candidate, engaged in every possible electoral strategy to win the next presidency.

Simultaneously, human rights once again caught the country's attention; in February 2006 a special prosecutor was appointed to tackle the mystery surrounding the escalating violent crime against women. United Nations groups criticized México over the unsolved murders of more than three hundred women in the border city of Ciudad Juárez. Also, sixty-five miners were killed in an explosion at a coal mine in Coahuila state. To this date, neither case has been successfully resolved.

In July 2006 PAN candidate Felipe Calderón was declared the winner of presidential elections with a razor-thin majority over his leftist rival, Andrés Manuel López Obrador, who challenged the result with mass street protests. The Federal Electoral Tribunal confirmed Mr. Calderón's win in September.

The Fox presidency ended in disappointment and the election of a new PAN President in 2006 was tarnished with accusations of election fraud. Whether the current political situation is a consequence of many years of enforced PRI party rule is yet to be determined. Mexicans have become much more involved in the election process. There has been an increase in political awareness, and the hope is for a continuation of the democratic process.

In October 2006, U.S. President George W. Bush signed legislation to build 1,125 kilometers – 700 miles – of high fencing along the U.S.-México border. México condemned plans for the barrier, which was intended to curb illegal immigration.

Heavy rains flooded the state of Tabasco in October of that year, and 500,000 were left homeless in one of the country's worst natural disasters. Severe flooding continues to be a huge problem in the low-lying states where there are many rivers.

Drug-related killings continued to soar. Murders linked to organized crime leapt to almost one thousand four hundred. Hundreds of thousands joined marches throughout México to protest against the continuing violence.

Faced with a drop in Mexican oil production, the government passed series of energy reforms. The package included controversial plans to allow private investment in some areas previously reserved for state oil giant Pemex.

I believe there is something very special about this country. Despite the political and social ills, the population is generous and happy. When hard times come along Mexicans are as philosophical and accepting as they can possibly be. They have the ability to enjoy life when they can. They live in the moment and have confidence that somehow the future will resolve itself.

Most who come here even once are intrigued by this delightful national characteristic and are lured back time and again. This explosive joy is the true *milagro mexicano* – the magical Mexican miracle.

OUR STATE & OUR CITY
A Short History of Yucatán & Mérida

Mérida and the Yucatán have always held a special fascination for outsiders, in part because of the Mayan culture, which is still very much alive. Many scholars believe the Mayan civilization was the most impressive of the Classic Mesoamerican societies. By about 250 C.E., their society was dominant in present-day southern México, Guatemala, western Honduras, Belize and northern El Salvador.

Throughout the Classic period—250 to 900 C.E.—they developed an intricate hierarchical society that was divided into classes and professions. Centralized governments, headed by a king, ruled the different territories. The borders changed as the various city-states gained and lost power. Sometimes called the Greeks of the Americas, the Maya had highly accurate astronomical charts and advanced engineering skills—their temples, pyramids, palaces, and observatories were all built without metal tools. The Maya discovered the concept of zero, and their artistic ability was impressive.

The Maya were skilled potters, weavers and highly productive farmers. They built large underground cisterns for the collection and storage of rainwater where groundwater was scarce. They were adept at building roads that facilitated extensive trade routes.

At the end of the 9th century C.E. the population of the principal Mayan centers of the Yucatán and Central America declined significantly and rapidly. This has been attributed to famine, drought, a slump in trade and political fragmentation, but no one can really know with certainty.

With the decline of the Mayan city-states as a political force in Mesoamerica power shifted northwards, first to the Toltecs and later to the Aztecs.

The similarities in architecture and iconography between the Toltec city in Tula and the Mayan sites of Chichén Itzá and Mayapán indicate that the Maya were particularly influenced by the Toltec between the 10th and 12th centuries C.E.

A noteworthy example of the Toltec cultural influence in the Maya world was the spread of the *Quetzalcóatl – Kukulkán* cult. The name Quetzalcóatl literally means Serpent with Feathers of the Resplendent Quetzal. The Yucatecan Maya knew this deity as Kukulkán; the Quiche Maya of Guatemala knew him as Gukumatz.

During the Post-Classic period—900 to the late 1400s C.E.—the three most important Mayan cities in the northern part of the Yucatán peninsula were: Chichén Itzá, headed by the Itzáes group; Uxmal, led by the Xiu clan and Mayapán whose rulers were the Cocom.

They lived in relative peace from 1000 to 1100 C.E.; then Mayapán overthrew the confederation and held supremacy for over two hundred years. In 1441 the Xiu, rulers of Uxmal, destroyed Mayapán, the city of their ancestral enemies, the Cocom. Then the Xiu abandoned their own capital, Uxmal, and founded a new one in Mani.

Perhaps the new capital of Mani would have been the setting of a Mayan Renaissance? Perhaps the Maya would have reclaimed their former greatness there? These questions will forever remain speculation because Christopher Columbus' arrival to the Americas in 1492 changed the balance of power and the Maya world was radically altered.

In 1511 a mariner named Gonzalo de Guerrero was part of the Spanish crew who were shipwrecked off the Yucatán coast. Only he and a priest, Friar Gerónimo de Aguilar survived. They were eventually found and taken to a Mayan village. In time, Gonzalo Guerrero married a Maya princess from Chetumal named Y'xpilotzama, and they became the parents of the first known *mestizos* – mixed-blood children born in the Americas, e.g., offspring of a European man and an indigenous woman.

Gonzalo Guerrero and Father Aguilar lived in the Mayan village for about eight years until 1519 when Hernán Cortés heard about their survival and went to find them.

They had both learned to speak Maya, but Gonzalo Guererro refused to go with Cortés, because he didn't want to leave his wife and three children: Gonzalo, Juan and Rosario. He had assimilated into the Mayan lifestyle and even had tribal tattoos all over his body. Cortés reluctantly left Guererro with the Mayan group, knowing that the former Spanish soldier could never integrate back into the Conquistador army.

But Padre Aguilar was anxious to leave the Mayan community and serve as a translator during the conquest of central México. At the time he was certainly one of the few Europeans who could speak a native language. When he arrived in Veracruz, he met Cortés' legendary mistress La Malinche, who was proficient in Maya and Náhuatal and eventually learned to speak Spanish as well.

After the Conquest of Tenochtitlán, Cortés, bypassing his nominal superiors in Cuba, sent several officers with treasure looted from the Aztecs directly to the King of Spain. One of the captains who went to Spain on Cortés's behalf was Francisco de Montejo *"el Adelantado"* – "the Elder" – who later requested royal permission to conquer "The Islands of Yucatán and Cozumel"—at the time, no one realized that the Yucatán was in fact a peninsula.

De Montejo the Elder and his army first arrived in Yucatán in 1527. They found a hot, humid, inhospitable land. They had to cut through dense underbrush and jungle in order to navigate the overgrown Mayan roadways. The Maya were not an easy people to dominate, and the subjugation took seventeen years. By this time, Francisco de Montejo the Elder was no longer a young man.

During most of the battles with the Maya he had been in San Cristóbal de las Casas in Chiapas, and his son and his nephew (both of whom were also confusingly named Francisco de Montejo) were in command of the Spanish troops in the Yucatán. The decisive battle was fought on 11th of June 1541.

After the Spanish victory, de Montejo the Elder returned to the Yucatán peninsula but the Spaniards found little of interest in the way of treasure—this was no Tenochtitlán with gold and other precious objects waiting for the taking. The Mayan civilization was in decline and the conquistadores found only the remains of formerly splendid cities. What Yucatán did offer were natural resources that were much-prized at the time: Campeche wood for the making of dyes; hardwoods such as mahogany; cotton and salt. The geographical position was also quite strategic and the enterprising colonials could see potential in the area.

Not just anyone could be successful in colonial Yucatán. These men possessed a sense of adventure and fearlessness and had a certain arrogance and self-assuredness. They needed to be in excellent standing with the most influential authorities and to have the good fortune of being accompanied by a wife who could withstand the hardships and hopefully bear many children. Robust health and not falling victim to the plagues or other health risks, was very important. So was the ability to procure laborers who would remain loyal and work hard. Drought was a constant threat as was invasion of one's property. The early colonials were a stalwart group, and by one means or another they prospered and laid the foundation of the Yucatán's culture.

One of the ruined Mayan cities the Spaniards came upon was Ichcanzihó—also called T'hó. On the 6th of January 1542, Francisco de Montejo *"el Hijo"* – "the Younger" – founded the new city of Mérida upon the ruins of T'hó. It is said that one of his soldiers, Francisco de Almaraz suggested the name Mérida because the ruined temples and palaces reminded him of the Roman ruins of Emerita Augusta near the city of Mérida in Spain.

The colonials laid their new city out on a grid using a cord as the measuring tool. Like most cities in New Spain, the streets were straight and the intersections were square. The axis was the main city square – *la Plaza de Armas* – the Plaza of Arms (weapons).

This hundred-meter-square, open-air meeting space had a much different function in colonial Yucatán than it does now. Once a year, the Conquistador or the governor of the region would call upon all the heads of the households to gather in the plaza with their horses, guns and ammunition. This way an accurate inventory of the city's defense resources could be compiled. During the early colonial period, rebel Mayan groups often attacked Mérida, and constant vigilance was necessary. It would be much later that the plaza took on the social functions it has today.

The Spaniards had no problem finding building materials and labor. The Mayan temples were demolished and they re-used the stones, yet vestiges of these buildings can still be found today. Mayan laborers were numerous and skilled. On the corner of 61st and 60th Streets you can see a section of wall where the plaster has been removed and the carved Mayan stones are exposed.

On the façades of many colonial walls and buildings you can also find and identify stones with Mayan motifs.

Mérida's San Ildefonso Cathedral, located on the eastern side of the plaza, is the oldest cathedral on mainland America. A magnificent example of Spanish colonial Franciscan architecture, its dimensions are colossal. It has been said that the plans for this building were actually drawn up for the city of Lima, Peru, but by some means they arrived in Mérida.

Construction began and the Cathedral was completed in 1598. The façade features rather austere detailing.

Most religious buildings in Yucatán were commissioned by the Franciscans. This order favored less ornate embellishment than the elaborately ornamented churches that the Dominican and Jesuit clergy built in other colonial cities. Located next to the Cathedral was the residence of the Bishop of Yucatán.

The Municipal Hall of Mérida was not built until 1736. However, in Mérida's earliest years, there were other buildings constructed on the western side of the plaza. These were the residences belonging to the colonial elite, and some, like the one found on the corner of Calles 62 and 61, are still in use today.

Las Casas Reales – the governor's offices, the market and the jail – were located on the northern side of the plaza. These were simple, functional, one-storied buildings and open-air spaces. It was not until 1892 that the Governor's Palace as we know it today was constructed. Other lands were set aside for more churches with their respective plazas.

The extraordinary building on the southern side of the *zócalo* – the main square – is the Montejo family home. Completed in 1547, the palace was built by Francisco de Montejo the Younger. *La Casa de Montejo* is acknowledged by many historians as the finest privately owned example of the Spanish Plateresque style in all of New Spain.

From the zócalo, the city continued four blocks to the north, south, east and west. Each block (measuring approximately 10,000 square meters) was divided into quadrants. These large pieces of land were given to the highest officers in de Montejo's small army. Among these men were: Alonso de Rosado; the earlier-mentioned Francisco de Almaraz; Cristóbal de San Martín; Hernando de Bracamonte; Alonso López de Herrero and Gaspar Juárez de Ávila.

In each quadrant, there would be a principal home. These were mostly of a standard design, featuring a flat façade with little adornment. The main doorway and perhaps one or two narrow barred windows were all one could see from the street. The façades of the homes were nearly impossible to scale, and high walls that were impossible to climb over were constructed all around the perimeter of these properties, keeping the inhabitants safe from any intruders. One could come through the front entrance on foot or on horseback or by wagon, as it was wide enough to allow wagons to be driven inside.

The compounds featured a central courtyard with high-ceilinged rooms built around the four sides. There would often be flowers and ornamental shrubs, perhaps even a fountain that lent a peaceful ambiance to the living quarters.

Behind the family's dwelling, there were *tres patios* – three enclosed open-air spaces. In the first there was always a well and the poultry coops. Here, the laundry and cooking were done and herbs and spices were cultivated. The second enclosure was a garden for vegetable production and fruit trees. In the back area, the stables for the horses and other animals were to be found.

In this section there were also storage areas. Indeed, each family compound was self-sufficient and could withstand a siege.

Because there were no valuable objects to be taken, some members of the conquering army decided to flee the hot, oppressively humid, new colony, but most remained, and their descendants are found at every level of modern-day Yucatecan society.

Other young cities, such as Campeche and Valladolid, vied with Mérida for pre-eminence. Campeche, being the only authorized port, had easier access to Cuba and Spain. Valladolid was closer to the rich forests where the trading commodities were harvested. Despite the city's challenges and disadvantages, Mérida became the See of the Dioceses of Yucatán in 1562.

Friar Diego de Landa Calderón was the Franciscan provincial superior, and he would hold the position of Bishop of Yucatán from 1573 to 1579. Like many of the Franciscan missionaries, he learned to speak Maya and was a keen observer of daily life. He was an extremely influential member of the religious community and spurred on the construction of many Catholic churches, convents, missions and monasteries.

He convinced the master craftsmen from Europe to teach the Mayan stone masons, carpenters, painters and sculptors. These were soon producing impressive buildings and beautiful artwork for the new religious centers.

Much has been written about Bishop de Landa. To some historians, he was a fanatical cleric who wreaked havoc amongst the citizenry and destroyed precious Mayan manuscripts and artwork. Others see him as a man of his time who held fast to his duty and position, in the process establishing a much-needed order of conduct in the new colony. For all his notoriety, his book, *Relation of the Things in Yucatán*, stands today as one of the most authoritative texts on Mayan customs and beliefs in the 16th Century.

Unlike the English colonials who recoiled from the idea of intermarriage with the natives, the Spaniards who did not have European wives set up housekeeping with local women and had families.

By 1600 about three hundred Spanish citizens, along with a couple of generations of their descendents, were living in Mérida. The city spread out to areas such as Santiago, where the Maya and other indigenous workers lived and Santa Catalina, the site of Mérida's first university. In all there were nineteen districts or *cacicazgos* – today we would call these *colonias* or *barrios*.

The Church was the institution that held most sway over the people and their daily lives. A code of conduct was established by Catholic authorities and severe penalties were paid by those who did not absolutely adhere to it. There were certainly clerics who were more liberal, and these individuals established a few training, language and music schools for the Mayan residents of the city. They also ran rudimentary hospitals and orphanages.

It was mandatory that the head of the city, town, village, or settlement reside there; he could not absent himself except when requested to do so by higher officials. In fact, no one was permitted to travel from one place to another without authorization. This enforced a consistent lifestyle and maintained strict vigilance over the population.

Absolute obedience to civic and religious authorities was enforced; crimes such as adultery were punished by one hundred lashes. Under no circumstances was the native population allowed to plant fields, build homes or churches, move or marry without permission. Nor could they absent themselves from twice-daily religious observance, and certainly they could not practice pagan rites. Taxes and tributes had to be paid promptly and in full. A demand to donate time and labor for community services could not be turned down by anyone.

Campeche and Valladolid, the two other important colonial centers each had approximately eighty Spanish residents. Although great rivalry existed between the cities, the colonials supported one another. Failure to do would have meant rapid annihilation by the much more numerous, antagonistic Mayan groups.

At the beginning of the 17th century, the Yucatán was not an extremely prosperous or important holding of the Spanish crown. There were no gold or silver mines; in fact, there was no metal of any kind. Mérida was surrounded by unproductive land, with no rivers or lakes. In the agriculture-based economy of the time, this part of the peninsula was not very desirable. Valladolid, Tizimín and Campeche had much more arable land. Mérida's great advantage was its central location; from the city, one could travel in any direction to the other districts.

The provincial Governor, Carlos Luna de Arellano, ordered the repair and amplification of the Mayan causeways that connected Campeche, Mérida, Bacalar and Valladolid in 1604; this important system of communication was called, *el Camino Real* – the Royal Road. Luna de Arellano also fortified the city of Campeche to defend it against pirate attack.

The mortality rate from pestilence reached epidemic proportions in 1648, and the hierarchy of Mérida pleaded for divine intervention. Religious icons, such as that of *la Vírgen de Izamal* (a very beautiful statue of Mother Mary) were believed to have miraculous powers, so she was brought in procession to Mérida. Her absence from the convent in Izamal was only authorized for a period of two weeks. During the nine days and nights that *la Vírgen* remained in Mérida, she was paraded through the streets, and citizens would throw open their doors, so they could thrust their sick in her path. The plague did abate and *la Virgen* was attributed a miracle.

Famine raged through the peninsula in 1650. The unsuccessful efforts of the governor, Count de Peñalba, to alleviate the suffering combined with accusations of hoarding resulted in his assassination in 1652.

Attack from the Maya (sporadically supported by the British colonials from the territory known today as Belize) was not the only one of the Spanish colony's principal preoccupations. Piracy was commonplace in both the Gulf of México and the Caribbean.

French, Dutch and English swashbucklers repeatedly sacked ports such as Campeche, Isla de Tris (now known as Ciudad del Carmen) and Cozumel. After a particularly devastating incursion by a pirate army led by Laurent Graff, the construction of a city wall was accelerated in 1685 to strengthen the fortifications of Campeche; this reduced the frequency of attacks against the only officially authorized port of colonial Yucatán. Parts of this great wall still stand firm in the port city.

There were sporadic revolts throughout the colonial period; a very important one occurred in 1761. Jacinto Canek, a young Campeche-born Mayan man, worked as a baker in Mérida's barrio de Santiago. Living conditions were deplorable, so he led an uprising against the colonial forces that culminated not only with his torture and execution in Mérida's main square, but also the total destruction of the village where Canek had been given shelter. Jacinto Canek lives on in the collective memory of Yucatán and is considered to be an early martyr for indigenous rights.

Despite the dangers, the system of roads and paths between the major centers and even the most remote holdings was mapped and policed by the colonial overseers. Trade between the local settlements was extensive, and authorized market places were laid out.

The diet of the colonial and the indigenous population was good; there was game and domestic meat, fish and fowl; grains and legumes were grown and fruit was plentiful. Despite poor and spare soil the fields produced a fair yield if not over-exploited. However, the crops were entirely dependent on rainfall. It can't be stressed enough that drought was about the worst calamity that could befall the Yucatán. Unfortunately, drought did occur with some regularity, followed by famine and disease.

By the close of the 18th century, Yucatán had diversified its agrarian production. Most of the livestock brought from Spain flourished, provided it could be supplied with sufficient water. Extracting the water from the underground sources was a problem at first, but a design for *las norias* – waterwheels – brought from Andalusia in Spain, solved this problem. The wheels were turned by horses or mules and brought forth the vital liquid from the deepest wells.

Crops such as corn, sugar cane and cotton flourished, but wheat and grapes, which were native to more temperate regions, did not do well in the hot, humid Yucatecan climate.

There were many forests of precious hardwoods that were harvested for timber. The dyes extracted from plants and insects indigenous to the Yucatán were held in great esteem in Europe and demand for them was high. The Maya also introduced the colonials to *chicle* – the resin used in the original chewing gum – and the rubber trees of the region.

The tanneries in Mérida processed a large number of hides that were exported; only the excess was made available to the local population. Salt was harvested annually from the coastal areas, and this too was an important trade item.

Once the Spaniards realized how useful sisal – the fiber from the leaves of the *sisal agave* plant (called *henequén* in the Yucatán) – was for making rope, sacks and other storage containers, they cultivated it for this purpose. Shipbuilding was introduced on the coast, but this activity was heavily regulated because the authorities did not want the population to have too much mobility.

The Mayan women proved themselves to be skilled at spinning, weaving, sewing, embroidery, hammock-making and pottery. The Mayan men mastered the European style of carpentry, stonemasonry and wood carving. The Maya also proved to be fine silversmiths, painters, sculptors and strong blacksmiths. Some of the Mayan household staff became excellent cooks and bakers; they developed innovative new dishes that blended European and indigenous ingredients and techniques.

For the elite, colonial Mérida was a fine place to live; there was a large labor force and this allowed their enterprises to grow and prosper. The native population lived a very different reality. For the most part, they were poorly treated and were subject to the whims of their colonial masters.

Dr. Juan Leandro Gómez de Parada y Mendoza, a learned man from Guadalajara, was named Bishop of Yucatán in 1716. He deplored the exploitation of the indigenous people and issued an edict for reform. The local governors, businessmen and even the friars were shocked by his unconventional humanitarian attitudes and did what they could to have him ousted from his position.

The King of Spain received their complaints and summoned the bishop to his court. Upon hearing of the exaggerated abuse that was being perpetuated by many of the hacienda owners and other men in powerful positions, the king reconfirmed his confidence in Gómez de Parada, and actually appointed him to head the government in the Yucatán. The Bishop never assumed that position—for reasons still unclear—and a short time later was transferred to Guatemala.

During the mid 18th century Mérida was still growing, and more educational opportunities for the young men were needed. The first institute of higher learning, *el Colegio de San Javier* had been founded in 1624 but only granted degrees in philosophy, theology, and canon (Church) law; those with religious vocations were satisfied with this option. In 1711, *el Colegio de San Pedro* was established and offered more secular instruction. In 1867 this school would become *el Instituto Literario*, the forerunner of the Autonomous University of Yucatán.

At the time of *el Grito* in 1810, the Yucatán was geographically isolated and in fact not even part of México. The region was politically dependent on the governorship of Guatemala (as was Chiapas). Nonetheless, the movement was so transcendental that it had immediate and far-reaching effects throughout all of the Spanish colonies.

Since 1805 *los Sanjuanistas* – a group of liberal reformists – had been meeting regularly in Mérida. The leader, a Catholic priest named Vicente María Velásquez, and his young followers were fervent supporters of the independence movement in México. The Sanjuanistas distributed many pamphlets that explained the new edicts of the Constitution of Cádiz and urged their implementation.

The governor at the time had no recourse but to adhere to the law. Municipal governments were elected in due course, and indigenous peoples' rights that had been called for by the Sanjuanistas were established. Up to this point there had been no civil rights for the Maya, and it was mandatory for them to give freely of their labor when ordered to do so by "citizens".

This unfair practice was abolished, and lands to be cultivated for their own families' use were given to married Mayan men.

Despite his own personal sentiments and distrust of the Mexican federal government, the Governor of Yucatán—which encompassed all of the Yucatán peninsula at that time—Juan María Echeverría, understood that the will of the people was to become part of the independent new country. After drafting the terms for the annexation, Echeverría sent an envoy to Mexico City who could hopefully come to an agreement with Iturbide. To avoid confrontation between himself and rival factions, Echeverría slipped quietly out of the country from the port of Sisal and returned to Spain.

The first political constitution of Yucatán was written in April 1825. For the first time, human rights were included in a formal document of this importance; these were eventually added to a later federal constitution as individual guarantees.

Geographically and politically isolated from the rest of Mexico, the Yucatán often went its own way. From 1841 to 1843, during of one of Santa Ana's presidential terms, Yucatán actually declared itself an independent republic because Santa Ana's federal government had perpetuated unacceptable injustices and misunderstandings.

The Yucatán rejoined the Republic when Antonio López de Santa Ana allowed the state to retain its political and fiscal autonomy—a constitution and customs laws—something that differentiated Yucatán from the rest of México.

The Yucatán became independent again when these privileges were revoked but rejoined after the Mexican-American war. That war, which cost Mexico a third of its northern territory nearly cost the country the southeastern portion as well. The Yucatecan Maya, who had been subjugated since the Conquest of México, launched a major uprising in July 1847. This was the start of *la Guerra de Castas* – the Caste War.

The Mayan forces, armed with guns from the English in Belize, attacked numerous cities and villages. They occupied all of the Yucatán peninsula except the cities of Campeche and Mérida. The Caste War continued sporadically for decades, ending only upon the federal army's defeat of the Mayan forces in 1901 at the rebel capital of Chan Santa Cruz, the town known today as Felipe Carrillo Puerto in the State of Quintana Roo.

During the French intervention, the Empress Carlota, cognizant of her imperial duties, travelled to many outposts in her husband Maximiliano's new domain, including the Yucatán frontier during December of 1864. While there, she stayed at the home of the wealthy Galera family.

Although there were sporadic Mayan uprisings during Maximiliano's short reign, his French backers saw great potential in the Yucatán. Along with a group of Yucatecan investors and land owners, they began to experiment with the intensive commercial cultivation of the sisal agave. The strong, sinuous fiber extracted from the leaves of the plant had gained fame throughout the world as a most durable fiber for the manufacture of high-quality rope and other products. The plants grew well in the hot, humid climate and huge tracts of land were consolidated for growing sisal; these were to become known as the great haciendas of the Yucatán.

Because the Caste War had decimated the local population, there was not a large enough work force to meet the demands of the new industry, so laborers were brought to the Yucatán peninsula from other parts of México and also from Korea, China and the Canary Islands. The problem of the labor intensive stripping of the sisal fibers from the plant's leaves was resolved by a local invention, *la Rueda Solis* – a barbed wheel that could strip leaves very quickly. The addition of steam-powered engines to turn the Solis wheels allowed the annual production of sisal fiber to grow to 200,000 tons by 1916. The first group of Lebanese immigrants arrived in Yucatán in the 1880s. They would prosper and in time become the rich merchant class. The sisal industry generated great fortunes, and this brought enormous progress and growth in the city of Mérida.

The Yucatán was still geographically isolated from the rest of México. Travel to the interior of the country was not carried out on a regular basis. The peninsula had strong commercial ties to France, and the local society greatly admired the gastronomy, music, art, fashion, architecture, culture and education of the European republic. Many members of the social elite spoke French and sent their young men to France for professional studies.

The sisal wealth in the Yucatán caused a construction boom. There was huge competition among the prominent families to own homes in Mérida and on their haciendas that would rival the chateaux of *la Belle Époque de la France.* In Mérida, the most prestigious addresses at the end of the 19th century were on 59th Street, around the main city plaza, and in the San Juan neighborhood. The buildings, which featured elegant lines, classic appointments and rich ornamentation, were the product of European builders and craftsmen who came to Yucatán, expressly to work on the projects. Some of these projects were enormous and took many years to complete.

The Governor's Palace on the northern side of the Main Plaza was inaugurated on September 15, 1892. The Peón Contreras Theater—known at the time as one of México's three jewels—was completed in 1908. The elegant, *paseo de Montejo,* patterned after the *Avenue des Champs-Élysées* in Paris, was also built at the turn of the nineteenth century.

Many of the ornate mansions along this avenue, such as *la Quinta Montes Molina, las Casas Cámara, la Casa Vales* and *el Palacio Canton*, were constructed by the *hacendados* – hacienda owners – of the time. Architects have named this type of construction *Porfiriano*, after the Mexican president of the period, who favored the style.

What we know today as Yucatecan cuisine was actually developed during this period. When Yucatecan families returned from extended stays in France and other European countries they instructed their cooks to duplicate the recipes for foods they had enjoyed there. Many ingredients were not available in the Yucatán, so the inventive kitchen staff would substitute local foods and condiments, creating a wonderful fusion of Mayan, Spanish-colonial and contemporary European culinary styles.

French music, fashion and fine arts were favored by society, and elegant balls, concerts and art exhibitions were held in the city's theaters and salons. Most of the doctors of the time were French-educated, and the university preparatory school system was modeled on the French *lycée*.

Although there were approximately one thousand haciendas in Yucatán, 90% of the production and commerce was controlled by about thirty families. This elite group was known as *la Casta Divina* – the exalted class. The main buildings of their haciendas were as elegant as their city homes.

These families were very adept at their businesses and because of the high demand for sisal products, their fortunes ascended to previously unheard-of amounts. So renowned was the wealth in Yucatán that Henry Ford travelled to Mérida in search of financial backing for his fledgling automotive industry.

Sisal agave growing at a hacienda in Yucatán

Although no actual armed conflict took place in Yucatán during the Mexican Revolution, the peninsula played a large role. Tariffs on exports and taxes imposed on the rich sustained the federal government.

In order to enforce the ideals of *la Revolución*, General Salvador Alvarado was sent by the new federal government to assert a strong military presence in Yucatán. The ruling class in Yucatán was greatly incensed when the revolutionary principles were introduced into the area by Alvarado. The local power elite tried unsuccessfully to stop the advance of his federal troops, and bloody battles were waged at Halacho and Blanca Flor, but the defenders' foot soldiers—young, inexperienced students and employees of the wealthy class—were no match for the professional forces. The Mexico City contingent entered Mérida, established the new rules, and after two years General Alvarado returned to the Capital. Life quickly reverted back to the way it had been. The Yucatecan elite enjoyed their many privileges and did not intend to allow imposed, central Mexican government edicts to alter their lifestyle.

In 1922, the young governor, Felipe Carrillo Puerto, a political protégé of the revolutionary president General Obregón, renewed attempts to help the impoverished Maya and mestizos in Yucatán with widespread reforms. He supported archaeological exploration by the Carnegie Institute and the incipient tourism industry as well.

He promoted Yucatán internationally and invited foreign journalists to report on the area. Among these was an American writer, Alma Reed, who was later immortalized in the most famous Yucatecan ballad, "Peregrina". This beautiful song was composed by Ricardo Palmarín and Luís Rosado Vega. Carrillo Puerto was assassinated by his political enemies in 1924; he is still mourned by the Yucatecan people.

During Cárdenas' presidency—1934 to 1940—the government expropriated and redistributed millions of acres of hacienda land to campesinos, principally in the states of Yucatán and Jalisco. The agrarian reform affected Yucatán in a fundamental way. Most of the great haciendas and the sisal fiber manufacturing plants were divided among the workers of the area, causing economic ruin for many of the state's prominent families.

Local cooperatives – *ejidos* – were formed and Banrural – a government owned bank – was established to give technical and economic support to the cooperatives.

The good intentions of the redistribution of the wealth did not bear the expected results. The uneducated farm workers did not have the necessary expertise to maintain the productivity of the fields. Little by little, their lands were bought back by the former owners. Yet most of the property has not reverted to agriculture. Homes have been built on the land, especially around Mérida, and many of the haciendas are now tourist attractions.

After his presidential term Cárdenas continued to speak out about international political issues, and in favor of greater democracy and human rights throughout Latin America and elsewhere. In the Yucatecan countryside he is still known as *Tata*, an affectionate indigenous term reserved for authority figures and elders who have earned the utmost respect.

In 1940 the Cárdenas presidency ended. Cárdenas became Secretary of Defense and there were German submarines operating in the Gulf of México throughout World War II. In order to improve access to the region in case of attack, the U.S. Army military engineers built the airports in Campeche, Mérida, Isla Mujeres and Cozumel…something that Cárdenas watched with a skeptical eye.

Because of the world wide conflict there was a renewed demand for sisal products. The agrarian reform had broken up many of the huge land holdings but the former owners of the haciendas consolidated their holdings and in some cases formed partnerships with the ejidos and began replanting. Sisal was called "green gold" because it brought renewed prosperity to the region.

In the early 1950s, a different industry boomed—tourism. It very quickly became one of the primary employers in the Yucatán peninsula. The President of México from 1947 to 1952 was Miguel Alemán, who was a great supporter of tourism as a source of income for México. During his term in office new infrastructure was built, and Mérida was finally connected by railroad to the central part of the country. Many new highways were built, including one that eventually connected Mérida to the Caribbean coast.

Chichén Itzá, one of the New Seven Wonders of the World

It is difficult to think of this corner of México and not think of tourism. Since the early 1950s Yucatecan businessmen have invested heavily in the industry. The many Mayan ruins are a primary attraction. Chichén Itzá, Uxmal and all of the other one thousand six hundred registered Mayan sites have an undeniable appeal to people from all countries.

They are special because they are a visible link to our universal past. Whether the tourists come from Scandinavia, Canada or China, no one can look at the remains of the former civilization and fail to feel a sense of wonder.

The climate of Yucatán, while very hot in the summer, is absolutely perfect in the winter months when it is freezing in the northern part of the hemisphere. People need to see the sun and feel its warmth, so they flock to southeastern México's beaches and ruins…just like the birds do!

The culture, folklore, music, cuisine and the colors of the Yucatán peninsula are extremely attractive to people from more austere societies and promote a certain abandonment of their everyday restraint. México has something for every type of tourist and a service infrastructure that fits any budget.

The fifties marked a serious decline of the sisal industry. With the introduction of synthetic fibers, the natural ones no longer were in high demand. The epoch of green gold had come and gone. Mérida's population was about 100,000, and the city was not really a major player, even on the national scene. It was during this period that the state gained its reputation as a quiet, tranquil, tropical oasis – *la ciudad blanca* – with its windmills, unique cuisine, *jarana* dancers and archaeological wonders. It was considered to be one of México's most exotic and romantic tourist destinations.

National theater troupes, the circus, and cabaret groups came to Mérida periodically and were always well-received. But mostly, people made their own fun; many Yucatecans play a musical instrument, and still more can sing beautifully. The extended family would get together frequently and serenade one another. There were also dances organized by a large number of social clubs.

Baseball was the preferred sport, and there were teams in every neighborhood and hamlet. Even the smallest settlement had a baseball diamond, and games would be played between the different villages. After the game there would be either a celebration, or the drowning of sorrows—either way, a great time was had by all the fans; there was certainly none of the commercialism or violence seen at sporting events today.

Most of the population lived right downtown and in the barrios of Santiago, Santana, Santa Lucía, San Sebastian, San Juan, Mejorada and San Cristóbal. There were a few sparsely populated suburbs such as Chuminopolis, García Ginerés, Itzimná and the newly developed colonias, México and Alemán. Each neighborhood had a plaza for social gatherings, a large Catholic church, a small public market, offices, a school and shops. There were houses of every description and the neighborhoods were populated by diverse socioeconomic groups. The more affluent would help their poorer neighbors; there was a great sense of belonging. Most of the children attended classes in small government or private schools. They could walk there unaccompanied and were never at risk.

As well as professionals like lawyers, doctors and bankers, there were many tradesmen: builders, electricians, plumbers and carpenters. There were a host of services that were offered door-to-door such as knife sharpening and the repair of metal pots, hammocks, shoes and cane furniture. Most people had their clothes made by the many seamstresses and tailors.

General staples such as bread, milk, flowers, ice, charcoal and produce were delivered right to the residences. Whatever could not be found on the doorstep or in the local markets was surely available at the main market, *el mercado Lucas de Gálvez*, on Calle 56.

The market was a hub of activity from daybreak until the early afternoon. Little was for sale afterwards because without refrigeration the state of the fresh produce could not be guaranteed. Many items were for sale in the market that we rarely see today – venison and other wild game, iguanas, turtles, animal pelts, *copal* – a hardened tree sap used as incense in México – herbs, charms and amulets. The community was very self-sufficient. Although it was a very provincial society, the citizens had all the services and the commodities they needed.

Because of the insular environment, Mérida's citizenry was quite naïve. They were suspicious of outsiders and of new technology. Jorge tells a story about one of his neighbors. This particular lady was very elderly; her well-past-middle-aged son lived with her, and she fussed over him as though he was still a little boy. When he would arrive home after work she would have a chocolate drink waiting for him. At the time, the chocolate had to be beaten by hand and this required more strength than the old lady possessed, so my mother-in-law performed this chore for her.

One day, a new innovation arrived at the Rosado household; my mother-in-law had been given a blender. The new appliance could beat the chocolate faster and more efficiently, but when Mrs. Rosado offered to prepare the customary drink using *la licuadora*, the neighbor was extremely suspect of "the contraption". She eyed my mother-in-law and said, "Fine Bertha, make the drink using that machine, but you give some of it to one of your children first." She was afraid the blender would somehow poison Junior's chocolate drink.

There was a definite rhythm to the city, and few broke with the established traditions. People would rise early, the children would get off to school and the women would commence their daily chores—cleaning house, washing clothes, shopping, preparing the midday meal and so on. The men would go off to work but usually took an hour off, mid-morning, to have coffee with their friends at a local café. Most of the gentlemen had a preferred spot where they would always go.

What we would call a late lunch, Yucatecans call *almuerzo* – the main meal of the day – referred to as *comida* in most other parts of México. At the time, it was always eaten *en familia*, and afterwards everyone in the household would have a siesta.

No shops or offices remained open between 1 p.m. and 4 p.m. My mother-in-law still says, "Decent people do not leave the house at mid-day!"

When it got a little cooler, people would bathe again and dress for the afternoon. They would use this time of the day to run errands or visit family and friends. Many ladies would do intricate hand-work as they chatted, and the children would complete their homework or attend additional classes in music, English, French or some other subject. There were no organized sports teams or other vigorous activities for children.

All of the hard play was reserved for the two week Easter vacation and the summer months of July and August. During these two periods, families would migrate en masse to the beach towns for *la temporada* – the season. The children would spend their days barefoot on the beach, and they would go to the small carnivals in the evenings. The adolescents would stroll the boardwalk flirting with one another—but this courting ritual was supervised; young women did not go anywhere without a chaperone.

In the early 1960s, Yucatán was granted a loan by the Inter-American Development Bank, and deep irrigation wells were dug in the southern part of the state; this allowed the citrus agro-industry to get started. The road from Mérida to Villahermosa was completed in 1965, and Mérida was finally connected to the rest of the country by all modes of transport. The federal government founded Cordemex in 1961, an enterprise that was designed to revive the failing sisal industry.

Already in the first decade of the new millennium hurricanes have done tremendous damage in the Yucatán peninsula. Hurricane Isadora was particularly destructive to Mérida on September 23, 2002. In 2005 Emily, Katrina, and Wilma veered north and Yucatán was spared but Cancún was not that lucky. The destruction from Wilma was extensive, so the 60,000 tourists who were in the area were bused to Mérida. The city's authorities, business sector and private citizens did a heroic job of looking after the unexpected throng, and everyone was on their way back home within three days.

Yet in the face of the continued struggle, the Mexican people always find something to renew their energy and optimism… such as the designation of the Mayan archaeological site Chichén Itzá as one of the seven new wonders of the world.

Since the mid 1970s México has experienced a succession of serious economic and social challenges, but because of tourism and the constant influx of capital Yucatán has not suffered as greatly as have other parts of the republic. More than 2.5 million visitors now come to the Yucatán peninsula every year. With Chichén Itzá's new fame this is expected to increase. Investment in the region has grown in every sector of the economy, and improved infrastructure has enriched the quality of life for the inhabitants.

During the past twenty years and especially during the last ten, Yucatán has experienced a large influx of new residents from abroad. The international press is full of unflattering portrayals of the country and truthfully, many issues are unresolved. But this has not deterred the new arrivals.

Despite what the headlines say, Yucatán suffers very little from the social problems found in other parts the country.

Foreigners are attracted by the laid-back lifestyle of the state, and this, combined with el centro's plethora of run-down colonial homes just waiting for restoration, presents an attractive retirement option. This group is very interested in home renovations.

The city of Mérida offers many of the amenities that international residents require: an international airport, state-of-the-art medical centers, good shopping, available household help, a rich cultural life and definitely...**no** cold weather!

A TIME LINE OF SIGNIFICANT EVENTS

I: Pre-Columbian México

20,000 B.C.E.: Ancestors of the México's indigenous groups crossed the Bering Strait.

5000–1500 B.C.E.: Archaic Period: Settled habitation begins in México.

1500 B.C.E.–300 C.E.: Pre-classic Period: The first highly-developed civilization, the Olmec, is established in Veracruz and Tabasco.

250 C.E.: The Maya are predominant group in southern México, Guatemala, western Honduras, Belize and El Salvador.

250–600 C.E.: In central México, Tula is founded and becomes a major center.

250–900 C.E.: Classic period: Maya civilization is at its peak.

700–1000 C.E.: In central México, Teotihuacán is the major city-state.

750–1000 C.E.: The Toltec culture from its capital in Tula expands its influence throughout the country.

900 C.E.: There is a serious decline in the Mayan population of Central America, attributed to drought and famine. The Maya civilization re-establishes its power base in northern Yucatán.

900–late 1400s C.E.: Post-classic period: Uxmal, Mayapán and Chichén Itzá are the prominent city states.

1100–1300 C.E.: Mayapán overthrows the Confederation and becomes the dominant city state. The Toltec culture strongly influences the Mayan in northern Yucatán, and the cult of Quetzalcóatl is embraced, even though the Maya call the god Kukulkán. The Maya from northern Yucatán extend their influence into northern Veracruz.

1441 C.E.: Uxmal defeats Mayapán's rule and establishes new capital, Mani. The defeated Cocom clan returns to the Peten area of Guatemala.

II: The Colonial Period

1492: Christopher Columbus arrives in the Americas.

1511: Gonzalo de Guerrero and Friar Gerónimo de Aguilar are shipwrecked off the Caribbean coast of the Yucatán peninsula. Guerrero fathers the first mestizos.

1519: Hernán Cortés lands in México at Veracruz.

1521: Hernán Cortés completes the conquest of Tenochtitlán (Mexico City).

During the following decade Cortés sends Bernal Díaz de Castillo and Pedro del Alvarado to conquer Oaxaca; Captain Niño de Guzman conquers Querétaro, Michoacán and Jalisco; Diego de Mazariegos leads an expedition to Chiapas.

1535: First Spanish Viceroy of México, Antonio de Mendoza appointed.

1542: The city of Mérida is founded by Francisco de Montejo the Younger.

1550: Approximately two thousand Spaniards are living in central México.

1553: The first university in colonial México (and in North America) is founded in Mexico City.

1600: There are approximately three hundred Spanish citizens who have settled in Mérida.

1604: El Camino Real is begun. This road links Mérida, Campeche, Valladolid and Bacalar.

1648: Disease reaches epidemic proportions killing colonials and Maya in the Yucatán peninsula.

1664: Sor Juana Inés de la Cruz begins her literary career.

1711: El Colegio de San Pedro is established; it is the earliest forerunner of the Autonomous University of Yucatán.

1716: Dr. Juan Gómez de Parada, Bishop of Yucatán tries to institute laws to protect the indigenous population.

1761: Jacinto Canek, a Mayan martyr for indigenous rights is killed.

1800–1810: The Sanjuanistas, a group of Yucatecan reformers is organized by Friar Vicente María Velázquez.

1809: Napoleon Bonaparte ousts Fernando VII from the Spanish throne.

1810: Miguel Hidaldo initiates the independence movement with El Grito on the night of September 15 in the central Mexican town of Dolores.

III: Independence

1812: The Constitution of Cadiz brings reform laws to the Spanish colonies.

1814: Fernando VII is reinstated as King of Spain.

1821: México's Independence is declared on September 27th, ending the eleven year war of independence.

1822: Augustín de Iturbide is crowned Emperor of México on July 21st.

1823: Yucatán becomes a state of México.

1825: Yucatán's first Constitution is written.

1833–1855: Antonio López de Santa Ana is President of México (on and off for eleven times).

1846: The Mexican-American war begins

1847: The Caste War begins in Yucatán; it doesn't end until 1901.

1848–The Mexican-American War is formally over with the signing of the Treaty of Guadalupe Hidalgo.

1855–1864: Benito Juárez is President of México.

1860: The beginning of the large-scale sisal industry in Yucatán. It is the dominant industry until the end of WW II.

1862: The French intervention in México – *Cinco de Mayo*

1864–1867: The Hapsburg monarchy rule.

1867–1872: Benito Juárez is once again President of México.

1876–1911: Porfirio Díaz is President of México.

IV. The Revolution

1910: The *Revolución* begins

1916: The American intervention – called The Punitive Expedition by the U.S. government – to try and arrest Pancho Villa begins. It fails to capture Villa and is eventually recalled.

1917: General Salvador Alvarado arrives in Yucatán to enforce the ideals of the Revolution and is meets great resistance from *la casta divina*.

1922–1924: Felipe Carrillo Puerto is governor of Yucatán. He is assassinated by political enemies.

1929: The *Partido Nacional Revoluconario* (PNR) is formed. It rules the country until 2000, although the name (and some of its "platform") was changed to the *Partido Revolucionario Institucional* (PRI) in 1949.

V. The Era of the PNR and PRI in México

1934–1940: Lázaro Cárdenas is President of México.

1938: Foreign-owned oil interests are expelled from México and PEMEX is incorporated as México's national oil company. Also, the Mexican railroads are nationalized.

1939–1945: World War II. Airports are built in Mérida, Campeche, Isla Mujeres and Cozumel.

1947–1952: Miguel Alemán is President of México. The tourism industry grows rapidly in Yucatán and the rest of the country.

1950s: Synthetic fibers are used with increased frequency, reducing the demand for sisal products.

1960s: Yucatán begins a citrus agro-industry in the southern part of the state.

1968: Tlaltelolco student massacre on October 2nd in Mexico City. The Mexico City Olympic Games are held the same year.

1970: Development of Cancún and the Riviera Maya begins.

1976: The first major currency devaluation occurs; this trend continues for nearly three decades.

1980–1990: Globalization expands to México.

1985: The earthquake in Mexico City.

1988: Hurricane Gilberto damages much of Mérida's infrastructure. Donaldo Colosio, the PRI presidential candidate is assassinated.

1990: The North American Free Trade Agreement (NAFTA) is signed between México, the U.S.A. and Canada.

1994: On January 1st the Zapatista rebel group occupies San Cristóbal de las Casas in the state of Chiapas and the federal army is dispatched. NAFTA goes into effect.

1994–1996: México is near bankruptcy and President Ernesto Zedillo instates austere economic policies.

2000: The PRI candidate is defeated in federal elections and the *Partido Acción Nacional* (PAN) candidate is elected.

VI. The Twenty-first century in México

2002: Hurricane Isadora

2005: Hurricane Wilma

2006: President Vicente Fox's popularity declines, yet the PAN candidate Felipe Calderón is elected president. Drug wars and violence escalate.

2008: Economic crisis once again hits México.

2009: H1N1 influenza virus causes travel advisories and further damage to the Mexican economy.

2010: On September 15th, México commemorates the 200th Anniversary of Independence from Spain and the 100th Anniversary of the Mexican Revolution.

¡Viva México!

BIBLIOGRAPHY
for Our Country, State and City

Ayuntamiento de Mérida. *Haciendas forjadoras del oro verde.* Editorial del Ayuntamiento de Mérida, 1998–2001.

Grabman, Richard. *Gods, Gachupines and Gringos: A People's History of Mexico.* Mazatlán, Sinaloa: Editorial Mazatlán, 2008.

Lara Navarrete, Ileana B. *Estilos arquitectónicos de Mérida.* Editorial Dante. 1998.

Molina Solís, Juan Francisco. *Historia de Yucatán, Tomo I: dominación española.* Consejo Editorial de Yucatán, A.C., 1978

Orosa Díaz, Jaime. *Historia de Yucatán.* Universidad de Yucatán, 1984

Quiñones, Sam. True *Tales From Another Mexico.* University of New Mexico Press, 2001.

Redfeld, Robert. *The Folk Culture of Yucatán.* The University of Chicago Press, 1941.

Rosado G. Canton, Alberto. *Historia de Yucatán, Tomo Tercero.* Universidad de Yucatán, 1978

_____. *Historia de Yucatán, Tomo Cuarto.* Universidad de Yucatán, 1978

Solís Robleda, Gabriela & Bracamonte y Sosa, Pedro. *Historias de la conquista del Mayab 1511–1697.* Universidad Autónoma de Yucatán, 1994.

TTT courtyard on 57th Street, Mérida, Yucatán, México

The TTT Story

Retrospect is a comfortable barometer. From the safety of the present, one can look back and see quite clearly which decisions were smart and which were foolhardy. Oddly enough, some of the choices we make end up filling both criteria!

IN 1990 JANUARY 13TH fell on a Saturday. Jorge and I were taking a walk in the *Parque de las Americas* and enjoying the cooler winter temperatures. As we trotted around the four block perimeter, we would wave at almost five-year-old Maggie and not quite nine-year-old Carlos who were playing happily on the jungle-gym in the childrens' playground area. With the exception of 1982's one year hiatus in Canada, I had lived for the past fourteen years in Mérida. I lifted my hair up off the back of my neck and tied it into a ponytail. "Let's run the next lap," I suggested.

Pointing to an empty bench, Jorge said, "No, let's sit here for a while. I have something I want to talk to you about."

After a decade and a half together, I could catch every nuance in his voice and at that moment, he sounded grave. What was he going to say? I plunked down onto the proffered concrete seat and listened hard.

Since returning from Canada seven years ago, Jorge had worked at a local university. The professional Tourism Administration program he'd developed was well respected, and the graduates had good career prospects. He'd gained a lot of experience and chose this day to tell me that he felt the time had come for us to have our own business.

"You know that being completely independent has always been my dream," he said. "There's certainly a market for another tourism college, and I think we should go for it."

I felt so relieved that he wasn't telling me he had some deadly disease or that he was having an affair, so I really didn't take in the ramifications of what he was proposing, but I readily supported him and urged him to move on this as quickly as possible. The new school year would begin in just nine months.

He made enquiries and found out what the legal requirements were. The Secretariat of Education gave him a great thick pile of terms, conditions, legal responsibilities, stipulations and provisions. He would have to satisfy every one of them before an authorization was given. The first of the hurdles was finding a place to start up the school.

It had been two years since Jorge's father's death and his mother no longer wanted to live downtown. Her house would be a perfect building for a college and she wanted to rent it to us. But once we got down to crunching the numbers, no matter how we cut corners and scrimped, we saw that we'd have a hard time financially.

We had enough savings to pay the rent for a year, renovate the necessary space and cover the initial operating costs, but supporting the new business and our family would be a stretch. We wracked our brains trying to come up with a solution.

We realized we'd have to approach our mothers for help… just for a year. We asked my mom if she'd be willing to have the children and I live with her in Canada, and we asked Jorge's mother if she'd be agreeable to moving in with him, so we could use her house for the school.

It was definitely an unconventional way to resolve the issue but bless their hearts, our mothers said yes immediately and we began planning in earnest.

The fact that Carlos, Maggie and I would be out of the picture meant Jorge would be able to devote all his energies to getting the college going, but he knew he'd miss us so much and vice versa. Was it worth it to risk our family's happiness on a business venture we had no guarantee would pan out?

We ultimately chose to take the gamble, but I seriously doubt we would have if we'd known all that was coming down the pike. There were people who did not want us to have a college and tried to use their influence to stop our application process. Fortunately we had friends of our own, and the opposition was thwarted.

Programs had to be designed and written, all the infrastructure needed to be put in place, teachers hired, a logo designed, paperwork filed and a name chosen. Jorge ultimately decided on *Tecnología Turística Total*, a long moniker, but I liked the acronym TTT.

Now all we needed were students!

Gabriela Esquivel was the first one to register. Petite, bright and enthusiastic; she got us off to a great start. One by one, more came through the door, and by September 1st, when Jorge opened the school, we had seventy young people, all keen to learn about working in the tourism industry.

The expenses we had incurred were much higher than we estimated, so in order to cover the cost we had to divest ourselves of all our assets (except for our house and the '75 VW Beetle).

In midsummer 1990 I left for Canada with the children. Jorge and I wrote to one another a lot, and we spoke on the phone as often as we could afford to, which wasn't very frequently. We shared our news, but it certainly was difficult having our family separated.

Jorge lived, breathed and dreamed to the rhythm of the school that year. He and his mom got along well and *Tecnología Turística Total* (TTT) had a strong first year.

In September our kids started school in Canada, and I took a job as a waitress.

My position at a popular European style restaurant was quite enjoyable and it paid for our expenses. The Dutch couple who owned the place was very exacting and sometimes I was reprimanded for being "careless".

A placemat that was not set as precisely as they liked it; a customer who had to wait more than thirty seconds for me to sedately walk over and take their order; a pastry not artfully placed on the plate...these things were all defined as huge offences.

At the time I thought my bosses were over reacting, but after we'd had our own business for a few years, I realized that they were not at all *über*-exacting. They were business owners, and their success depended partly on me doing an absolutely perfect job.

I enjoyed my year at Mom's home, so did Carlos and Maggie. They got to really know their grandmother, aunts, uncles and cousins.

Jorge worked very hard, and ¡*Gracias a Dios*! the pieces were all falling into place. He came to visit us for two weeks at Christmas and again at Easter. Being together on these two occasions made it possible to be apart for the rest of the time.

The year passed quickly. I wanted to go back to Mérida but once again it seemed very hard to endure the pain of separating from my Canadian family.

When I arrived back in Mérida in 1991, we had a firmly launched college and a lot of work ahead of us. To say TTT operated on a shoestring budget during the first years would be an understatement in the extreme. Our expenses were barely covered by the students' tuition, and we had to save money all through the academic year in order to continue building new classrooms and other infrastructure when the students went on vacation in July and August.

The summer the kids and I came back from Canada saw us building the second floor on the original building; the next year we did the food & beverage lab and more classrooms; a third floor followed, and finally in our fourth summer we'd run out of room on the original property.

Jorge and I worked as hard as any two people could. We both taught classes, and with the help of one secretary (Silvia is still working with us) and a part-time accountant we did all the administrative work as well.

Our instructors were mostly friends from the tourism industry who went far beyond their job descriptions to see that the students received a good education.

The students themselves were incredible young people. Most came from working class families, and education was a top priority for them. Their families sacrificed a great deal in order to send them to college. The students also loved to have fun and they wanted lots of extracurricular activities; so we had to find time to fit these in as well.

Jorge and I went on field trips, held symposiums, hosted guest lecturers, organized big parties for the students and got involved in community service. There was always something going on.

One Christmas season, we went with the students to an elementary school in the countryside where we planned to host a Christmas party. To our dismay, when the little ones saw us driving up, they started crying and ran away.

One wee guy jumped up like a goat onto the top of the stone wall and scrambled down the other side. The teachers yelled in Maya, *"¡Ma–chuhuc!"* Roughly translated this means, "No, don't go, there's candy!"

Later, after their pupils had been corralled, the out-of-breath educators exasperatedly told us that last week a government health care team came and gave vaccinations to everyone. The doctors had shown up in white vans like ours, so today the kids thought they would be getting another bite of the needle. It took a while to assure the weeping preschoolers that no such thing would happen at our hands.

Our friends shook their heads. They thought Jorge and I had taken a huge risk in opening a college but they did what they could to help us and to divert our worries. I remember that during one particularly stressful period, Paul and Juanita, a couple we knew well called us up and invited us for dinner. Not unusual, but when we arrived at their house they had set up an elegant table on their roof garden with candles and flowers and served every exotic food they knew we liked. Wined and dined like royalty, we felt as though we had wandered into a five-star restaurant. Paul told jokes and Juanita said, "Enjoy yourselves. Let go of your worries!"

I'll never forget that night.

My teaching schedule was arranged so that I had a break and could slip out to pick up Carlos and Maggie from school and take them home to Estelita, our housekeeper. While I taught the second half of my daily classes she'd make their dinner, supervise baths and so on.

We arranged our routine so we could spend as much time together as possible. Our son and daughter came on the school outings with us and attended events. They would participate whenever and however they could. In very real ways, they too helped build TTT.

The campus is located right downtown in Mérida's historic center. It is comprised of four inter-connecting Spanish colonial buildings. Parts of these are very old and are actually recorded on the first maps of the city. Small gardens, arches and stairways link one building to the next. Although the classrooms are air-conditioned, the public areas have a wide-open, tropical ambiance. We endeavor to instill pride in our state's architectural heritage by conserving and enhancing the distinctive Meridano style.

Our personnel and teaching staff is an international mix of Mexicans, Central and North Americans and Europeans. About a third of them are young, and some are graduates of TTT. We find that these young instructors have an instinctive rapport with the current students and also have the energy needed to accompany the groups on organized excursions and activities. Professional practicums – the part of a course consisting of hands-on work in a particular field – outings and excursions to other cities and states are often dreamed up by this enthusiastic group.

The foreign teachers give our local students a wider perspective of the world and the experienced older ones add levity and

Jorge with TTT students at Chichén Ítza

focus to the relaxed atmosphere at our college. But at the heart of everything there is the student body.

I've had the honor to know so many amazing young people... kids with so much talent. They know that in México, a professional degree is the first ticket towards improving their lives. And some of them have done extremely well.

Many work while attending the four year course of studies, and many make long commutes to TTT from their villages. Some are already parents or have children during their studies. We give these students extra support and remind them their efforts are not just for themselves but for the future of their families. An inspirational book could certainly be written about the drive, determination, inventiveness and creativity of our students.

When working with your spouse, there's one aspect that can get awkward. Jorge and I spent almost every waking moment (and sleeping ones too) in each other's company. You know, there is such a thing as too much togetherness!

We both have strong personalities and it took effort for us to determine the area of school's operation that each of us was best suited to. Then the challenge became to not undermine one another's decisions.

We found too that all we did was talk, worry and plan about TTT or our children. So we started "dating" each other again because we realized if we weren't careful, our responsibilities would consume our entire life as a couple.

In June of 1994 our first Bachelor in Tourism group graduated. I will never forget that night. Jorge and I felt very proud of the students, our staff, our children and ourselves—we'd all done it together.

At the celebration, I looked around the assembled group of three hundred persons: students, teachers, parents, family and friends and thought to myself, *All this is happening because Jorge had that great idea!* At every graduation since, (there were 2,100 people at the last one!) I think the same thing. Our impact is huge…so is our responsibility.

1995 was a terrible year. The country was in serious recession and our new enrollment was very small. We were hard-pressed to keep our doors open, and our college only survived because we had no debts and were always able to (barely) cover the payroll and pay our bills.

But eventually things turned around, and I an idea about starting a high school promotional campaign. This was not a common practice in Yucatán, but I figured desperate times called for innovative measures! That year I visited about forty high schools throughout the state. I was very nervous about doing this public speaking *en español*, but I somehow managed to keep the students' attention. At the time very few college representatives went directly to the high schools, so the students enjoyed the break from their regular routine.

The following September, our enrollment more than doubled. We also registered enough students to start up a second bachelor – *licenciatura* – degree program, one in Modern Languages. From there, we never looked back. Our college has grown steadily ever since.

By 1999 we needed more space and were very fortunate to be able to buy another building that backed onto our existing one. The spring and summer of 2000 saw us renovating again; more classrooms, a larger office space, additional bathrooms and an outdoor cafeteria would be improvements appreciated by all.

With the new addition there was also more room to expand our international programs. Although I'd worked with a limited number of foreign students every year since 1992, I did not feel I could accommodate too many of them due to lack of infrastructure.

Now though, things could change. At present, our college offers semester-long programs every spring and fall and we host university field schools in April and May.

This adds another dimension to our campus. Canadian and American students are able to get to know the Mexican culture and learn Spanish. Our local students benefit from the opportunity to interact with their peers from other countries, and through agreements with Canadian and American partner institutions TTT students are able to study abroad.

At TTT, the reliability of internet communication has accelerated the internationalization of our campus. Our students are now in regular contact with their peers at partner institutions and they have a much wider view of the world. They meet on line to share research and make plans for when they'll visit one another. For many students, financial circumstances may limit actual travel; nonetheless this generation has a lot of virtual mobility without ever leaving home.

2005 marked TTT's fifteenth anniversary year. We celebrated our Quince Años at a local hotel with our closest friends and colleagues. We gave five, ten and fifteen year service awards to our staff. We laughed, cried and sighed while watching a video presentation that our son Carlos had made to document the story of our college, and we reveled in our accomplishment. It was a wonderful day.

Since then, our college has continued to innovate and change. The worldwide recession that began in 2008, the outbreak of H1N1 virus and the country's socio-economic instability curtailed expansion but every indication is that Tecnología Turística Total will continue to be a popular option for higher education in the state.

In 2010 Jorge and I retired from the directorship of the college, but we will always be involved in an advisory capacity. Our daughter Maggie is active in the day to day running of the campus, and one day she hopes to be at the helm. Our son Carlos lives abroad but still contributes with his multimedia skills and by promoting the international programs abroad.

When Jorge and I meet new people they often express surprise over the fact that we started our own college. To be truthful, we were extremely lucky. In 1990 the government had wanted many more new educational institutions. They didn't make it easy, but they were receptive, and TTT was only the third private college to open in our state. Since then the number has climbed to more than one hundred. Starting a new school nowadays is very, very difficult.

Tecnología Turística Total has provided Jorge and me with an extremely interesting professional career and many opportunities to serve our community. We feel grateful to all the people who helped us along the way, and we are extremely satisfied with the results of our efforts. "Nothing ventured, nothing gained," is a popular saying, but I like this quote from Thomas Jefferson, "I'm a great believer in luck, and I find the harder I work the more I have of it."

Joanna and Jorge on their Retirement Day

ACKNOWLEDGEMENTS

M Y DEEP APPRECIATION GOES OUT TO David Bodwell and Richard Grabman of Editorial Mazatlán. They believed in me, accepted my manuscript and, under David's patient tutelage and editing, *MAGIC MADE IN MEXICO* emerged.

And without the encouragement of the Mérida Writers' Group, I suspect this book would yet be languishing on my computer's hard drive. Thank you – Rainie, Marianne, Cherie, Bob, K., Marietta, Lorna-Gail, and Gwen.

The diverse vignettes that add humor and perspective to the book were generously provided by Marianne Kehoe, Maggie Rosado, Kurt Wootton, Sharon Helgason, K. Jack, Nancy Walters, Juanita Zak, Marietta Ackenbom, Janice Knight, Ellyne Basto, Rainie Bailie, Bob Jack, Lorna Gail Dalin, Debi Kuhn, Cherie Pittillo, Juanita Geraghty, John Brown, Theresa Gray, Larry McIntosh, Colleen Leonard, Reg Deneau, and Valerie Pickles . My gratitude to you all…

Gracias Carlos Rosado and Sam Woodruff for the preparation of the photos interspersed throughout the pages of the book, many of which are Carlos' original work.

I am also grateful to Jo Nuñez, Nancy Walters, Jan Morgan, Marianne Kehoe and Barb van der Gracht for reading and critiquing my first draft and encouraging me to publish it.

I am indebted to Loretta Scott Miller for allowing me to quote from her cook book; to my long-time friend Mary Lumby, who cheers from afar; to Harriet Riggs from the Merida English Language Library for her help in compiling the Recommended Reading list; and to Javier Cuevas, the computer whiz at our college, who gave me unending technical assistance.

My friends in my adopted country have shown me that color, music and magic are at the heart of our lives. They have also helped me to see that resilience, determination and patience are virtues we must employ every day. My mother-in-law, Doña Bertha Baeza de Rosado and I have learned from one another about diversity, acceptance, and quiet strength – I bless her for *hanging in there* with me! Indeed, I humbly thank everyone who has made me sure that I belong in México.

Yet, of all the good hearted people in my life, no one deserves more appreciation than my husband Jorge, and our children Carlos and Maggie – they support me in large and small ways – every single day.

Maya Angelou once said,

> *"I've learned that people will forget what you said, people will forget what you did, but people will never forget how you made them feel."*

Thank you to everyone who made me feel that I could and must write *MAGIC MADE IN MÉXICO*, and to my readers for making me glad that I did.

Joanna
Mérida, Yucatán, México
October 2010

JOANNA'S RECOMMENDED READING LIST

If you would like to read more about Mexico and Latin America, the following is a list of books that you might enjoy:

LATIN AMERICAN AUTHORS (TRANSLATED WORKS)

Allende, Isabel
HOUSE OF THE SPIRITS
Translated by Magda Bogin
Black Swan Publishing

Allende, Isabel
INES OF MY SOUL
Translated by Margaret
    Sayers Peden
Harper Collins Publishing

Esquivel, Laura
LIKE WATER
FOR CHOCOLATE
Simon & Schuster

Esquivel, Laura
MALINCHE
Simon & Schuster

Fuentes, Carlos
OLD GRINGO
Farrar, Straus & Giroux

Fuentes, Carlos
AURA
Translated by Lysander Kemp
Farrar, Straus & Giroux

Garcia Marquez, Gabriel
LOVE IN TIME OF
CHOLERA
Translated by Edith
    Grossman
Vintage International Press

Garcia Marquez, Gabriel
ONE HUNDRED YEARS
OF SOLITUDE
Translated by Gregory
 Rabassa
Harper Perennial Modern
 Classics

Paz, Octavio
SOR JUANA
Translated by Margaret
 Sayers Peden
Harvard University Press

HISTORY, ARCHAEOLOGY & ANTHROPOLOGY

Byrd Simpson, Lesley
MANY MEXICOS
University of California Press

Coe, Michael
THE MAYA
7th Editon, Thames &
 Hudson

Fash, William L.
SCRIBES, WARRIORS &
KINGS
Thames & Hudson

Foster, Lynn V.
HANDBOOK TO LIFE
IN THE ANCIENT
MAYA WORLD
Oxford University Press

Freidel, David & Schele, Linda
MAYA COSMOS
William Morrow

Gilbert, M. Joseph
REVOLUTION FROM
WITHOUT
Duke University Press

Grabman, Richard
GODS, GACHUPINES
AND GRINGOS:
A People's History of Mexico
Editorial Mazatlán

Lewis, Oscar
THE CHILDREN OF
SANCHEZ
Vintage Books

Mayo, C.M.
THE LAST PRINCE
OF THE MEXICAN
EMPIRE
Unbridled Books

Redfield, Robert
THE FOLK CULTURE
OF YUCATAN
University of Chicago Press

Redfield & Villarojas
CHAN KOM
University of Chicago Press

Reed, Nelson A.
THE CASTE WAR OF
YUCATAN
Stanford University Press